WELL WOMEN

This book is dedicated to the memory of Dr Abla Mayss. Abla, who died in September 2000, was a valued member of the Feminist Legal Research Unit at Liverpool. Not only was she an able scholar who felt strongly about the position of the women and children who figured in her research – she was also a warm, generous and supportive colleague. The members of the FLRU, and others who knew her, miss her both professionally and personally.

Well Women

The gendered nature of health care provision

Edited by
ANNE MORRIS
SUSAN NOTT
University of Liverpool, UK

Ashgate

Published by
Ashgate Publishing Limited
Gower House
Croft Road
Aldershot
Hants GU11 3HR
England

Ashgate Publishing Company
131 Main Street
Burlington, VT 05401–5600 USA

Ashgate website: http://www.ashgate.com

British Library Cataloguing in Publication Data

Well women : the gendered nature of heath care provision
  1. Women - Health and hygiene 2. Medical personnel
  I. Morris, Anne E., 1952- II. Nott, Susan M.
  613'.04244

Library of Congress Control Number: 2001099674

ISBN 1 84014 720 2

Typeset by Bournemouth Colour Press, Parkstone.
Printed and bound in Great Britain by TJ International Ltd, Padstow, Cornwall.

Contents

Notes on Contributors

Dr Faye Boland is a lecturer in law at the University of Liverpool. She lectures on criminal law and criminal evidence. She was awarded a PhD by the University of Leeds in 1996. She has written extensively on mental condition defences and Irish mental health law. She is the author of *Anglo-American Insanity Defence Reform: The war between law and medicine* (Ashgate, 1999).

Kirsty Keywood LL.B, LL.M is a lecturer in the School of Law, University of Manchester. She is also a member of the Centre for Social Ethics and Policy at the University of Manchester and a fellow of the Institute of Medicine, Law and Bioethics. Her research and teaching interests lie in the field of health care law, human rights and feminist theory. She has undertaken research for the Joseph Rowntree Foundation on the practice of health care decision-making by, with and for adults with learning disabilities and has contributed to a number of Department of Health publications on the health needs of people with learning disabilities. She has published numerous articles on health care law.

Dr Judith Laing is a lecturer in law at Cardiff University. Her areas of expertise are medical law, mental health law and criminal law and justice, and she has published numerous articles in leading journals on these topics. She was awarded her PhD by the University of Leeds in 1996 and her thesis was published by OUP in 1999 entitled *Care or Custody? Mentally Disordered Offenders in the Criminal Justice System*. She has recently co-edited a book entitled *Criminal Justice, Mental Health and the Politics of Risk* (Cavendish, 2001). She is Assistant Editor of the *Medical Law Review* and Recent Cases Editor of the *Journal of Social Welfare and Family Law*.

Dr Melanie Latham is a senior lecturer at Manchester Metropolitan University Law School. Her specialisms lie in the area of medical law and comparative law and politics. She has published numerous articles on women's health care law, particularly on the subject of women's reproductive rights. She is the author of *Regulating Reproduction: a century of conflict in Britain and France* (Manchester University Press, 2002).

Ellie Lee is based in the Department of Sociology and Social Policy at the University of Southampton. She is currently a research fellow working on a Joseph Rowntree Foundation study investigating differences in rates of abortion in England, Wales and Scotland among women under the age of eighteen. Previously she taught sociology at Southampton and Kent Universities. She is the editor of *Abortion Law and Politics* (Palgrave), a co-editor of *Real Bodies* (Palgrave, 2002) and the co-ordinator of Pro-Choice Forum (www.prochoiceforum.org.uk). She is currently working on a book comparing the abortion debate in the USA and Britain.

Anne Morris is a founder member of the Feminist Legal Research Unit and a senior lecturer in law in the Law School at the University of Liverpool. She lectures on medical law, employment law and law and the sexes. She has written on gender issues in both medical law and employment law. She is co-author, with Susan Nott, of *All My Worldly Goods: A feminist perspective on the legal regulation of wealth* (Ashgate, 1995).

Susan Nott LL.B, BCL is a senior lecturer in law at Liverpool Law School, Liverpool University. She is also a founder member of Liverpool University's Feminist Legal Research Unit. She lectures on public law, private international law and law and the sexes. She has written extensively on the strategies used to promote gender equality, particularly gender mainstreaming, as well as on the law relating to working women. She is the co-author, with Anne Morris, of *All My Worldly Goods: A feminist perspective on the legal regulation of wealth* (Ashgate, 1995) and edited, with Fiona Beveridge and Kylie Stephen, *Making Women Count* (Ashgate, 2000). She has also been the recipient, together with fellow members of the Feminist Legal Research Unit, of a number of research grants to investigate the workings of gender mainstreaming.

Dr Kylie Stephen was, until 1999, a researcher based at Liverpool University's Feminist Legal Research Unit. Before that she worked as senior research assistant at the University of Queensland and as a part-time lecturer at the University of Kent. She holds a political science degree and gained a doctorate in feminist theory and political science from the University of Queensland (Australia). Her research interests are in the fields of feminist theory, theories of citizenship, reproductive technologies and gender mainstreaming. She is the co-editor, with Susan Nott and Fiona Beveridge, of *Making Women Count* (Ashgate, 2000). She is currently working for the UK government's Women's Unit.

Preface

The collection of essays that appear in this book are the product of many people's efforts over a rather longer time frame than was originally envisaged. Anyone with interests in the area of health care law and ethics will appreciate that it is a fast moving and ever-changing field which pays little attention to editors' deadlines. Particular sympathies must be extended to Faye Boland and Judy Laing who saw their chapter affected by proposals for wholesale changes in the provision of mental health care. We believe that each of the essays has a valuable contribution to make to the exploration of the impact that gender has within medicine and health care. It was a deliberate policy to include topics which are not immediately seen as 'women's issues' since we wish to challenge the idea that women are affected by medical decisions only in those areas of their lives which are, stereotypically, seen as their primary concern or function, namely reproduction and its consequences. On the other hand, it would be artificial in the extreme to refuse to acknowledge that it is women's biological/reproductive capacity which has shaped the attitude of medical men (*sic*) and the provision of medical care.

Hence several of the essays set out to examine the influence of gender in those areas where women are traditionally most likely to meet the medical profession. Kylie Stephen thus looks at the access HIV+ women have to fertility treatment, and the 'reasons' for denying them such treatment, while Melanie Latham continues the theme of the regulation of assisted conception by focusing on the status afforded to the embryo. Anne Morris then examines some of the underlying factors at play in the assessment of the competence of pregnant women and the supposed conflict between woman and foetus. Kirsty Keywood takes as her theme sterilization – most often looked at in the context of the sterilization of women with learning disabilities – but here set in the context of the medico-legal discourse, with particular reference to the impact of the first male sterilization case faced by the courts. The idea of coercion and control is also reflected in the Boland and Laing chapter on the treatment of women within the mental health systems of Ireland and England and Wales. Susan Nott and Anne Morris in their introductory chapter draw together the various themes by assessing the contribution of feminist theory to improving health care for women and some of these issues are further developed in Susan Nott's chapter on the World Health Organization.

Introduction

Well Women takes as its central proposition the notion that the provision of health care is gendered. The essays that make up the collection argue that gender is a crucial factor in all aspects of health care, and the very diversity of the topics considered in *Well Women* is a testimony to how pervasive a factor gender is. Not only does gender influence the treatment that women receive from the medical profession, but it also affects the role they play as health care providers.

Some of the topics that are dealt with in *Well Women* are more familiar than others. On the one hand, it would be artificial in the extreme to refuse to acknowledge that it is women's biological/reproductive capacity which has shaped the attitude of medical men (*sic*) and the provision of medical care. Several of the essays, therefore, examine the influence of gender in those areas in which women are traditionally most likely to meet the medical profession. On the other hand, *Well Women* also analyses topics such as women's treatment by the mental health system and the contribution of the World Health Organization to improving women's access to health care. It was a deliberate policy to include subjects which are not automatically perceived as 'women's issues' since the object is to challenge the idea that women are affected by medical decisions only in those areas of their lives which are, stereotypically, seen as their primary concern or function – namely, reproduction and its consequences. Finally, while some of the contributions in *Well Women* focus exclusively on the provision of health care within the United Kingdom, their message is neither narrow nor nationalistic. Indeed, these essays call attention to the importance of listening to women and their experiences of the health care system whether they are providers or recipients of health care. The differences which these essays highlight between women's and men's experiences, even though they occur within a particular national context, illustrate the inequalities and stereotypes that lurk behind the apparent gender neutrality of the laws, agencies and policies which govern health care provision. Whilst the particulars of health care vary from country to country, the impact of gender is a universal theme.

It is sometimes said to be a failing of books such as *Well Women* that, whilst each individual contribution is of interest in its own right, they are fragmented and do not offer their readers a comprehensive narrative. The editors of this book have addressed this potential criticism by using the notion of gender as the organizing theme of the collection. The opening essay is devoted to an exploration of this key concept and its utility as a mechanism for feminist analysis. What emerges from that exercise is an account of the strengths and weaknesses of gender as a means of exposing discrimination against women. One of the principal criticisms of gender is that it carries the risk of essentializing women – in other words, assuming that all women are affected by gender in the same fashion and that there is a single solution to gender bias. For this reason, some feminist commentators question the use of gender as a meaningful tool for analysis. Whilst the contributors to *Well Women* are familiar with these arguments, it is their belief that gender, for all its essentializing tendencies, does expose the injustices, unfairness and inequality in the provision of health care that masquerade as gender-neutral behaviour. Moreover, the fact that some women, by virtue of their colour or their educational background, will experience these disadvantages differently or, in some circumstances, not at all does not seem to justify abandoning gender as a mechanism for analysis. Rather, it presents a challenge. More particularly, it means that, in attempting to devise solutions to gender bias, such insights have to be part of the answer.

The search for solutions is a secondary theme of the essays in *Well Women*. All too often, books devoted to the analysis of gender bias, in whatever context, paint a picture of women as victims suffering at the hands of male legislators or a male-dominated medical profession. Clearly, the effect of gender is to institutionalize unhelpful stereotypes of women in such a way that aspects of society, such as the provision of health care, may work to women's disadvantage. This does not mean, however, that change is impossible. There are numerous ways of tackling gender inequality, some of which are more successful than others. The contributors to *Well Women* take seriously the notion that it is central to the feminist project to secure change. Their essays, therefore, consider what strategies to improve the situation of women are available and their likely chances of success.

A third theme identified in the book is the international dimension of women's access to health care, which displays itself in a number of ways. First, many of the effects of gender experienced by women in the United Kingdom are also experienced by women in other jurisdictions. Comparisons of how these problems arc tackled elsewhere can draw attention to possible solutions that might be employed in the United Kingdom – subject, of course, to the rider that transplanting a means of addressing gender inequality from one jurisdiction to another may not succeed unless the particular 'legal transplant' is adapted to its new situation. Yet, as long as this is borne in mind, there is much to gain from learning how a particular issue is dealt with elsewhere. Second, the provision of medical treatment is itself an international undertaking. Drugs developed in one country will be tested and marketed worldwide. Members of the medical profession may seek employment abroad either by choice or from necessity. Indeed, the existence of the Internet may have increased the internationalization of health care by allowing individuals in whatever country they are situated to seek information regarding disease, its treatment and any potential side effects. Finally, international organizations, such as the World Health Organization, have set international standards for the provision of health care whilst other international bodies have established the right to health as an international human right. These international aspects of health care can both benefit and disadvantage women. On the one hand, international organizations can apply pressure to states to eliminate gender inequality from their health care services. On the other hand, international drug companies or employment agencies recruiting health care staff from abroad can exploit and discriminate against women and perpetuate existing stereotypes.

'Gender' is neither a perfect tool of analysis, nor a perfect solution to a problem, but we hope that these essays, in their examination of the role it plays, will shed light, stimulate debate and – maybe – provoke change for the better.

Chapter 1

All in the Mind: Feminism and Health Care

Susan M. Nott and Anne Morris

One of the most fertile areas for feminist research has been women's health and their treatment by the medical profession. Issues of particular importance to women such as abortion, pregnancy, contraception, assisted reproduction and sterilization have rightly been a focus of feminist analysis.[1] More generally, feminist scholarship has exposed the assumptions regarding women and their health which have permeated the medical profession and coloured that profession's attitudes towards women, their access to health care and subsequent treatment.[2] What has been revealed is the presence of deep-rooted prejudice against women whether they are the recipients or providers of health care. This situation has been further complicated by the long-standing alliance maintained between the legal and the medical profession. While the medical profession may turn to the law in order to resolve 'hard cases' or to establish an appropriate framework within which medical treatment or intervention is to take place, lawyers, for their part, have deferred to the medical profession by taking refuge in the shibboleth of 'clinical judgment'.[3] Feminist scholarship has demonstrated, however, that the content and application of the law is prejudicial to, and prejudiced against, women.[4] Hence the powerful partnership between law and medicine produces a health care system which is particularly resistant to women's needs, views and opinions.

The studies featured in *Well Women* reveal the extent to which women are discriminated against in particular health care contexts. In this essay, however, the focus is on the contribution that feminism and feminist theory can make towards reversing this situation. There is a considerable literature devoted to feminist theory and feminist discourse regarding women's bodies.[5] From that literature emerge various explanations for women's subordination. The question posed in this chapter, however, is what practical impact has such theorizing had in altering the treatment women receive and how they are perceived? By addressing this issue, the assumption is made that one of the purposes of feminist analysis is to bring about substantive change. Arguably, feminist theory has no need to justify its existence by pointing to some change for the better for which it is responsible. Yet, from its inception, feminism has sought to question tradition and to challenge accepted ways of thinking. The task of feminism is seen as threefold: '... dedicated first, to describing women's subordination – exploring its nature and extent; dedicated second, to asking both *how* – through what mechanisms, and *why* – for what complex and interwoven reasons – women continue to occupy that position; and dedicated third to change'.[6] Thus the notion of transformation and reconstruction is at the heart of feminism since, whatever disagreements exist among feminists, the fact of women's long-standing subordination, oppression and disadvantage is a constant. Since that is the case, it seems perfectly legitimate to consider what are feminism's practical achievements in a particular context – namely, securing women better access to, and treatment within, the health care system.

It is not possible, in a single chapter, to discuss the entire range of feminist theory. The list ranges from liberal feminism via cultural, difference and radical feminism to postmodernism.[7] Within these various schools of thought emphasis is placed on different concepts, such as gender, and different techniques, such as deconstructionism. Some feminist theories are contradictory. In the context of feminist legal theory, for example, radical feminists such as Catherine MacKinnon have urged women to construct a feminist theory of law and state (a feminist jurisprudence).[8] On the other hand, postmodern feminists reject such grand theorizing and highlight the significance of the particular.[9] Postmodernism, with its emphasis on discourse, stresses that words, such as 'equality' for example, rather than carrying some overarching and constant meaning, depend on their context for coherence and value. Thus:

> … in place of certainty, there is uncertainty, contingency, fragmentation, diversity. In place of the "big story", there are only "little stories". Not only is the meta-narrative denied, but the uncertainty produced is one which is accepted: there is *no meaning, no truth*, beyond the fragmented, the incoherent.[10]

As a consequence, the faith placed in ideas such as equality to provide a practical solution to women's subordinate status is undermined.

In order, therefore, to assess the contribution (if any) that feminist theory has made to improving women's access to health care, this chapter will take as its focus the notion of gender. The title of this book, *Well Women: The gendered nature of health care provision*, is based on the proposition that gender is a key factor in understanding women's access to health care. Moreover, gender is a cross-cutting concept which is used by feminists in general, though not necessarily in an identical fashion, rather than by one particular 'school' of feminism. Barnett has observed that 'gender has been, and remains, an organising focus for feminist analysis. The gender question is thus central to all schools of feminist thought, whether liberal, Marxist-socialist, cultural, radical or postmodern.'[11] The question is whether the insights provided by the idea of gender have produced changes for the good and have improved the situation of women, particularly in relation to health care.

Exploring Gender: The Theoretical Dimension

The term 'gender' is a familiar one. Among feminists it is used to emphasize the fact that 'however "natural" and common sex differences may seem, the differences between women and men are not biologically compelled; they are, rather, "socially constructed"'.[12] This process of social construction can take a variety of forms. The images of men and women in the media, the manner in which children are socialized and educated and legal rules have all played a part in forming and informing gender stereotypes. Yet the process does not end with the creation of gender stereotypes – for example, identifying men with qualities such as logical thought and women with emotionalism. Feminists have drawn attention to gender's role in creating the division between the public and the private sphere.[13] Men were regarded because of their 'male qualities' as the appropriate occupants of the public sphere of government and the market. Women, however, were perceived as suited to performing those caring tasks associated with the private sphere of home and family. A major consequence of this division between men and women was that men's role in society attracted greater respect and reward. Even when women were eventually allowed access to the public sphere, it was on men's terms and with the expectation that women would continue to perform their caring role. In this respect, therefore, gender is seen as offering an explanation, though not necessarily the whole explanation, for the imbalance of power between the sexes.

Once the process of constructing distinct and different social roles for men and women is under way it permeates all aspects of society. The phenomenon of gender feeds upon itself. In a legal context, for example, the content of laws may be shaped by gender presumptions (see, for example, Latham's essay, Chapter 5 of this volume). The manner in which the judiciary chooses to interpret the law may also be gendered (see, for example, Chapters 2 and 6 by Keywood and Morris respectively). Those gender stereotypes created by the law may then, in their turn, influence both how the medical profession views women patients and the treatment they receive.

The idea of gender 'stereotypes' points to the danger inherent in the concept, as in other heuristic devices – namely, that gender may be described as monolithic in its application so that all women may be regarded as affected in equal and identical ways. Apart from the fact this ignores the differences between women, it makes it possible for gender to be used in subtle ways. In particular it can operate in such a way as to reward or penalize female behaviour that is seen as commendable or reprehensible when judged from a male perspective.[14] For example, whilst women are, in general, associated with the task of caring for children, those who are perceived as 'good mothers' will be preferentially treated by the legal and medical professions. As a consequence, IVF treatment may be available to the woman who is in a stable, heterosexual relationship but not to the single woman, the lesbian couple or to a woman involved in prostitution.[15] As Michael Thomson remarks in relation to section 13(5) of the Human Fertilisation and Embryology Act 1990[16] which defines acceptable recipients for assisted conception:

> This section, which provides the clearest statement of appropriate recipient status, proves interesting in a number of ways. At its most immediate it is clear that the provision privileges a particular model of female sexuality – the stable, secure heterosexual. Yet perhaps more interesting is the explicit moral role that has been sanctioned for clinicians.[17]

This moral role permits the medical profession to construct its own paradigm of motherhood within the parameters established by the law. Whilst views on motherhood may vary from doctor to doctor, some feminist commentators believe that such views privilege certain women as opposed to others.[18]

Thus, while it is useful in uncovering inequality between the sexes, the concept of gender is not above criticism. In so far as its potentially monolithic quality results in women being treated as an homogeneous group, it can obscure the fact that other forces are at work creating and maintaining inequality. 'Gender is only part of what constrains women's experience, and it is often less critical than other factors, such as race, class and sexual orientation.'[19] A woman's access to health care may be adversely affected by how women in general are perceived (that is, by gender), but that adverse effect may be much reduced in the case of a well-educated, professional woman as compared with her working-class counterpart. Nor can it be assumed that the experiences of women from ethnic minorities are identical to those of other women. The context in which gender inequality occurs thus influences the precise extent and nature of its impact.

Another problem arising from an overemphasis on gender is the discounting of bodily differences between men and women. There has been a not unreasonable fear that a focus on biological differences would serve as an excuse to treat women differently:

> It is argued that notions of bodily difference are all too easily drawn upon to naturalize differences based on gender, 'race' or sexuality. As explanation, bodily difference legitimates social inequality as unavoidable, 'normal' or immutable. Differences among individuals are obscured, while one difference is exaggerated as the only one which counts. A focus on bodily-based difference goes hand in hand with essentialism and homogenization.[20]

Yet despite the dangers associated with identifying bodily differences, they can provide additional insights into the power that men exercise over women. In the context of health care, such insights can be particularly significant. On the one hand, it becomes possible to concentrate on women's own experiences and feelings regarding their bodies and how those feelings are often ignored or reinterpreted by men. Bodily processes such as pregnancy or the menopause, for example, have become medicalized conditions whose management has passed from women to the medical profession. On the other hand, it is also possible to draw attention to the fact that women's bodies are subjected to violence and exploitation by men. Not only that, but 'male' perceptions of 'female' beauty may persuade women to resort to cosmetic surgery, not least to undergo breast augmentation or reduction or to diet constantly. All of this raises a variety of issues, including the effects on women's health and well-being.

The criticisms directed towards the notion of gender are based on its essentializing of women and on the accusation that gender's domination of feminist theory has caused other sources of inequality to be neglected. Some critics of gender, however – particularly those who adopt a postmodern approach – take the argument regarding the reductionism associated with gender a stage further. They believe that the manner in which gender essentializes women makes the use of the concept dangerous.

'Postmodern feminists perceive the employment of group identities in mobilizing political solidarity as a dangerous exercise because, they argue, rather than bringing to light and celebrating some underlying authentic (unitary/fixed) self repressed by power, it involves the reiteration of identities which are themselves produced by the operations of power and are therefore not self-evidently emancipatory.'[21] Some, though not necessarily all, postmodern feminists consequently urge that the theories that have been constructed regarding gender be abandoned. Instead, attention should be focused on the particularities of women's lives.

The argument that the failings inherent in 'gender' are such that it should be abandoned as a means of exposing inequality between the sexes is clearly very extreme. It does, however, force those who are minded to use the concept to address the possibility that, rather than being a positive force for change, this central notion of feminist theory may do more harm than good. The analysis that follows explores the insights that gender has given into the character of the health care received by women. This serves as a preliminary step in assessing what practical impact such revelations have produced. If the conclusion is that very little has changed, then one possible explanation may be the shortcomings, already alluded to, that some feminists regard as inherent in the notion of gender.

Health Care and Gender

The insights offered by gender into the treatment of women at the hands of the medical profession are enhanced by an historical perspective. The manner in which women's biological differences from men have been socially constructed so as to marginalize, regulate and oppress women has a considerable history which must be appreciated to some extent in order to comprehend women's current situation. The Hippocratic Oath may suggest that contemporary Western doctors are part of a medical tradition stretching back in an unbroken line to the Ancient Greeks,[22] but the kind of modern, 'scientific' medicine with which we are now familiar is largely derived from the radical rethinking which occurred during the Enlightenment of the seventeenth and eighteenth centuries and which stressed an approach based on empiricism and rationalism. Nevertheless, some things remained constant. The supremacy of science did not alter the view taken of women – namely, that they were intrinsically associated with nature rather than with reason. Women were constructed as emotional, caring and dependent, while men were rational, responsible and independent. Women were perceived as deviating from the *male norm*. Women's biology, and in particular their reproductive capacities, were regarded as defining their destiny. Their role was to bear and care for children. Women who attempted to mimic men by refusing, consciously or not, to conform to the female stereotype (wife, mother, carer) were regarded as deviant and categorized as ill.

Quite how long this had been the situation can be judged from the history of hysteria. The word 'hysteria' is derived from the Greek word for uterus and the condition was considered to be physiologically based on a malfunctioning (or wandering) womb. Needless to say, this made it a condition peculiar to women. An early description of hysteria has been found in Egyptian sources dating from 1900 BC.[23] In both Egyptian and Greek traditions, hysteria was associated with a womb which had not fulfilled its natural function, which is to say it was suffered by women who had not been pregnant. Even when greater familiarity with human anatomy was achieved, undermining the earlier theories, including that of the wandering womb, it was still argued that hysteria – still perceived as exclusively female – was derived from what were seen as sexual abnormalities, but which were, more accurately, a failure to conform or comply with the prevailing expectation that women's main, if not only, role was to serve as bearers and rearers of children. As Turner notes:

> ... the very notion of hysteria carries with it a certain moral, evaluative and judgmental impact about women as a whole and about their role in society. Women were culturally considered to be the weaker sex, given to constitutionally structured fits of weeping, fainting and uncontrollable laughter. This tendency ... was particularly common among young single women, old widows, divorced women or women who abstained from marriage and normal sexuality in order to pursue careers in education or other professions.[24]

Hence gender, meaning those characteristics which are socially constructed rather than biologically determined, has an overwhelming importance in determining female (and male) experience of the world:

> Gender is inescapable. It is probably the most important determinant of any individual's life experience. For the two sexes exist in different social worlds with widely divergent pressures, rewards and expectations. In many areas of life there is no truly human experience. There is only female experience and male experience.[25]

Female experience was – for better or worse – inextricably linked to women's biology and what were perceived to be the consequences of their reproductive capacities. When, for example, women were excluded from the universities (and thus from the learned professions) the reasons advanced by their opponents were that their natural differences made them less capable of intellectual endeavour or that education would irreparably damage their health. Thus in *Jex Blake* v. *Senatus of Edinburgh University* (1873) the former attitude was adopted by Lord Neaves:[26]

> It is a belief, widely entertained, that there is a great difference in the mental constitution of the two sexes, just as there is in their physical conformation. The powers and susceptibilities of women are as noble as those of men; but they are thought to be different, and, in particular, it is considered that they have not the same power of intense labour as men are endowed with. If this be so, it must form a serious objection to uniting them under the same course of academical study. I confess that, to some extent, I share this view, and should regret to see our young females subjected to the severe and incessant work which my own observation and experience have taught me to consider as indispensable to any high attainment in learning.

His Lordship was not alone in these views. It was Darwin's view that: 'The chief distinction in the intellectual powers of the two sexes is shown by man's attaining to a higher eminence in whatever he takes up, than can women ...'[27]

The idea that women were also physically weaker than men was used to discourage their entry into higher education on the grounds that they would be unable to meet the demands it placed upon them and would thus not be strong and healthy enough to fulfil their role as childbearers. The same argument was used to exclude women from the workplace – their primary responsibility was to produce the next generation and they should not be exposed to factors which would sap their strength or compromise their capacity to bear healthy children.

Women were, therefore, trapped by their biology. Their very difference from men was used to categorize them as weak, intellectually less capable and – importantly in this context – prey to disorders which flowed, metaphorically and literally, from their sex. As a consequence, women were perceived as inferior to men. From this it is easy to appreciate the split that developed between the public sphere of men and the private (domestic) sphere of women. As Ussher comments:

> Biological difference and nature, specifically the capacity of women to reproduce, has been used for centuries in almost all societies to justify the subjugation of women. Women have been conceptualized as being ruled by their bodies, bodies which are seen as unstable and inherently weak.[28]

An understanding of gender, therefore, provides an insight into how inequality between the sexes became embedded in every aspect of society, including medicine and the medical profession. Indeed, medicine seems to have played a central role in producing those social and cultural constructs of women, women's bodies and women's behaviour that created that inequality. The problem is, however, that once these gender stereotypes have been created and institutionalized within society, a tremendous effort of will is required to remove them. Understanding the pervasiveness of gender and its capacity to marginalize women is one thing but attempting to resolve the problem is far more difficult. In the context of medicine, gender still continues to influence the standard of treatment women receive and the control they are allowed to exercise over their bodies. Moreover, the medical profession continues to be dominated by men and informed by male values. It is to the current relationship between women and medicine that this analysis now turns in order to explore to what degree gender and gender stereotypes still permeate the system.

The Medical Profession

The story of how medical practitioners transformed themselves and their business into one of the learned professions is itself a story of the marginalization of women. Even though women were (and still are) regarded as the natural carers within society, the increasing professionalism of medical practitioners demoted not only their 'natural' spheres of child care but also midwifery. In relation to the former, for example, women were to be instructed in the best ways of rearing children since they were prey to irrational and unscientific influences.[29] It was not acceptable that daughters should learn from their mothers and grandmothers how to care for infants and children; rather, they needed guidance from men of science. In midwifery, more than in any other area of practice, women were ousted from their position as the first resort of those in need. Oakley points out that female midwifery fitted easily into the overall caring function of women but that:

... onto this traditional fabric was then grafted the new imprint of the emergent medical profession. This laid its claim to fame not on caring ... but on technical expertise: science as opposed to love; forceps and the lying-in hospital as opposed to the purely domestic art of 'catching' babies at home.[30]

In order to justify their usurpation of a traditional female role, the 'scientific' male obstetricians discredited the midwife by describing her as ignorant and superstitious. In doing so, the obstetrician chose to define pregnancy and childbirth as a medical 'problem'. If it were not 'normal' then it required medical (rather than amateur) intervention. Oakley argues that:

> ... the rise of obstetrics and its eventual dominance over midwifery was achieved in part by the argument that those who care for childbearing women can only do so properly by viewing the female body as a machine to be supervised, controlled and interfered with by technical means.[31]

Childbirth had had to be 'mastered'.

> The male role in obstetrics paralleled the male cultural role; socialized to be masters of their own fates, families and environments, the same kind of impulse possessed the men who first took over childbirth from the traditional carers of women, midwives.[32]

Of course, the days are long gone when women were not allowed to study medicine at universities.[33] Nevertheless, despite increasing numbers now entering medical schools, women are scarce in certain specialities and at the upper levels of many. This discrepancy cannot be wholly explained by the historically lower number of women entering medical school.[34] In 1999, for example, only 5 per cent of consultant surgeons in the UK were women. The president of the Royal College of Surgeons suggested that specialities such as cardiothoracic surgery did not appeal to women because they require inflexible and long working hours. To combat this, it is usual to propose remedies which include increasing flexibility, by allowing job-sharing and part-time work. Whilst such moves should not be rejected (by women or men) it must be realized that 'the very structure of medical training creates a mystique of stamina, fierce dedication, and stoic endurance, so that deviation from the norm, however licensed, spells weakness rather than leadership potential'.[35] In other words, taking advantage of measures that are meant to make the job easier to combine with family life can be used as reasons for not promoting someone who is perceived not to be sufficiently committed.

It may be asked whether focusing on the absence or underrepresentation of women at all levels of the medical profession and in all specialities is in any way worthwhile or meaningful. Medicine, as with other professions, is generally acknowledged to be hierarchical. This hierarchy is not only dominated by men, it is also informed by male values, as is apparent from the chapters which follow. The way in which women are perceived as 'patients' is reflected in the profession's perception of its practitioners. Nowhere is this so apparent as in the sometimes uneasy relationship between doctors and nurses. For many, the mental images conjured up by 'doctor' and 'nurse' remain resolutely gendered. Doctors are men of science while nurses fulfil the traditional female role and 'care' for the patient and attend to his or her basic needs. Lest this be thought to be overstated or outdated, consider that in April 2000 the editor of the *British Medical Journal* wrote: 'Doctors and nurses are divided by gender, background, philosophy, training, regulation, money, status, power, and – dare I say it ? – intelligence (doctors are usually top of the class, nurses in the middle).'[36] Elsewhere the writer comments on the fact that the Secretary of State for Health had talked about liberating nurses and had told them that 'for too long you have had responsibility without power'. The writer interjects that the comment would have created 'in the minds of his mostly university educated audience an unfortunate resonance with prostitutes, who of course have the opposite combination'. A response[37] to this editorial suggests that perhaps the politician recognized that nurses (female) need to be liberated from the white, male, middle-class culture that has so dominated health care for the past century or more. She also points out that prostitutes have no power – that lies in the hands of 'the men who use them'. Perhaps it is not surprising that women are still underrepresented in the higher reaches of the medical profession, but it is depressing to learn that, apparently, men are discouraged from entering nursing by the 'stigma' of the job.[38]

The Medicalization of Women's Lives

Women's generally lowly status within the medical profession may have made them particularly prone to the effects of the creeping medicalization which has been a feature of medicine in the latter half of the twentieth century. Everything which touches upon reproduction seems to been taken over by the medical professions. Menstruation, contraception, fertility treatments, pregnancy, childbirth, postnatal depression and the menopause are all firmly within the province of the 'medical men'. It cannot be coincidence that these are (with the exception of contraception and fertility treatments)[39] exclusively female conditions. Indeed, everything which defines a woman's sex seems to be the site of a potential medical 'problem'.

Most women do not, initially, regard the natural functioning of their bodies as an illness. Women who become pregnant do not immediately think of themselves as patients. Neither menstruation nor the menopause is, by definition, an illness. And yet, in all these cases, women may well find themselves the recipients of medical treatment. This is all but inevitable in the case of pregnancy and increasingly so in the case of a menopausal woman. Once science has decided that menopausal symptoms experienced by some women to excess, may be treated, every menopausal woman is a potential patient. The message is that doctors can ameliorate symptoms (as they can with other illnesses). The same is true of menstruation which incapacitates some women and is coped with satisfactorily by the majority. Nevertheless, menstruation is categorized as a problem – a complaint. It should be noted that there are, admittedly, far more complex issues at play here, in relation to both menstruation – associated in many cultures with a variety of taboos – and the menopause, which may be seen as the end of a woman's 'useful' life. But, of course, these complexities are themselves indicators of the gendered nature of our societies. In short, women are problematic and need to be constrained in order to ensure the continuation of a male-dominated order.

The increasing medicalization of women's lives may well explain why, on the whole, women appear to be sicker than men: 'Women and men inhabit the same world but the world of women is different from that of men. Women live longer but suffer from more health problems during their lifetime....'[40] It seems generally accepted that women see themselves as ill more often than do men.[41] This raises issues with which medical sociologists, amongst others, have engaged. It is important to realize that 'health' is an elusive concept. Certainly, it is arguable that health is, for many people, more than just the absence of illness. To be in 'good health' implies, in that case, that there are emotional and psychological aspects to health (quite apart from any mental illness) which contribute to that state. In other words, there is more to health than a simply medical model:

> Certain textbooks in medical sociology now propose a neat and economic classification of human disorders into three distinct categories, namely, sickness, illness and disease. Whereas disease is a concept which describes malfunctions of a physiological and biological character, illness refers to the individual's subjective awareness of the disorder, and sickness designates appropriate social roles....[42]

Whilst this categorization is open to criticism[43] it highlights the fact that 'health' and 'illness' are conditions in which the perceptions, attitudes and stereotypical expectations of both patient and doctor have a role to play. A single mother with three children under school age, a low income and unsatisfactory housing visits her GP because she is constantly tired, has frequent headaches, and generally feels she 'can't cope'. The GP diagnoses her as suffering from depression and prescribes medication. Given the surrounding circumstances, her symptoms are understandable. It might be argued that the remedy is improved, affordable childcare, better housing and financial security. Because that is something the GP cannot provide, it is possible (even understandable) for the doctor to ignore the *causes* of her 'illness'. The woman entered the surgery as a victim of her circumstances and leaves it as someone who is 'ill'.

What this analysis of women's treatment at the hands of the medical profession reveals is the continuing use of medicine as a means of regulating and restraining women.[44] Hence medicine contributes to the power imbalance between the sexes. Women's biology and their reproductive capacity is seen as a source of weakness and inferiority which still affects their access to the workplace and their ability to remain in employment. As a matter of biology, only women menstruate and become pregnant. These biological facts have, however, been translated into social and cultural norms relating to women's behaviour and the role they should play in society. Moreover, the disadvantages that women suffer as a result of gender inequality, such as poverty or a lack of education, are translated into symptoms of ill-health.

It cannot be ignored, of course, that for many women their biology, in the sense of their reproductive capacity, does have a direct bearing on their health. Although maternal mortality generally is falling, it remains high in the developing world. Over half a million women die each year from causes related to pregnancy and childbirth, and 98 per cent of these are in developing countries. For each woman who dies, up to 100 survive but suffer from serious disease, disability or physical damage caused by pregnancy-related complications.[45] Many of the complications arise at childbirth, and many of these can be avoided or treated if there is a professional (nurse, midwife or doctor) in attendance, yet only 58 per cent of deliveries in the developing world occur with such assistance.[46] Conversely, in the developed world, pregnancy is less a risk to a woman's health than it is to her independence and autonomy. The medicalization of pregnancy and childbirth in wealthy countries has left women feeling that they must battle to choose how, and where, to give birth. If proof were needed of women's diversity and different needs, it can be found in the comparison of women who reject high-tech intervention and demand a home birth, with those who, experiencing repeated pregnancies and lack of medical care, may long for hospital care for themselves and their infants.

Gender as a Bar to Adequate Health Care

Gender influences both the role that women play in the medical profession and how that profession perceives women. Importantly, however, it also influences directly and indirectly the quality of health care (if any) that women receive. Gender determines how men and women experience life: more specifically, it influences their education, employment prospects and earning capacity, or lack of all of these.

Education has a central role to play in promoting the health of women and their families. Not only does education contribute to knowledge surrounding health issues – including family planning – but it tends also to increase women's confidence and autonomy.[47] Research shows that educating girls and women has positive effects on the health of the family, and especially on infant mortality. Craft comments that 'after other variables such as access to immunisations and to a supply of potable water have been controlled for, education emerges as the strongest influence on infant mortality'.[48] The global predominance of women amongst the illiterate and uneducated means that they and their children are disadvantaged.

All over the world – including the United Kingdom – women predominate amongst the poorest sections of society.[49] It has also been shown that, within poor families, women are frequently the poorest.[50] The fact that women are more likely to be classed as poor than men undoubtedly has adverse effects on their health. Their diet may be poor; the quality of the housing that they live in may be below average; and they may not heed public health warnings relating to smoking or alcohol consumption. Poverty can also affect their access to health care when they need it, particularly if a charge is made for such care. The World Health Organization, for example, has drawn attention to the fact that 'even in rich countries like the United States, poor women find themselves without access to health care more often than men from the same social group'.[51] Where health care is free, those areas of a city where the poor live may be less well provided for than more affluent areas. For example, GPs may be reluctant to practise in deprived inner city areas. In the countryside the cost of travelling to the doctor's surgery, always assuming that the individual in question has access to a car or public transport, may discourage those on low incomes or social security benefits from seeking medical help. The stress that individuals experience as a consequence of poverty can also produce adverse consequences for mental well-being. Once again, women are more likely to be affected in this way than are men.[52] 'Women in lower income groups suffer more stressful events more often: problems with debt, eviction, unemployment, illness, and having to deal with state agencies are more common occurrences amongst poor households, as a result of low income.'[53]

Gender inequality and women's inferior standing in society also has repercussions for the personal relationships between men and women. According to the World Health Organization, intentional and non-intentional injuries 'are among the major causes of morbidity and mortality for both men and women at all ages and across all societies'.[54] Such injuries are more commonly associated with men and 'masculine behaviour' such as alcohol consumption and driving at speed. However, for women, male violence and abuse, on the part of a partner or some other male family member, has very grave consequences for women's health including physical injury, death or psychological damage:

> Physical and mental abuse can also have deleterious effects on the well-being and productivity of women. Violence against women is widespread in all cultures and cuts across all age and income groups. Its consequences include unwanted pregnancy, infections with STDs, miscarriage, partial or permanent disability, and psychological problems such as depression and low self-esteem.[55]

Indeed, the World Health Organization quotes estimates from the World Bank that rape and domestic violence together account for 5 per cent of the total disease burden for women in developing countries and for 19 per cent in developed countries which is 'comparable to that posed by other risk factors and diseases such as HIV and TB'.[56]

Gender is a prime influence in determining what is appropriate sexual behaviour for men and women. If women are regarded as the subordinate or passive partner in any relationship they may find it difficult to refuse sex, including unprotected sex, with their partner. Moreover, poverty may force some women, and indeed children, into prostitution as a way of earning a living or simply surviving. The power imbalance which sanctions men's sexual domination of women and allows such behaviour to be regarded as 'normal' or a matter of choice by women poses a variety of threats to women's health. These include infection with HIV or the risk of contracting a sexually transmitted disease.

Gender Restrictions on Women's Contribution to Health Care Politics

The fact that women are less valued in society and exert less influence than men reduces their ability to make an input into the content of a state's health care policies and how a state allocates resources to health care. The same holds true of those laws that regulate issues of importance to women, such as the availability of contraception or abortion. In the world as a whole, the representation of men in state legislatures far exceeds that of women:

> In the political arena, women are one of the most underrepresented groups in the world. Women comprise more than 50% of the world's population, but hold a global average of only 12% of the seats in national legislatures.[57]

Indeed, in the developing world, it may not even be possible for women to hold elected office. Either way, this means that women's voices, and hence women's experiences, are, to a greater or lesser degree, missing from the decision-making process. There is some dispute among feminists as to what difference women's presence in politics can and does make.[58] Doubts have also been expressed on whether more women politicians mean a higher profile for women's issues.[59] Part of the explanation for the lack of impact made by women politicians may be the compromises that they are forced to make in order to succeed. As Rhodes notes:

> We cannot expect that women who take the positions now necessary for political success and who gain a stake in current structures will want to promote a transformative vision. Even those who wish to do so will confront powerful countervailing influences of money, seniority and old-boy networks.[60]

Women's underrepresentation in the legislative and executive branches of government is mirrored, in many states, by their relative absence from the judiciary. The extent to which gender influences the 'impartial' judge is, of course, controversial, but it is perhaps less contentious to observe that male judges cannot have the same insights into the most intimate areas of women's lives, including pregnancy.[61]

At an international level, women are also excluded from participating fully in the debates surrounding the creation of international agreements with a bearing on women's rights and women's health. Connors identifies a range of consequences arising from women's exclusion. These include: ignoring the effects of gender on statements of substantive human rights; not defining issues such as violence against women as human rights issues; perceiving human rights as relevant solely to the relationship between the state and its citizens rather than the relationships between individuals and allowing certain practices to be justified on grounds of religion, culture and ethnicity.[62]

Securing Gender Equality in Health Care

A gender analysis of women's access to health care reveals a contradictory state of affairs. On the one hand, women's biology, and in particular their reproductive capacity, is used as a reason for subjecting them to medical care. The ability of women to choose where to give birth, who attends the birth, whether to carry a foetus to term, or whether to resort to assisted reproduction has been restricted or removed. Women's autonomy has been overruled or ignored in favour of other considerations such as the well-being of the foetus or, indeed, the potential foetus. On the other hand, the quality of the medical care which some, though not all, women receive may be inferior because of gender inequality. Women's poverty or their lack of education or their lack of political power deny them the health care that is most appropriate to their needs.

There is, however, one constant factor in the discussion of gender inequality in the delivery of health care: it is a largely negative picture which emerges. Women are represented as victims – or at least as subjects – powerless to address or reverse the gender stereotypes that pervade the medical profession and the health care system. In some respects, gender conceals as much as it reveals. There are undoubtedly women with the education, the resources or indeed the sheer bloody-mindedness to take on the medical profession and win. Yet the very act of theorizing about the effects of gender in the context of health care, and more generally, seems to represent a double-edged sword. Undoubtedly, it draws attention to the discrimination faced by women or the ways in which their needs are misunderstood or overlooked, but it also categorizes *all* women as victims. This is problematic, not only because some women, such as those experiencing financial hardship, are at a much greater disadvantage when compared with their more prosperous sisters, but also because it accepts a categorization which, by definition, disempowers women.

Criticizing the essentializing qualities of gender does not, however, end here. Books and articles which theorize about gender inequality are quick to point out the problem but more reluctant to suggest a solution or a strategy for tackling it. If women are, to a greater or lesser extent, the victims of the medical profession, what should the response be? Clearly, any solution cannot be of a 'one size fits all' character since that, too, essentializes women. The fragmentation of women's experience suggests that a search for a solution to gender inequality is ill-conceived. Attempts by feminism to ensure that women receive the health care that they need, rather than the health care that men believe they need, seems condemned to fail. The situation is further complicated by the fact that, if it were possible to devise a strategy to secure gender equality in health care, some means would have to be found of ensuring that it was observed. The most obvious way of achieving this would be to make any strategy legally binding. Since, however, laws and legal systems are themselves gendered, the search for a feminist solution seems doomed from the outset.

Such a counsel of despair might be taken to imply that, since no solution is perfect, it is preferable to abandon the search. Yet feminism's strength is its belief that it has the power to transform and reconstruct. Its very practicality is the essence of its appeal. Now, however, some commentators accuse feminism of losing direction and of using language and concepts that make it inaccessible to the very constituency it is supposed to support. As Conaghan observes:

> ... we are being swept along by a tide of change, economic, technological, social, environmental, global. Every day we are witness to the lack of control we have over our own lives, unemployment, exploitation/abuse, homelessness, poverty, famine, ecological disaster, war, death. It is easy to believe we can do nothing about these things, to adopt the fashionable stance of the sceptic, to insist that all engagement must be oppositional in order to avoid seduction by the forces one is waged against. It is much harder to acknowledge that we can and must do something and that *what* we do might make some difference to *where* we end up. To deny this possibility is to engage in the worst kind of essentialism; to admit it is to recognize some value in utopias.[63]

Rather than doing nothing, feminism should adopt whatever strategy might best secure equality for women. Equality, however, is itself a problematic concept. To some, it means an absence of discrimination. To others, it means the empowerment of women so that their actual views and needs (rather than a stereotypical representation) are taken into account when decisions are made or policies instituted by government or other powerful agencies, such as the health care profession. Undoubtedly, how the term 'equality' is defined can have an effect on the success or failure of a particular strategy for eliminating inequality. Anti-discrimination legislation, for example, promotes equality between the sexes by outlawing discrimination and requiring men and women to receive equal treatment. In so doing, it is assumed that men's and women's experiences and society's expectations of them are identical, which clearly they are not. The extent to which anti-discrimination legislation can address gender inequality is, therefore, strictly limited.

An alternative strategy for promoting equality is the use of rights. At both national and international level there are legally binding statements of human rights which apply both to men and women. Feminist commentators have pointed out that such rights are often of little use to women,[64] since the content of these rights, and their application to women, can be undermined by the very gender inequality which they might be expected to address. Women may not have access to the resources – for example, the financial resources – needed in order to allow them to vindicate their rights. Moreover, the human rights that are guaranteed under the law may be of limited use to women since they do not deal with the issues that are important to them. In the past, rights have concentrated on civil and political issues, such as the right to vote, rather than on social, economic or cultural issues, such as the right to health. Although the situation has changed, reservations are still voiced on the extent to which human rights and human rights law have been 'feminized' or whether those rights are still 'built on typically male life experiences and in their current form do not respond to the most pressing risks women face'.[65] Even when human rights appear to focus on those issues which are of significance to women there is no guarantee that women's lives will change as a consequence. The right to life, for example, could be interpreted to offer women protection against domestic violence, and yet the courts may interpret this right as one which operates solely in the public sphere and protects men and women from violence at the hands of the state. Moreover, the self-same right to life may be used as a justification for denying women access to abortion facilities.

There are feminists who would argue that, despite the possible pitfalls associated with a rights strategy, human rights can be used to women's advantage. The discourse of rights is very powerful, and to identify certain forms of behaviour as a breach of human rights can be a very potent weapon in securing change. At the same time, this is coupled with the realization that the ability of a rights strategy to transform women's lives may vary from society to society. The acknowledgement that rights could be seen as inconsequential in the face of poverty, starvation and epidemics such as AIDS may have provided the impetus for devising alternative ways of addressing women's needs and eradicating gender inequality.

Within those international organizations concerned with economic development, efforts were made to integrate gender into the policy-making process. This initiative, known as mainstreaming, has been seized upon by women's organizations and featured prominently in the women's conference held at Beijing in 1995. As well as being accepted by international organizations, such as the United Nations, national governments have also committed themselves to this strategy. Mainstreaming undoubtedly has considerable potential to tackle gender inequality, although some feminists have expressed the view that the eagerness with which mainstreaming has been seized upon by governments and international organizations is a sign that, whilst these bodies have adopted the rhetoric of mainstreaming, they are not committed to the procedures which must be put in place if this strategy is to succeed. Putting aside such scepticism, however, there is an aspect to mainstreaming which may answer the criticism that some women's lives are more affected by race or disability than gender. Mainstreaming can be used to address a range of inequalities rather than gender alone, as has been done by the new assemblies in Scotland, Wales and Northern Ireland, for example. Not surprisingly, some feminists warn against using mainstreaming to tackle inequalities, since each example of inequality is seen as having a very specific character. As yet, however, the jury is out on whether such a broad strategy can succeed.

In analysing the provision of health care to men and women, gender is a key factor in determining whether both sexes benefit to the same degree. If they do not, then a suitable strategy (or strategies) has (have) to be selected for eliminating those instances of gender inequality that have been identified. There is also the possibility that, although gender inequality in respect of health care is a universal phenomenon, the best way to eliminate it may vary from culture to culture and that there is no single solution to the problem. The essays which follow seek to identify and to shed light on some of the areas in which gender has a role to play.

Notes

1   See, for example, Bridgeman, J. and Millns, S. (eds) (1995), *Law and Body Politics: Regulating the Female Body*, Aldershot: Dartmouth.

2   For example, Bridgeman, J. (1995), 'They Gag Women, Don't They?', in Bridgeman, J. and Millns, S. (eds), *Law and Body Politics*, op. cit., n.1, p. 23; Foster, P. (1995), *Women and the Health Care Industry: An Unhealthy Relationship?*, Milton Keynes: Open University Press; Lee, C. (1998), *Women's Health: Psychological and Social Perspectives*, London: Sage, ch. 1; Oakley, A. (1993), *Essays on Women, Medicine and Health*, Edinburgh: Edinburgh University Press; Sheldon, S. (1997), *Beyond Control: Medical Power and Abortion*, London: Pluto Press.

3   As illustrated, for example, by the judicial application of the *Bolam* test for medical negligence: *Bolam* v. *Friern Hospital Management Committee* [1957] 2 All ER 118. See, for example, *Sidaway* v. *Board of Governors of the Bethlem Royal Hospital* [1985] AC 871, *per* Lord Scarman: '...the law imposes the duty of care but the standard is a matter for medical judgment.' See also Sheldon, S. (1998), 'Rethinking the *Bolam* Test' in Sheldon, S. and Thomson, M. (eds.) *Feminist Perspectives on Health Care Law*, London: Cavendish; and Keywood, Chapter 2 of this volume.

4   There is a wealth of writing on the gendered nature or maleness of law. Amongst the most well known are: Smart, C. (1989), *Feminism and the Power of Law*, London, Routledge; MacKinnon, C. (1989) *Toward a Feminist Theory of the State*, Cambridge, MA: Harvard University Press; idem (1987), 'Difference and Dominance: On Sex Discrimination', in *Feminism Unmodified: Discourses on Life and Law*, Cambridge, MA: Harvard University Press; West, R. (1988) 'Jurisprudence and Gender', *University of Chicago Law Review*, **55**(1) at p. 58.

5   See, for example, Bordo, S. (1993), *Unbearable Weight: Feminism, Western Culture and the Body*, Berkeley: California University Press; Brook, B. (1999), *Feminist*

Perspectives on the Body, London: Longman; Keywood, K. (2000), 'More than a Woman? Embodiment and Sexual Difference in Medical Law', *Feminist Legal Studies*, **8**, p. 319.

6   Dalton, C. (1987), *Berkeley Women's Law Journal*, **3**, p.1, quoted in Freeman, M. D. A. (1994), *Lloyd's Introduction to Jurisprudence* (6th edn), London: Sweet and Maxwell, p. 1028.

7   For a discussion of the various 'schools' of feminism and of feminism in general see Beasley, C. (1999), *What is Feminism?*, London: Sage.

8   MacKinnon, *Toward a Feminist Theory of the State*, *op. cit.*, n.4.

9   Smart, *Feminism and the Power of Law*, *op. cit.*, n. 4.

10 Barnett, H. (1998), *Introduction to Feminist Jurisprudence*, London: Cavendish, p. 179.

11 Ibid., p. 14.

12 Frug, M. J. (1992), 'A Post-modern Feminist Legal Manifesto (an Unfinished Draft)', *Harvard Law Review*, **105**, p. 1045 at 1048.

13 Pateman, C. (1987), 'Feminist Critiques of the Public/Private Dichotomy' in Phillips, A., *Feminism and Equality*, Oxford: Basil Blackwell.

14 Smart, C. (1992), 'The Woman of Legal Discourse', *Social and Legal Studies*, **1**, p. 29.

15 See *R* v. *Ethical Committee of St Mary's Hospital (Manchester) ex parte Harriott* [1988] 1 FLR 512.

16 S. 13(5): 'A woman shall not be provided with treatment services unless account has been taken of the welfare of any child who may be born as a result of treatment (including the need of that child for a father), and of any other child who may be affected by the birth.'

17 Thomson, M. (1998), *Reproducing Narrative Gender, Reproduction and the Law*, Aldershot: Dartmouth, p. 181.

18 Millns, S. (1995), 'Making "Social Judgments That Go Beyond the Purely Medical": The Reproductive Revolution and Access to Fertility Treatment Services', in Bridgeman and Millns, *op. cit.*, n. 1, p. 79.

19 Rhode, D. L. (1999), *Speaking of Sex: The Denial of Gender Equality*, Cambridge MA: Harvard University Press, p. 241.

20 Davis, K. (1997), 'Embody-ing Theory', in Davis, K. (ed.), *Embodied Practices*, London: Sage, p. 8.

21 Beasley, *What is Feminism?*, *op. cit.*, n. 7, p. 88.

22 The historical importance of the Oath is open to argument. See, for example, Thompson, I.E. (1987), 'Fundamental Ethical Principles in Health Care,' *British Medical Journal*, **295**, p. 1461.

23 Turner, B. S. (1995), *Medical Power and Social Knowledge* (2nd edn), London: Sage, p. 92.

24 Ibid., p. 91.

25 Rohrbaugh, J.R. (1981), *Women: Psychology's Puzzle*, Reading: Abacus, pp. 3-4, quoted in Nicolson, P. (1992), 'Towards a Psychology of Women's Health and Health Care', in Nicolson, P. and Ussher, J. (eds), *A Psychology of Women's Health and Health Care*, Basingstoke: Macmillan.

26 (1873) 11 M. 784.

27 Sayers, J. (1982), *Biological Politics: Feminist and Anti-feminist Perspectives*, London: Tavistock, at p. 94, quoted in Ussher, J.M. (1989), *The Psychology of the Female Body*, London: Routledge, at p. 2.

28 Ussher, *The Psychology of the Female Body*, London: Routledge, p. 1.

29 William Cadogan, in 'Essay on Nursing' (1748), stated that 'the Preservation of Children should become the Care of Men of Sense'. See Jordanova, L.J. (1999), 'Natural facts', in Samson, C. (ed.), *Health Studies: A Critical and Cross Cultural Reader*, Oxford: Blackwell.

30   Oakley, *Essays on Women, Medicine and Health, op. cit.*, n. 2, p. 68.

31   Ibid., p. 71.

32   Ibid.

33   Debates about discrimination against ethnic minorities – and, indeed, against men – in admissions to medical schools continue. See McManus, I.C. (1998), 'Factors Affecting Likelihood of Applicants Being Offered a Place in Medical Schools in the United Kingdom in 1996 and 1997', *British Medical Journal*, **317**, p. 1111.

34   McManus, I.C. and Sproston, K.A. (2000), 'Women in Hospital Medicine in the United Kingdom: Glass Ceiling, Preference, Prejudice or Cohort Effect?', *Journal of Epidemiology and Community Health*, **54**, p. 10.

35   Showalter, E. (1999), 'Improving the Position of Women in Medicine,' *British Medical Journal*, **318**, p. 71.

36   Smith, R. (2000), *British Medical Journal*, **320**, 15 April at <http://www.bmj.com/cgi/content/full/320/7241/0>.

37   Lunn, J. (2000), *British Medical Journal*, **321**, p. 698.

38   As reported in *The Independent*, 17 April 2000. See Royal College of Physicians (2000), *Hospital Doctors under Pressure: New Roles for the Healthcare Workforce*, London: RCP. Cf Oakley, A. (1992), 'On the Importance of Being a Nurse', in Roberts, H. (ed.), *Women's Health Matters*, London: Routledge.

39   Even here, the 'treatments' available to men are generally less invasive, risky and/or sophisticated. Compare the pill/sheath; IVF treatment/donor insemination.

40   Miles, A. (1991), *Women, Health and Medicine*, Buckingham: Open University Press, p. 1.

41   Ibid., ch. 1, 'Patterns of Ill Health in Women'. See also Popay, J. (1992), '"My Health is All Right, But I'm Just Tired All the Time": Women's Experience of Ill Health', in Roberts, *Women's Health Matters, op. cit.*, n. 38. Cf. Moynihan, C. (1998), 'Theories of Masculinity', *British Medical Journal*, **317**, p. 1072.

42   Turner, *Medical Power, op. cit.*, n. 23, p. 2.

43   As Turner points out, 'the division between physical and mental illness corresponds to a cultural division between mind and body, which is in fact philosophically and sociologically very problematic' (ibid., p. 3).

44   Ibid., p. 19.

45   Sioncke, J. and Domay, F. (2001), Maternal Mortality update 1998–1999: A Report on UNFPA Support for Maternal Mortality Prevention, New York: UNFPA. The lifetime risk of maternal death ranges from 1 in 16 in Africa, to 1 in 65 in Asia, 1 in 130 in Latin America, and 1 in 1,800 in all developed countries (ibid).

46   Ibid.

47   World Bank (1994), *World Development Report 1993 – Investing in Health*, New York: Open University Press.

48   Craft, N. (1997), 'Women's Health: Life Span: Conception to Adolescence', *British Medical Journal*, **315**, p. 1227, citing Caldwell, J. and McDonald, P. (1982), 'Influence of Maternal Education on Infant and Child Mortality: Levels and Causes', *Health Policy and Education*, **2**.

49   It has been estimated that 70 per cent of those living in poverty (as defined by the UN) are women: *United Nations Development Programme. Human Development Report*, (1995), New York: Oxford University Press.

50   See, for example, Morris, A.E. and Nott, S.M. (1995), 'Wealth Within the Family', *All My Worldly Goods: A Feminist Perspective on the Legal Regulation of Wealth*, Aldershot: Dartmouth, ch. 6.

51   World Health Organization (1998), *Gender and Health: Technical Paper*, Geneva: World Health Organization, p. 37.

52 Graham, H. (1997), 'Budgeting for Health: Mothers in Low Income Households', in Glendinning, C. and Millar, J. (eds), *Women and Poverty in Britain in the 1990s*, Brighton: Wheatsheaf; Snape, D. *et al.* (1999), *Relying on the State, Relying on Each Other*, DSS Research Report No. 103, London: Corporate Document Service, p. 51.

53 Payne, S. (1991), *Women, Health and Poverty*, Hemel Hempstead: Harvester Wheatsheaf, p. 176.

54 World Health Organization, *Gender and Health, op. cit.*, n. 51, pp. 25–26.

55 World Bank, *World Development Report 1993, op. cit.*, n. 47, p. 25.

56 World Health Organization, *Gender and Health, op. cit.*, n. 51, p. 28.

57 Baldez, L. (1998), 'Gender Quotas and Women's Representation: International Perspectives', *Women's Progress: Perspectives on the Past, Blueprint for the Future*, Washington, DC: Institute for Women's Policy Research, p. 38 (footnote omitted).

58 Rhode, *Speaking of Sex, op. cit.*, n. 19, pp. 245–50.

59 For example, Margaret Thatcher holding the office of Prime Minister in the United Kingdom for over ten years did not move women's issues higher up the political agenda.

60 Rhode, *Speaking of Sex, op. cit.*, n. 19, p. 247.

61 This is not to dismiss the role of male judges in adjudicating 'female' matters, but to observe that all institutions can benefit from diverse views of those with diverse experiences. Whether female judges bring a distinctive voice is open to debate, see Baldez, 'Gender Quotas and Women's Representation', *op. cit.*, n. 57.

62 Conners, J. (1997), 'General Human Rights Instruments and their Relevance to Women' in Byrnes, A., Conners, J. and Bik, L. (eds), *Advancing the Human Rights of Women*, London: Commonwealth Secretariat, p. 29.

63 Conaghan, J. (2000), 'Reassessing the Feminist Theoretical Project in Law', *Journal of Law and Society*, **27**, p. 351 at 383 (footnotes omitted).

64 Smart, *Feminism and the Power of Law, op. cit.*, n. 4, pp 138–40; Kingdom, E. (1991), *What's Wrong With Rights? Problems for Feminist Politics of Law*, Edinburgh: Edinburgh University Press; Beveridge, F. and Mullally, S. (1995), 'International Human Rights and Body Politics', in Bridgeman and Millns, *Law and Body Politics, op. cit.*, n. 1.

65 Cook, R.J. (ed.) (1994), *Human Rights of Women*, Philadelphia: University of Pennsylvania Press, p. 59.

Chapter 2

Disabling Sex: Some Legal Thinking about Sterilization, Learning Disability and Embodiment

Kirsty Keywood

Introduction

For many years, English law's engagement with medicine has traditionally been characterized by its deference to medical knowledge. This medico-legal alliance has been subject to rigorous critique for its failure to recognize patients' rights and interests in formulating the scope of a doctor's duty of information disclosure.[1] Other criticisms revolve around law's failure to address expressly and systematically ethical questions concerning the moral value of life[2] and economic considerations, such as resource allocation, and the role these should play in medical decision-making.[3] Feminist critiques have sought to demonstrate the implications of law's relationship with medicine for female[4] and, more recently, male subjectivity.[5] Through the valorization of dominant medical discourses on the frailty of the human body, English law has shown itself unwilling to challenge the dominance of what are complex, fragmented and often highly contested accounts of human development and identity.

In recent years, however, law has witnessed some important shifts in its relation to medicine. In a series of cases concerning the sterilization of adults with learning disabilities, the courts have called into question the proper place of medical expertise in the courtroom. Through an examination of these cases, this chapter profiles the changes to law's relationship with medicine in the light of the recent judicial attempts to rework established legal principles. Whilst the implications of the deferential relationship between judges and medical practitioners have been noted by many feminist commentators,[6] the mechanisms, structures and processes that have produced this medico-legal alliance remain largely unexplored. After providing an outline of the development of the sterilization case law, this chapter proceeds to offer a 'systems theory' analysis in order to examine at a macro-level law's relation to medicine. Claims that law is an autonomous 'closed' system have been developed by theorists seeking to understand law's communicative potential with other discursive systems and to explore the possibilities for a greater degree of reflexivity within the legal system.[7] Teubner, for example, claims that law is an autopoietic system, dependent on its own internal structures for its viability, rules of operation and self-production:

A system operates to produce its elements, structures and processes, its boundaries and unity in a circular way. This presupposes that systems seek the fixed points of their mode of operation in themselves and not in the environmental conditions to which they adapt themselves as best they can. These fixed points are sought in a self-description which in turn functions as a programme of internal regulation, organising the system in such a way that it corresponds to this self-description.[8]

Using Teubner's model of autopoietic law as an heuristic device has considerable appeal when seeking to examine law's relation to medicine in the context of the sterilization cases. By conceptualizing law as an organizationally closed network of internally constituted norms, structures and processes, we are able to consider in a new light the nature of law's of engagement with medicine. In particular, the theory of autopoietic law may help us understand why law's efforts to incorporate medical knowledges result in reductionist, oversimplified accounts of human development, which bear little relation to the complex array of medical (and, indeed, non-medical) knowledges concerning learning disability and sexed embodiment. Autopoietic theory reveals the limitations of law's reconstruction of medical discourses within the courtroom, which obscures from consideration broader social questions concerning the status of disabled people in society and, significantly, omits an examination of the consequences of its judicial pronouncements for sexed subjectivity.

This analysis of the interaction of law and medicine at the level of discourse and organizational systems has enormous potential for feminist legal scholarship, for it offers important insights into how legal and medical 'thinking' produces sexed identity. Such an analysis of the sterilization cases, developed in this chapter, supports the contention that learning-disabled subjects are represented as failing to conform to those sexed identities that 'matter' in legal, social and cultural life.[9] In other words, women and men with learning disabilities do not conform to the culturally sanctioned traits of 'women' and 'men' in contemporary society. They are represented as being of no sex. In making sense of how law 'thinks' about sterilization and exploring the limitations of law's 'thinking' about medicine generally, this chapter contributes to the feminist project of 'sexing' the subject[10] and exposes some of the institutional structures and discursive processes which produce the legal subject as sexed.

Setting the Scene: Law's Engagement with Medicine in the Sterilization Cases

Beginning with Bolam

Medical judgement has come to occupy a privileged place in legal doctrine and this has been facilitated in the common law by the development and extension of the *Bolam* principle.[11] The courts' reification of the *Bolam* principle meant that, for many years, judicial opportunities to challenge medical thinking were narrowly circumscribed. Should a judge wish to challenge the validity of medical knowledge concerning diagnosis, treatment or information disclosure in the context of a medical negligence suit, he or she would have to be satisfied that such knowledge could not be supported by a 'responsible' body of medical opinion. In this way, legal academics came to lament the 'rise and rise' of the *Bolam* principle[12] and proclaim that *Bolam* protected all but the 'complete maverick' in the exercise of that which was regarded as falling within the remit of a doctor's clinical judgement,[13] leaving judges impotent to challenge the legitimacy of medical knowledge and its application in a range of legal contexts.

Indeed, few domains of health care law seemed immune from the powerful effects of *Bolam*. Whilst the privileging of medical discourse(s) occurred without formal application of the *Bolam* principle in some areas,[14] *Bolam* was extended further to enable medical knowledge effectively to determine the lawfulness of treatment provision for mentally incapacitated adults. In *F* v. *West Berkshire Health Authority and another (Mental Health Act Commission intervening)*,[15] the House of Lords was called upon to consider the lawfulness of a sterilization, to be performed upon a 36 year-old woman with severe learning disabilities. The House upheld the ruling of the Court of Appeal and confirmed that the proposed sterilization was lawful. Their Lordships ruled that medical treatment could lawfully be performed upon a mentally incapacitated adult, provided that the treatment was in the patient's best interests. Furthermore, they ruled that the best interests of such patients were to be determined by reference to the *Bolam* principle.[16] In other words, if the view that the proposed treatment was in the patient's best interests was supported by a responsible body of medical opinion, that treatment would not (and, indeed, could not) be declared unlawful. In so doing, the House of Lords handed over to the medical profession the power to determine what treatments could lawfully be given to vulnerable patients unable to provide a legally effective consent.[17]

The judicial recourse to the *Bolam* principle in determining best interests had a number of consequences for adults whom it was proposed should be sterilized. First, it prevented judges from subjecting medical opinions in favour of sterilization to rigorous examination. Once the judge was satisfied that the views of those in favour of sterilization were in accordance with a responsible body of opinion, then the judge would be prevented, on a strict interpretation of *Bolam*, from declaring the medical treatment to be contrary to the patient's best interests. Indeed, in *F* v. *West Berkshire Health Authority*, Lord Goff was clear that 'there is a high degree of likelihood that they [medical opinions] will be accepted'.[18] A second and related consequence was that a strict application of the *Bolam* principle required no detailed, comparative evaluation of the evidence in favour of sterilization against evidence that the best interests of the adult patient demand some other form of intervention.[19] The *Bolam* principle makes clear that a judge cannot rule against a defendant practitioner merely because there is another body of medical opinion expressing a contrary view. For example, in the case of *Re W (Mental Patient) (Sterilisation)*,[20] conflicting medical opinions were presented to the court as to whether sterilization would be the best course of action for W, a 20 year-old woman with severe learning disabilities. A number of expert witnesses supported the sterilization procedure, whilst a consultant obstetrician and gynaecologist recommended the fitting of a coil. In confirming the lawfulness of the proposed operation, Hollis J did not attempt to evaluate the relative clinical benefits of either treatment for W, nor did he contemplate seriously the possibility that W should be provided with no contraceptive treatment since she was not presently sexually active and the chances of her becoming pregnant were described as 'minimal'.[21] What the court was, in fact, being called upon to determine was not the patient's best interests, objectively determined, but rather the medical practitioners' non-negligent assessment of the patient's best interests.[22]

The retreat from Bolam

The 1990s witnessed an increased judicial willingness to subject medical judgement to closer scrutiny. The House of Lords' decision in *Bolitho (Deceased)* v. *City and Hackney Health Authority*, for example, signalled that, in determining whether the defendant clinician had fallen below the standard of care expected of a reasonably competent clinician in the exercise of diagnostic skills or the provision of medical treatment, judges could rightly examine whether the defendant's practice was capable of withstanding logical analysis.[23] Although Lord Browne-Wilkinson acknowledged that medical judgement would only rarely fail on this analysis, *Bolitho* paved the way for increased judicial scrutiny into medical practice and expertise.[24] Furthermore, in the context of a doctor's duty to disclose information about risks and side effects inherent in medical procedures, the courts' traditional adherence to the *Bolam* principle[25] has given way to a recognition that information disclosure in the context of medical treatment raises key questions about a patient's moral claim to autonomy. In determining whether a doctor has fallen below the standard of care in failing to provide information about risks, side effects and alternative treatments, consideration must be given to what the reasonable patient would wish to know and not simply to what a doctor, in the exercise of her clinical judgement, deems it appropriate for the patient to be told.[26]

Similarly, judicial concern over the proper role of medical expertise in the courtroom came to be expressed in cases concerning the sterilization of mentally incapacitated adults. The first judgment which declined to follow the logic of *Bolam* was the case of *Re LC (medical treatment: sterilisation)*.[27] L was described as an 'attractive' women aged 21 years, who had recently moved to a new residential service for people with learning disabilities. She had been sexually assaulted by a member of staff at her former residential home and her mother was concerned that she would remain vulnerable to sexual abuse. The local authority applied to the High Court for a declaration that it would be lawful to sterilize L. There was support for the sterilization from L's mother, two medical practitioners and also from the area manager of the social services department. Significantly, Thorpe J made no reference to *Bolam* in his judgment. On a strict interpretation of *Bolam*, he would have been unable to refuse the declaration unless the medical opinions in favour of surgery could be said to be irresponsible or unreasonable. Significantly, he did not suggest that the views of medical expert witnesses were anything other than responsible in this case, yet nevertheless he declined to grant the application. Thorpe J showed himself willing to evaluate the medical evidence submitted and weigh it in the balance against other relevant factors. He attempted to evaluate the degree of risk that L would become pregnant and was satisfied that it was not sufficiently great to warrant bodily interference. Further, he acknowledged the relevance of other non-medical factors such as the quality of social care that L was receiving and her level of vulnerability to sexual abuse in her residential home.

Noting that the case raised issues that were beyond the scope of medical judgement, he made reference to the need to consider societal values which are called into question by the practice of sterilizing people with learning disabilities.

Whilst the case of *Re LC* marked a positive move towards greater judicial scrutiny of professional judgement, the case raised many questions. Were the courts willing to banish *Bolam* from the realms of decision-making and restrict its application to matters of treatment and diagnosis? In the case of *Re X (adult: sterilisation)*, Holman J explained that the task of determining whether sterilization was in the best interests of a woman with learning disabilities rested with the judge and not with medical opinion.[28] Bennett J was more explicit in his judgment in *Re Z (medical treatment: hysterectomy)*.[29] In declaring lawful the sterilization of a 19 year-old woman with Down's syndrome in order to eliminate her heavy periods and the risk of pregnancy, he was clear that medical expertise should not determine the best interests of the patient: 'In making my assessment the responsibility for that assessment falls on the court alone. Experts are what they are – experts. They must be listened to with respect, but their opinions must be weighed and judged by the court.'[30]

Some months later, the Court of Appeal took the opportunity to clarify the proper relationship between *Bolam* and an adult's best interests. For the first time, a case was brought concerning the proposed sterilization of a man with Down's Syndrome. In *Re A (medical treatment: male sterilisation)*,[31] Butler Sloss LJ declined to grant the application requested by A's mother and took the opportunity to place limits around the role played by professional judgement in such cases. She rejected the claim, advanced by the Law Commission (1995), that the best interests test had become conflated with the *Bolam* principle. Instead, she argued, the two principles remained separate and imposed distinct obligations upon professionals. In the case of *Re SL (adult patient) (medical treatment)*, Butler Sloss LJ went further and stated that, in the context of the sterilization cases, it is for the court to determine whether sterilization is in the adult patient's best interests.[32] For Butler Sloss LJ, the decision-making process seems to break down into two distinct elements. First, a doctor's responsible exercise of clinical judgement may lead her/him to nominate a range of procedures that would be beneficial to the patient, and it is here that the *Bolam* principle would apply. Second, from this range of treatments, the one which best meets the patient's needs must be selected. At this stage, the best interests of the patient must be determined objectively and not by reference to a responsible body of medical opinion.[33] At first instance, Wall J had attempted to determine the best interests of the adult woman with learning disabilities strictly by reference to the responsible body of medical opinion in favour of sterilization.[34] Butler Sloss LJ made plain that he was wrong to do so and thereby effected a dislocation of best interests from *Bolam*.

Thinking about how Law 'Thinks': A Systems Analysis

Although the cases outlined above demonstrate that judges are willing to examine more rigorously the evidence of expert witnesses both in favour of and against sterilization and weigh clinical factors against broader ethical and policy considerations, this falls short of a critical interrogation of the core foundations of medical knowledge and their appropriateness to determining the best interests of vulnerable adults. A detailed examination of law's engagement with medicine in the sterilization cases suggests that the recent retreat from *Bolam* has not led to a constructive 'dialogue' between law and medicine for, even in the most recent sterilization cases, English law persists in its uncritical adherence to a medicalized conception of the learning-disabled subject.

One approach to understanding the nature of the dialogue between law and medicine is to examine the legal system's institutional autonomy. Adopting such an approach, the development and application of the *Bolam* principle can be seen as the product of a legal system which represents itself as impervious to non-legal critiques and functionally incapable of engaging in direct communication with other discursive systems. This is not to diminish the significant role that *Bolam* has played in law's engagement with medicine; it undoubtedly effected a stabilizing influence over law's relationship with medicine, providing normative support for law's apparent deference to medical knowledge. It must be remembered, however, that law's deference to medicine occurred in legal domains which remained, strictly speaking, untouched by *Bolam*.[35] Thus, law's deference to medical knowledge can be understood not as the result of the application of a legal principle, but as evidence of how law, as a system, retains institutional and discursive authority over the lives of its subjects. Read in this light, English law's retention of a deeply medicalized conception of learning disability suggests that law's deference to medicine is currently an integral feature of our legal system, rather than a by-product of it.[36]

For Teubner, law's normative function is to code all acts and communications as either legal or illegal, and the criteria for determining legality or illegality are produced by reference to law's internally constituted elements.[37] Conceptualizing law as an operatively closed system does not mean that law is unable to communicate with other forms of knowledge; it means, rather, that there can be no direct, unmediated access by law to other epistemes. When law comes into contact with other knowledges which conceptualize acts and communications along different lines, using different methodologies and in the furtherance of different objectives, law's engagement with those knowledges will take a variety of forms.[38] In the sterilization cases, law's engagement with medicine is effected through two very different strategies. Both strategies, explored below, expose the central role occupied by medical discourse in the constitution of the learning-disabled, legal subject.

The 'medicalization' of legal authority

The early sterilization cases indicate a surrender of legal authority to medical discourse, evidenced by the courts' adherence to the *Bolam* principle in determining the best interests of an adult who lacks mental capacity. The conceptualization of law as functionally incapable of communicating directly with medical and other knowledges means that law is unable to evaluate 'truth' claims from medical discourse. When law comes into contact with medical discourses, as in the sterilization cases, it may seek to withdraw from its substantive engagement with medical knowledge by delegating to medicine the authority to determine the legality or illegality of legal communications. The once powerful effects of *Bolam* in such cases as *Re W (mental patient) (sterilisation)*[39] and *F* v. *West Berkshire Health Authority*[40] can be read as law's early attempts to retain its institutional integrity whilst at the same time confronting those medical knowledges which purport to speak the truth about the learning-disabled 'condition'. The inclusion of *Bolam* in the courts' elaboration of the best interests of the mentally incapacitated adult afforded law a way out of this epistemic confrontation, through conferring upon medical knowledge the legitimacy to determine the lawfulness or otherwise of surgical intervention. However, when the legitimacy of legal knowledge becomes dependent on validation by information drawn from other discourses, a loss of epistemic authority for law necessarily ensues. In the early sterilization cases, law's role was limited to satisfying itself that those medical opinions in favour of sterilization were in accordance with a 'responsible' body of medical opinion. Hence, medical claims that sterilization was in the learning-disabled woman's best interests went largely unchallenged, and the role of the judiciary became almost one of 'rubber-stamping' applications for declaratory relief.[41]

This renunciation of epistemic authority may, indeed, have provided a short-term solution to law's confrontation with medicine, but law's reluctance to engage more effectively with medical knowledge produces other conflicts that threaten law's integrity. Law not only has to accommodate medical knowledges in its judgments, but inevitably encounters other discursive communications, such as ethical discourses on justice, rights and self-determination. In the context of the sterilization cases, law has also had to contend with the emerging discourses of self-advocacy and normalization, which seek to guarantee the equal status of people with learning disabilities and ensure their social inclusion.[42] Law, having conceded epistemic authority to medical knowledge, has no way of defending itself against claims from other epistemes which assert that the sterilization of women with learning disabilities constitutes a violation of the right to reproduce and prevents them from living socially valued lives. A renunciation of legal authority in favour of medical knowledge serves to mire legal discourse further in Teubner's 'epistemic trap'.

The 'legalization' of medical knowledge

In recent years, law has sought to reassert its discursive and institutional authority over the lives of learning-disabled men and women by reclaiming and reconstituting medical knowledges within legal discourse. This alternative strategy witnesses law's reconstruction of medical knowledge within its own organizational domain in a bid to retain institutional and discursive authority. Law does not incorporate concepts directly from other discourses into legal thinking, but reconstructs them so that they are rendered intelligible within the legal setting.[43] Such a process inevitably alters the meaning of concepts as they are reproduced within different discourses but, for Teubner, this is an inevitable consequence of law's organizational closure. The strategy is not without its faults, however, as the reconstruction of non-legal knowledges into the legal system results in the oversimplification of concepts and, according to Teubner, can produce 'hybrid artefacts with ambiguous epistemic status and unknown social consequences'.[44] For example, King and Piper's critique of child law offers a powerful illustration of the effects of law's enslavement of other discourses, whereby complex accounts of child development in the welfare sciences are reconstructed to produce oversimplified conceptions of child welfare in judicial discourse.[45]

Judicial recourse to *Bolam* to determine the best interests of mentally incapacitated adults provided law with a short-lived reprieve from potential conflict with medical knowledge. Judicial engagement with medical knowledge in recent sterilization cases – in particular, *Re SL (adult patient) (medical treatment)* and *Re A (medical treatment: male sterilisation)* – indicates law's readiness to engage more directly with medical issues in an attempt to reassert discursive authority over the lives of its learning-disabled subjects. In the case of *Re SL (adult patient) (medical treatment)*, for example, Wall J at first instance declared the performance of a hysterectomy lawful on the basis that such a procedure, whilst not in the best interests of the learning-disabled woman, did fall within the scope of the *Bolam* test.[46] The Court of Appeal roundly criticized the approach taken at first instance and confirmed that the role of the judge is to undertake an objective assessment of the medical evidence and decide whether to accept or reject it.[47] At first glance here, law might appear to be collaborating *with* medicine in determining the best interests of the woman with learning disabilities. On closer examination, however, law is engaged not in a collaboration with medicine but in a crude, simplistic reconstruction of medical knowledge. In the sterilization cases, as in other domains of health care law, complex, contested and often fragmentary medical accounts of human development are represented in judicial discourse as monolithic, universal and incontestable.[48]

Law's investment in reconstituting medical knowledge lies in its desire to strengthen its own institutional integrity through the furtherance of its normative function of coding behaviour as either legal or illegal. Inevitably, in the furtherance of its objectives, law is functionally incapable of replicating the complexity of the knowledges it purports to reconstitute. In the sterilization cases, this has two primary consequences which are examined below. First, law's engagement with medicine is premised on a grossly oversimplified account of medical knowledge, which is used to construct a medical 'model' of disability and which obscures from consideration pressing social and ethical questions concerning the status of people with disabilities in contemporary society. Second, the terms of law's engagement with medicine operate to produce subjects of legal discourse who are not located within that privileged domain that produces bodies as sexed. They are not, in Judith Butler's phrase, 'bodies that matter'.[49]

Reconstituting the Medical Model of Disability

Major shifts in social and economic life during the industrial age meant that many disabled people who were unable to demonstrate their economic productivity were placed in institutional confinement. The admission of the medical profession into institutional settings, such as asylums, gave medical practitioners an opportunity to strengthen their own professional status by extending their expertise to diagnose and treat the 'feeble-minded', the mentally ill and those with physical impairments.[50]

Despite the recent emergence of the 'social model' of disability which conceptualizes the social environment as disabling those with different physical and intellectual capacities,[51] English law retains a deeply medicalized understanding of the potentialities and experiences of people with learning disabilities. Conceptualizing people with physical or learning disabilities primarily in terms of their dysfunction, as lacking that which constitutes 'normal' health and well-being represents an outdated, crude attempt to position them within a medical model of sickness, incompleteness and abnormality. Defining people with learning disabilities in terms of their pathology – their cognitive dysfunctions – remains a persistent feature of the courts' treatment of such people, even though these practices have been subject to challenge by self-advocacy movements in the United Kingdom and elsewhere.[52] The courts have long construed the corporeal and intellectual self of the person with learning disabilities as the source of their impairment, dysfunction and vulnerability.[53] In the most recent sterilization case, *A National Health Trust* v. *C*,[54] Cazalet J granted a declaration that it was in C's best interests to be sterilized. C was a 21 year-old woman with Down's syndrome who had been taking the contraceptive pill since the age of 14, when she had been discovered in a 'sexually compromising situation' with a fellow pupil. Cazalet J noted that the residential college that C currently attended made every effort to protect vulnerable students from sexual 'activity'. 'Accordingly', he pointed out 'many female students do take the oral contraceptive pill. There has never in fact been ... a student pregnancy.' It would appear that Cazalet J's concern is that C's learning disability is the cause of her vulnerability and since that disability cannot be improved, she must be prevented from the physical consequences of any sexual abuse. Studies of sexual abuse perpetrated against men and women with learning disabilities suggest that the risk of abuse is a very real one, made possible by the interaction of various factors, including institutional arrangements (a lack of continuity of care, inadequately trained personnel and the placement of known offenders in services), economic factors (inadequately funded services that cannot keep people safe) and policy considerations (a lack of collaboration between criminal justice agencies and learning disability services) which all contribute to compound the vulnerability of such people.[55]

Law's reductionist reconstruction of medical knowledge has a further consequence – it operates to obscure from consideration other questions that are relevant to the sterilization of men and women with learning disabilities. In most cases, the courts have been confronted with conflicting views over the most appropriate form of contraception. What remains unexplored by the courts are questions concerning the ability of learning-disabled men and women to lead fulfilling sexual lives and the opportunity for them to become parents. The nature of sexual behaviour engaged in by the subjects of the sterilization cases is rarely known and is frequently discussed in ambiguous terms. In the case of *Re A (medical treatment: male sterilisation)*, A was described as engaging in 'affectionate incidents of a sexual kind'.[56] In *Re X (adult patient: sterilisation)* X was reported as occasionally acting in a 'sexually provocative way'.[57] There is little in the reported cases that suggests that courts are concerned to ensure that learning-disabled men and women are supported to lead sexually pleasurable lives, and less still that they may be considered as potential parents; the focus is generally on the suitability of alternative contraceptive regimes for women with learning disabilities.[58] Furthermore, research reveals that the sexual lives of men and women with learning disabilities are rarely supported by families[59] or social services.[60] Indeed, the sexual lives of many women with learning disabilities are so compromised that they do not identify themselves as sexual beings. Their accounts of their sexual behaviour reveal abusive sexual practices, the performance of sexual acts often in return for money, and sexual encounters devoid of non-penetrative activities that many non-learning-disabled women find pleasurable.[61] Further, for many people with learning disabilities, parenting is simply not a reproductive choice that they[62] or others[63] perceive as available to them. It is noteworthy, for example, that in *Re A (medical treatment: male sterilisation)* Butler Sloss LJ envisaged no meaningful role for A as parent, in the highly unlikely event that he should father a child. She observed that '[n]either the fact of the birth of a child nor disapproval of his conduct is likely to impinge on him to a significant degree…'.[64]

The diversity and complexity of the circumstances surrounding the lives of men and women with learning disabilities remain unacknowledged by the Court of Appeal. Autopoietic theory would suggest that an understanding of the complex 'dynamic of disability'[65] is simply not necessary to further law's objective of coding behaviour as either legal or illegal.[66] Law's primary function as an organizationally closed discursive system is not to effect changes to social institutions, nor to rework economic and social policy in order to improve the well-being of vulnerable people. Hence, law's intervention in the sterilization cases is limited to declaring the legality or illegality of the performance of a surgical procedure upon the learning-disabled subject. This reinforcement of doctrinal integrity, however, has meant that there has been no acknowledgement of the complexity of the processes which shape our understanding of subjects as (dis)abled and has left intact a crude, biomedical model of impairment and identity.

Disabling the Question of 'Sex'

In feminist and disability theory, the body became regarded as a 'natural' entity, on to which socially constructed 'understandings' of disability and gender were grafted. In attempting to rework the social constructions of disability and gender, the transformative potential of the body remained largely unexamined. Thus, the body, understood as a biological entity, already sexed, already (dis)abled, was allocated to the realm of the natural (as opposed to cultural) and the private (as opposed to public), facilitating the perpetuation of dualisms which underpin our system of social organization. The gains made by advocates of the 'social model' of disability were significant in that they compelled service providers to examine the disabling effects of the social environment on those with different physical and intellectual attributes, although the social model left intact a biological understanding of the body which constituted people as either ablebodied or disabled.[67] Similarly, feminist theory omitted from its political project an examination of the body as a sexed entity and focused its efforts on reworking the social constructions of male and female biology. In recent years, feminist theorists have drawn attention to the need to examine how bodies, both physical and metaphorical,[68] become understood as sexed and the consequences that the processes of sexing have on questions of individual responsibility, identity and freedom.[69] Likewise, the sociology of disability has sought to reclaim the body as a site of possible transformations in the understanding of disability and its interaction with the social environment.[70] Recent attempts to theorize biologically sexed and disabled bodies focus on reclaiming key elements of phenomenology to articulate embodied experience and existence, together with a poststructural conception of the body as a semantic artefact. Such projects represent attempts to enable subjects to speak *through* the body, to produce a plurality of embodied identities which resist containment by the dualistic conceptions that currently constitute subjectivity in legal, social and cultural life.[71] In examining the processes through which bodies become understood as sexed, raced, classed and (dis)abled, we are able to examine how bodily forms, represented as natural, untheorizable entities, are put to use in the deployment of disciplinary mechanisms to produce privileged bodily forms – bodies that matter – and to contain those bodily forms that do not correspond to culturally sanctioned body types.

Despite the emergence of a collection of research exploring the potentialities of the body for reworking subjectivity, the corporeal, sexed selves of people with learning disabilities have largely escaped theoretical examination. Learning-disabled people are rarely understood as sexed subjects; they are regarded instead as 'disabled first and disabled second'.[72] If being male or female is an effect of discourse, rather than an immutable characteristic of a biologically determined body, we must examine what is at stake in the representation of bodies as sexed. Butler explains that the sexing of subjects as either male or female has as a powerful objective the normativization of heterosexual desire.[73] Given that people with learning disabilities are rarely valued as (hetero)sexually desiring – still less desired – beings, it should come as no surprise to find that they are not commonly understood as sexed subjects. Hence, learning-disabled men and women are excluded from the domains of sexed subjectivity and find themselves caught between two contradictory stereotypes. On the one hand, they are construed as eternal childlike beings, innocent and in need of protection from any sexual advances. On the other, they are figured as animalistic creatures, with dangerous sexual appetites that cannot be controlled.[74] Indeed, in the sterilization cases, both stereotypes are well represented. The vulnerability of the women in the sterilization cases is compounded by the courts' conflation of their experiences and capabilities with their mental age, together with a failure to acknowledge that their vulnerability is not an intrinsic, immutable feature of their disability.[75] The learning-disabled woman's innocence and vulnerability is often understood as necessitating a surgical solution to keep her safe. This image can be contrasted with the conceptualization of the learning-disabled woman as possessing a sexual appetite that is 'unknowable' and in need of restraint.[76] Despite an alarming lack of clarity as to what sexual acts learning-disabled men and women are engaged in, the courts have construed their sexual desire as potentially dangerous to others. Of course, animalistic conceptions of the sexuality of men and women with learning disabilities are well-established outside legal discourse, finding support in the clinical literature of the early twentieth century[77] and in the self-descriptions of people with learning disabilities.[78] Both conceptions of people with learning disabilities, whilst radically opposed, have at root the denial of sexed identity.

It is in the case of *Re A (medical treatment: male sterilisation)*, that the sex of the learning-disabled legal subject was expressly acknowledged by the Court of Appeal. The case represented the first attempt to obtain a declaration as to the lawfulness of sterilizing a man unable to give a legally effective consent, although undoubtedly men with learning disabilities had been sterilised in the past without judicial intervention. Butler Sloss LJ noted that A's sex was relevant to the court's determination that a vasectomy would not be in A's best interests. She noted that 'sexual intercourse for a woman carries the risk of pregnancy which patently it does not for a man. Indeed, there is no direct consequence for a man of sexual intercourse other than the possibility of sexually transmitted diseases.'[79] She conjured up the spectre of the paradigmatic male bodily form – that contained, bounded entity, capable of separation from other objects and bodily forms through rational, self-directed action. The male body is said to occupy a privileged space in legal discourse, as it constitutes the metaphorical representation of the paradigmatic legal subject[80] and underpins the foundational legal norms for human action and responsibility. This male bodily form is premised on an abstract conception of a male heterosexual body, against which the particularities of other bodily forms will be measured. Those who fail to conform to the attributes of the paradigmatic male bodily form find themselves 'othered', and their otherness becomes the justification for their differential treatment in law.[81] Indeed, the insertion of the paradigmatic male form by Butler Sloss LJ operates as a contrast to the attributes of A. Whilst a 'normal' man might choose to assume parenting responsibilities for any child conceived, we are told that '[i]n the case of a man who is mentally incapacitated, neither the fact of the birth of a child nor disapproval of his conduct is likely to impinge on him to a significant degree other than in exceptional circumstances'.[82] A, unlike many women with learning disabilities in the reported cases, escapes law's corrective effect of non-consensual sterilization, but finds himself deprived of that which would identify him with the paradigmatic male form and render him intelligible as a sexed subject in legal discourse. A's maleness has no significance for him, for he is unable to possess his bodily form in accordance with the Kantian conception of rational man.[83] Lacking the requisite intellectual capacity to engage in self-directed action – to effect his separation from, or association with, other bodily forms – he is distinguished from the paradigmatic male form.

Conclusion: Rethinking Law's Engagement with Medicine

Law's reconstruction of medical knowledge in the sterilization cases has positioned people with learning disabilities beyond the realms of sexed subjectivity and has located them in a biomedical model of impairment which oversimplifies the processes through which identity is produced. Law's relation to medicine in the context of the sterilization cases thus far reveals law's reluctance to incorporate the complexities of medical and other knowledges, producing crude, medicalized 'thinking' about learning-disabled subjectivity. Teubner seeks to explain the terms of law's engagement with other knowledges by reference to law's autopoietic nature. For law to attempt a greater degree of 'understanding' and cooperation with medical knowledge risks a loss of epistemic authority for law. It is important to recognize, however, that law's efforts to retain epistemic authority have been secured at the expense of a detailed theorization of sexed identity and disabled subjectivity.

Teubner's theoretical model serves as a useful analytical device to examine law's relation to medicine at the level of discursive and organizational systems. It provides a compelling explanation as to why law's engagement with medicine in the sterilization cases fails to accommodate the complexities and contradictions within medical and other discourses, producing instead an unsophisticated, medicalized understanding of learning disability and ignoring questions of sexed subjectivity. Teubner argues that law's failure to replicate the complexity of other epistemes within legal 'thinking' is an inevitable consequence of law's attempts to engage with other knowledges whilst at the same time retaining epistemic authority,[84] although whether he is correct in this assertion remains to be tested empirically. Nevertheless, he hypothesizes that, in order for law to respond more effectively to the complexity of other epistemes, law must provide 'norms of procedure, organization, and competences that aid other social systems in achieving the democratic self-organization and self-regulation…'.[85] He acknowledges that other social subsystems may be more apt to determine complex social and moral questions and envisages a limited regulatory role for law, whereby '… as a precondition for the incorporation of social knowledge, the legal system defines certain fundamental requirements relating to procedure and methods of cognition'.[86]

Whilst law's 'thinking' about medicine in the sterilisation cases has produced some disquieting perspectives on sexuality, learning disability and sexed identity, there is cause to resist law's withdrawal from its substantive engagement with medicine along the lines suggested by Teubner's 'legal reflexivity'. First, there is no evidence to suggest that the well-being of men and women with learning disabilities would be improved in the absence of substantive legal engagement with medical and other discursive systems. Indeed, recent research suggests that decision-making practices in the health domain do not serve people with learning disabilities well. In those areas of health care decision-making which are not currently subject to judicial involvement, stereotypes concerning the infantilized, asexual identities of people with learning disabilities continue to prevail.[87] Second, there is some evidence to suggest that law's engagement with medical knowledge can be reworked to produce a more integrated, collaborative response to the complex issues that surround the lives of learning-disabled men and women. Carney and Tait's analysis of the decision-making practices of Australian guardianship tribunals demonstrates that a decision-making body, vested with the power to determine the lawfulness of proposed interventions, can act responsively to the needs of vulnerable adults.[88] Systemic solutions are proposed where individual well-being is compromised by administrative or institutional changes and medical knowledges are recognized as offering only a partial explanation of a person's capabilities, which need to be weighed against evidence from other relevant sources, including the vulnerable adult and his/her carers. If such interactions between law and medical knowledge result in a loss of epistemic authority, as Teubner predicts, that loss of authority appears to have no detrimental impact on the lives of vulnerable adults. Furthermore, if Teubner's thesis about law's autopoietic nature is correct, then law's epistemic weakness must be exposed and exploited in order for questions of sexed subjectivity to be addressed. Law's substantive engagement with other epistemes, if reworked to acknowledge that such knowledges offer partial, complex and often contested accounts of human development, enables an unmasking of the processes through which legal subjects are constituted as sexed, raced, classed (dis)abled and opens up a possible space within which to reconfigure legal subjectivity. If a loss of epistemic authority ensues, this may well prove to be a small price to pay.

There are undoubtedly dangers involved in resorting to law in order to rework the identity of vulnerable legal subjects such as people with learning disabilities. Smart's observations that legal discourse's claim to scientificity and truth 'positions law on a hierarchy of knowledges which allows for the disqualification of "subjugated knowledges"' rightly caution feminist legal scholars against resorting too readily to law in order to reconfigure subjectivity.[89] Law's claim to 'truth' and institutional autonomy is, after all, responsible (at least in part) for the exclusion of adults with learning disabilities from the domains of sexed subjectivity. It has been rightly observed, for example, that 'women with disabilities have fallen through the gaps of definition, theory and consciousness'.[90] Further, the sexed identities of men with learning disabilities have been meaningful only insofar as they have been 'understood' in legal and social science discourses as abusers or as a victims of sexual abuse.[91] The extent to which law can engage with adults with learning disabilities with a self-critical awareness of the epistemic weakness not only of its own pronouncements but also of the partiality and contingency of the foundational categories upon which it constitutes identity must be explored further. If this form of reflexivity (as opposed to the Teubnerian model of reflexive law) can be fostered within the legal system, let us hope that law will begin to 'think' differently about the (non)sexed, embodied subjectivities of people with learning disabilities.

Acknowledgements

My thanks to David Booton, Mandy Burton and Marie Fox for their helpful comments on earlier drafts of this chapter.

Notes

1 Jones, M. (1999), 'Informed Consent and Other Fairy Stories', *Medical Law Review*, **7**(2), p. 103.
2 Keown, J. (2000), 'Beyond Bland: A Critique of the BMA Guidance on Withholding and Withdrawing Medical Treatment', *Legal Studies*, **20**(1), p. 66; Finnis, J. (1993), 'Bland: Crossing the Rubicon', *Law Quarterly Review*, **109**, p. 319.
3 Alldridge, P. and Morgan, D. (1992), 'Ending Life', *New Law Journal*, **142**(6575), p. 1536.
4 For example, Bridgeman, J. (1995), 'They Gag Women, Don't They?', in Millns, S. and Bridgeman, J. (eds), *Law and Body Politics: Regulating the Female Body*, Aldershot: Dartmouth, p. 23; Sheldon, S. (1997), *Beyond Control: Medical Power and Abortion*, London: Pluto Press; Jackson, E. (2000), 'Abortion, Autonomy and Prenatal Diagnosis', *Social & Legal Studies*, **9**(4), p. 467; Thomson, M. (1998), *Reproducing Narrative: Gender, Reproduction and the Law*, Aldershot: Dartmouth.

5   For example Sheldon, S. (1999), 'Reconceiving Masculinity: Imagining Men's Reproductive Bodies in Law', *Journal of Law and Society*, **26**(2), p. 129.

6   In the context of health-care decision-making see, for example, Sheldon, S. (1998), '"A Responsible Body of Medical Men Skilled in That Particular Art ...": Rethinking the *Bolam* Test', in Sheldon, S. and Thomson, M. (eds), *Feminist Perspectives on Health Care Law*, London: Cavendish, p. 15; on access to abortion services see, for example, Sheldon, *Beyond Control*, *op. cit.*, n. 4, and Jackson, 'Abortion', *op. cit.*, n. 4; on reproductive technologies see, for example, Thomson, *Reproducing Narrative*, *op. cit.*, n. 4, and Millns, S. (1995), 'Making "Social Judgements That Go Beyond the Purely Medical"' in Millns and Bridgeman, *Law and Body Politics*, *op. cit.*, n. 4; on eating disorders see, for example, Bridgeman, 'They Gag Women', *op. cit.*, n. 4. These works offer an impressive range of critiques of the medical and legal discursive regimes which produce sexed subjects in English law.

7   For example, Teubner, G. (ed.) (1988), *Autopoietic Law: A New Approach to Law and Society*, Berlin: Walter de Gruyter. Luhmann, N. (1990), *Essays on Self-Reference*, New York: Columbia University Press. Teubner, G. (1993), *Law as an Autopoietic System*, Oxford: Blackwell Publishers. King, M. and Piper, C. (1995), *How the Law Thinks about Children*, Aldershot: Ashgate Publishing (Arena).

8   Teubner, *Law as an Autopoietic System*, *op. cit.*, n. 7, at p. 15.

9   Butler, J. (1993), *Bodies That Matter: On the Discursive Limits of 'Sex'*, London: Routledge.

10 For example, Butler, J. (1990), *Gender Trouble: Feminism and the Subversion of Identity*, London: Routledge; Grosz, E. (1994), *Volatile Bodies: Towards a Corporeal Feminism*, Indianapolis: Indiana University Press; Naffine, N. (1997), 'The Body Bag' in Naffine, N. and Owens, R. (eds), *Sexing the Subject of Law*, Sydney: Sweet & Maxwell.

11 'A doctor is not guilty of negligence if he has acted in accordance with a practice accepted as proper by a responsible body of medical men skilled in that particular art': *Bolam* v. *Friern Hospital Management Committee* [1957] 2 All ER 118, *per* McNair J at p. 122.

12 Keown, J. (1995), 'Doctor Knows Best: The Rise and Rise of the Bolam Test', *Singapore Journal of Legal Studies*, p. 342.

13 Brazier, M. (1990), 'Down the Slippery Slope', *Professional Negligence*, **6**(1), p. 25, at 27.

14 See, for example, the medicalization of adolescent autonomy: Brazier, M. and Miola, J. (2000), 'Bye-bye *Bolam*: A Medical Litigation Revolution?', *Medical Law Review*, **8**(1), p. 85, at 93.

15 [1989] 2 All ER 545.

16 '... if the professionals in question have acted with due skill and care, judged by the well-known test laid down in *Bolam* v. *Friern Hospital Management Committee* ... they should be immune from liability in trespass, just as they are immune from liability in negligence': ibid., *per* Lord Bridge at p. 549.

17 Note that where sterilization was the proposed medical treatment, the House of Lords recognized that whilst the involvement of the court in such cases was highly desirable and good practice, it would not be necessary. See, for example, Lord Bridge, p. 548; Lord Brandon, p. 551; Lord Goff, p. 568, ibid.

18 Ibid. p. 569.

19 Note, for example, in the case of *F* v. *West Berkshire Health Authority*, that the court did not question whether the patient would have benefited from the fitting of an intra-uterine device.

20 [1993] 1 FLR 381.

21 Ibid. p. 384.
22 Indeed, the legitimizing effects of medical knowledge were taken a stage further in the case of *Re GF (Medical Treatment)* [1992] Fam. Law 63, where Sir Stephen Brown P. opined that, where sterilization was proposed for the purposes of menstrual management (as opposed to contraception), and where the proposed treatment was supported by two registered medical practitioners as being necessary for therapeutic purposes, in the best interests of the patient, and there were no less invasive means of treatment, court involvement was not necessary.
23 [1998] AC 232.
24 A breach of a clinician's duty of care in the course of diagnosis and treatment has been established where clinical judgements could not stand up to logical analysis. See, for example, *Glicksman* v. *Redbridge Healthcare NHS Trust* (2000) unreported; *Walsh* v. *Gwynedd Health Authority* [1998] CLY 3977; *Marriott* v. *West Midlands Regional Health Authority* [1999] Lloyd's Rep. Med. 23.
25 Note, for example, that the amount of information provided to patients was to be determined in accordance with a responsible body of professional opinion, irrespective of whether the procedure was therapeutic or whether information had been specifically solicited by the patient. See *Gold* v. *Haringey Health Authority* [1987] 2 All ER 888; *Blyth* v. *Bloomsbury Health Authority* [1993] 4 Med. LR 151.
26 *Pearce* v. *United Bristol Healthcare NHS Trust* (1999) 48 BMLR 118.
27 [1997] 2 FLR 258.
28 [1999] 3 FCR 426, p. 428.
29 [2000] 1 FCR 274.
30 Ibid., p. 286.
31 [2000] 1 FCR 193. The case is significant for a further reason. One of the features of Down's syndrome in men is a very low sperm count. See Horan R.F., Beitins I.Z. and Bode H.H. (1978), 'LH-RH Testing in Men with Down's Syndrome', *Acta Endocrinologica*, **88**(3), p. 594. The first instance judgment is not reported, yet the Court of Appeal states that A is fertile.
32 *Re SL (adult patient) (medical treatment)* [2000] 2 FCR 452.
33 Ibid., p. 464.
34 *Re SL (adult patient) (medical treatment)* [2000] 1 FCR 361, p. 376.
35 The series of cases concerning the sterilisation of young girls with learning disabilities parallels very closely the approach adopted by the courts in relation to learning-disabled adults, demonstrating an uncritical deference to medical knowledge and a reluctance to challenge expert medical testimony in favour of sterilization. See, for example, Lee, R. and Morgan, D. (1988), 'Sterilisation and Mental Handicap: Sapping the Strength of the State?', *Journal of Law and Society*, **15**(3), p. 229. Brazier and Miola, 'Bye-bye Bolam', *op. cit.*, n.14, p. 93, speak of a 'covert *Bolam*isation' in operation to make sense of law's willingness to abandon the task of determining a minor's best interests to the medical profession, even though *Bolam* plays no formal role in this task.
36 This is not to suggest that law's deference to medicine is an immutable feature of our legal system. Law's uncritical engagement with medicine reflects a strategy currently adopted by the legal system in order to retain its institutional autonomy.
37 Teubner, *Law as an Autopoietic System, op. cit.*, n. 7, p. 33.
38 For a more detailed discussion of law's engagement with other social subsystems, see, for example, Teubner, G. (1989), 'How the Law Thinks: Towards a Constructivist Epistemology of Law', *Law & Society Review*, **23**(5), pp. 727–57.
39 [1993] 1 FLR 381.
40 [1989] 2 All ER 545.
41 Keywood, K. (1998), 'Hobson's Choice? Reproductive Choices for Women with Learning Disabilities', *Medicine & Law*, **17**, p. 149.

42   For example, Brown, H. and Smith, H. (1992), *Normalisation: A Reader for the Nineties*, London: Routledge; Sutcliffe J. and Simons, K. (1993), *Self Advocacy and Adults with Learning Difficulties: Contexts and Debates*, Leicester: National Institute of Adult Continuing Education.

43   Teubner, *Law as an Autopoietic System, op. cit.*, n. 7, p. 58.

44   Teubner, 'How the Law Thinks', *op. cit.*, n. 38, p. 747.

45   King and Piper, *How the Law Thinks about Children, op. cit.*, n. 7, p. 132.

46   [2000] 1 FCR 361, p. 376.

47   [2000] 2 FCR 452, p. 464.

48   For example, Keywood, K. (2000), 'My Body and Other Stories: Anorexia Nervosa and the Legal Politics of Embodiment', *Social & Legal Studies*, **9**(4), p. 495, at 497.

49   Butler, *Bodies That Matter, op. cit.*, n. 9.

50   For example, Foucault, M. (1961/1995), *Madness and Civilization: A History of Insanity in the Age of Reason*, London: Routledge; Ryan, J. and Thomas, F. (1987), *The Politics of Mental Handicap*, London: Free Association.

51   For example, Oliver, M. (1990), *The Politics of Disablement*, London: Macmillan.

52   For example, Sutcliffe and Simons, *Self Advocacy, op. cit.*, n. 42.

53   Although in *Re A* and *Re LC* the courts were clear that sterilization would not eliminate any possibility of sexual exploitation.

54   The transcript is available via Westlaw and Lexis.

55   Lyall, I., Holland, A.J. and Collins, S. (1995), 'Offending by Adults with Learning Disabilities: Identifying Need in One Health District', *Mental Handicap Research*, **8**(2), p. 99. Lyall, I., Holland, A.J. and Collins, S. (1995), 'Offending by Adults with Learning Disabilities and the Attitudes of Staff to Offending Behaviour: Implications for Service Development', *Journal of Intellectual Disabilities Research*, **39**(6), p. 501. Brown, H., Stein, J. and Turk, V. (1995), 'The Sexual abuse of adults with learning disabilities: Report of a second two-year incidence survey', *Mental Handicap Research*, **8**(1), pp. 3–24; McCarthy, M. (1999), *Sexuality and Women with Learning Disabilities*, London: Jessica Kingsley.

56   [2000] 1 FCR 193, p. 195.

57   [1999] 3 FCR 426, p. 429.

58   An exception to this is the judgment of Thorpe LJ in *Re A (medical treatment: male sterilisation)* [2000] 1 FCR 193, at p. 205: 'The obligation of society is to minimise the consequence of disability by vouchsafing for the disabled wherever possible the rights and freedoms vouchsafed to the majority who have been spared disability. If there are opportunities of replacing with reality the fantasies that stimulate A's isolated masturbatory sexual activity then they should be grasped.'

59   Shepperdson, B. (1995), 'The Control of Sexuality in Young People with Down's Syndrome', *Child Health and Development*, **21**(5), p. 333; Bambrick, M. and Roberts, G.E. (1991), 'The Sterilisation of People with a Mental Handicap: The Views of Parents', *Journal of Mental Deficiency Research*, **32**, p. 353.

60   Clements, J., Clare, I. and Ezelle, A. (1995), 'Real Men, Real Women, Real Lives? Gender Issues in Learning Disabilities and Challenging Behaviours', *Disability and Society*, **10**(4), p. 425.

61   McCarthy, *Sexuality and Women with Learning Disabilities, op cit.*, n. 55.

62   Keywood, K., Fovargue, S. and Flynn, M. (1999), *Best Practice? Health Care Decision-Making By, With and For Adults with Learning Disabilities*, Manchester: NDT, p. 48.

63   Brantlinger, E. (1992), 'Professionals' Attitudes Towards the Sterilisation of People with Disabilities', *Journal of the Association of Persons with Severe Handicaps*, **17**(1), p. 4.

64   [2000] 1 FCR 193, at p. 203.

65   Carson, D. (1993), 'Disabling Progress: The Law Commission's Proposals on Mentally

Incapacitated Adults' Decision-making', *Journal of Social, Welfare and Family Law*, **5**, p. 304, at 309.

66   Teubner, 'How the Law Thinks', *op. cit.*, n. 38, at p. 741. Similarly, in the context of child welfare law, family dynamics are stripped away to produce the child as semantic artefact – as witness, as rights-bearer, as victim of abuse: see King and Piper, *How the Law Thinks about Children*, *op. cit.*, n. 7, ch. 4.

67   Hughes, B. and Paterson, K. (1997), 'The Social Model of Disability and the Disappearing Body: Towards a Sociology of Impairment', *Disability and Society*, **12**(3), p. 325.

68   Gatens, M. (1996), *Imaginary Bodies: Ethics, Power and Corporeality*, London: Routledge.

69   For example, Butler, *Gender Trouble*, *op cit*, n. 10; idem, *Bodies That Matter*, *op. cit.*, n. 9; Grosz, *Volatile Bodies*, *op. cit.*, n. 10; Naffine and Owens, *Sexing the Subject of Law*, *op. cit.*, n. 10.

70   Wendell, S. (1996), *The Rejected Body: Feminist Philosophical Reflections on Disability*, Routledge: New York; Hughes and Paterson, 'The Social Model of Disability', *op. cit.*, p. 325.

71   In disability theory, there is a growing body of literature developing a sociology of impairment (Hughes and Paterson, The Social Model of Disability', *op. cit.*, n. 67, p. 325), or a sociology of pain (Wendell, *The Rejected Body*, *op. cit.*, n. 70). In feminist politics, there have been similar calls to theorize an 'embodied existence'. See Lacey, N. (1997), 'On the Subject of Sexing the Subject', in Naffine and Owens, *Sexing the Subject of Law*, *op. cit.*, n. 10, p. 65; O'Donovan, Katherine (1997), 'With Sense, Consent or Just a Con? Legal Subjects in the Discourse of Autonomy', in Naffine and Owens, *Sexing the Subject of Law*, *op. cit.*, n. 10, at p. 47; Diprose, R. (1994), *The Bodies of Women: Ethics, Power and Corporeality*, London: Routledge.

72   Baum, S. and Burns, J. (2000), 'Editorial. Waiting to be Asked: Women with Learning Disabilities', *Clinical Psychology Forum*, **137**, p. 4.

73   Butler, *Gender Trouble*, op. cit., n. 10.

74   Craft, A. (ed.) (1987), *Mental Handicap and Sexuality: Issues and Perspectives*, Tunbridge Wells: Costello. Ryan, J. and Thomas, F. (1987), *The Politics of Mental Handicap*, London: Free Association.

75   See, for example, *Re LC (medical treatment: sterilisation)* [1997] 2 FLR 258 where Thorpe J describes L as 'attractive, demonstrative and therefore vulnerable' (p. 262). This echoes the observations of Lord Hailsham in *Re B (a minor) (wardship: sterilisation)* [1988] AC 199, at p. 212, that B 'is vulnerable to sexual approaches'.

76   In *Re B (a minor) (wardship: sterilisation)*, n. 75 *supra*, we are told that B's developing sexual awareness would render her 'a danger to others', p. 213. Such conceptions of the sexuality of people with learning disabilities are prevalent in more recent cases. See, for example, *Re A (medical treatment: male sterilisation)* [2000] 1 FCR 193: Butler Sloss LJ notes at p. 203 that A's female sexual partners would be 'the object of protection rather than A'.

77   'The sexual desires are exaggerated in proportion to the animal over the physic forces', Barr and Maloney (1921), p. 14, cited in Craft, *Mental Handicap and Sexuality*, *op. cit.*, n. 74.

78   Note the explanation of a woman with a learning disability who had been sterilized: 'It's too late now, I've been done': Scior, K. (2000), 'Women with Learning Disabilities: Gendered Subjects After All?', *Clinical Psychology Forum*, **137**, p. 6 at 8). In my own research I have spoken to many women with learning disabilities who describe their (injected) contraception regime as 'being on the needle'.

79   [2000] 1 FCR 193, pp. 202–203.

80 O'Donovan, 'With Sense, Consent on Just a Con?', *op. cit.*, n. 71, p. 47.
81 This is not to recreate an essentialist conception of the paradigmatic male subject of legal discourse. Such a subject finds himself on shaky epistemological ground, as feminist theory has revealed him to be not one bodily form endowed with fixed attributes, but a contradictory figure, whose features shift in place and time and operate to 'other' male and female bodily forms (for example, Lacey *op. cit.*, n. 71, p.65).
82 [2000] 1 FCR 193, p. 203.
83 Naffine,'The Body Bag', *op. cit.*, n. 10, p. 81.
84 Teubner, 'How the Law Thinks', *op. cit.*, n. 38, p. 749.
85 Teubner (1983), 'Substantive and Reflexive Elements in Modern Law', *Law & Society Review*, **17**(2), p. 233, at 275.
86 Teubner, 'How the Law Thinks', *op. cit.*, n. 38, p. 751.
87 Keywood *et al.*, *Best Practice?*, *op. cit.*, n. 62.
88 Carney, T. and Tait, D. (1997), *The Adult Guardianship Experiment: Tribunals and Popular Justice*, Sydney: The Federation Press, p. 88 *et seq.*
89 Smart, C. (1995), *Law, Crime and Sexuality: Essays in Feminism*, London: Sage at p. 72.
90 Chenoweth, L. (1996), 'Violence and Women with Disabilities: Silence and Paradox', *Violence Against Women*, **2**(4), p. 391, at 394.
91 Cambridge, P. and Mellan, B. (2000), 'Reconstructing the Sexuality of Men with Learning Disabilities: Empirical Evidence and Theoretical Interpretations of Need', *Disability & Society*, **15**(2), p. 293.

Chapter 3

Infertility Treatment and the HIV Positive Woman: Old Moral Prejudices Disguised as New Ethical Dilemmas

Kylie Stephen

Introduction

> The sexual potentialities of the body have been integrated into a vast range of different social contexts ... some cultures have seen no connection between sexual intercourse and conception; others have seen only justification for sex in reproduction. Some cultures have made little distinction between heterosexual and homosexual forms, concentrating rather on age or class of the partner; our culture has made the distinction of prime social significance. In some societies, sex is a simple source of pleasure, a key to the glorification of the erotic arts; in others it is a source of danger and taboo, of mortification of the flesh.[1]

As this quote suggests, the interrelated concepts of sex, sexuality and sexual behaviour have always been value-laden, but not always in the same way. In Western culture we give supreme importance to sex in our individual and social lives because of a history that has assigned central significance to all things 'sexual'.

The context for feminist consideration of sexuality has been, and remains, the meanings attributed to women's bodies and women's sexual behaviour. Foucault suggests that power operates through the construction of particular knowledges. And it is through the constructed knowledge of sexuality that control over individuals is exercised. Foucault's idea that sexuality is not a natural quality of the body but, rather, the effect of historically specific power relations[2] has provided feminists with a powerful analytical framework by which to explain how women's lives are controlled by culturally determined images of female/feminine sexuality. These assumptions are in turn developed and reinforced in law, as legislation recognizes and reflects the current political and social structures of society. Thus, cultural stereotypes of appropriate/inappropriate sexual behaviour for women are directly and indirectly regulated by the reinforcing power of law. Foucault's work directs us to investigate the role of certain knowledges in shaping our conceived notions of sexuality and sexualized bodies. We are starting to question the eternal validity of social roles, and we now recognize that the way in which we define masculinity and femininity, motherhood and fatherhood, are culturally specific and not simple products of biology.[3] The apparatus of sexuality is of central importance in the modern play of power. But what are the concrete mechanisms and practices through which power is exercised?

Society's concern with the spread of sexually transmitted diseases, and women, namely prostitutes, as harbingers of such diseases, is not new. The Contagious Diseases Acts of 1864, 1866 and 1869 all sought, on the surface, to prevent the spread of venereal disease in the armed forces. This was achieved, however, by the identification of women as 'common prostitutes' who were then forcibly examined for venereal diseases. If these women were found to have a venereal disease they were confined to Lock Hospital. Men, however, were not subject to similar treatment. The regulation of women with, or believed to have, sexually transmitted diseases (STDs) aimed to control a group of women whose sexual activity was deemed inappropriate and, by association, such behaviour was deemed to be a threat to society as a whole.

While these 'old laws' are no longer in operation and this direct regulation of women's sexual behaviour no longer exists, examples can be found in contemporary society whereby the female body and female sexuality are constructed and regulated according to socially accepted norms. The increased attention devoted both medically and publicly to the development of new reproductive technologies and the identification of HIV and AIDS has altered the public interest in sex, sexuality and sexual practices. This has been accompanied by an array of arguments around the ethical, moral and social dilemmas that accompany both these issues, one of which is the regulation of access to reproductive technology. I will examine the legal provisions relating to *access* to reproductive technology in the United Kingdom and Australia and the debates surrounding their implementation. The aim of this essay is not to make arguments for or against reproductive technology in general, but to investigate the 'orientation and direction of that technology, more specifically by challenging the ideology underpinning who is deemed a suitable recipient'.[4] It will be argued that stereotypes surrounding ideas of infertility, disease and motherhood form what is perceived to be a social, moral and legal basis on which to regulate access to infertility treatment. This in turn directly discriminates against some women's access to infertility treatment – in particular, those with sexually transmitted diseases – and indirectly regulates the sexual activity of all women.

The first section establishes why reproductive technology, and access to infertility treatment in particular, is an area in which the legal regulation of women takes place. The following two sections highlight how the social stereotypes described in the first section impact directly on women's access to infertility treatment in the United Kingdom and Australia. The next section highlights how, through such legislation, women's sexual and gendered behaviour is regulated in contemporary society and women are defined by specific sexualized meanings attributed to infertility, sexually transmitted diseases and notions of the 'suitable mother'. The final section presents the conclusions.

Infertility and the Sexually Active Woman: Cause and Effect?

The advent of the oral contraceptive pill and legalized abortion in the 1960s demolished the idea that having sex inevitably meant having babies. In vitro fertilization (IVF) and reproductive technology in general seemed to sever once and for all the tie between sex and parenthood. However, the perception of a growing technological separation of the biological processes of reproduction and sex should not fool us into thinking that in the uses of artificial reproduction there are no important connections between attitudes towards sexuality and procreation. Arguments about the pros and cons of whether or not reproductive technology should be available at all have largely been superseded by arguments about who should have access to it. Or, more specifically, much of the remaining antipathy towards the use of artificial reproductive technology is based on the apprehension that 'unsuitable' persons may be allowed to use it to become parents. As Liu makes clear:

> The question of eligibility in the context of artificial reproductive methods ... touches on the interplay between private morality and the complex matrices of public policy, the importance of marriage and the family as the fundamental unit of society, and society's perception of what is in the best interests of children.[5]

Screening for parenthood takes place in many contexts in Western society, most notably in the case of adoption, and the adoption model, whereby intending parents are carefully assessed for their suitability to care for a child, seems to have been taken on in relation to access to infertility treatment. It has been suggested that where medical resources are scarce, society may well be entitled to set priorities for their allocation, although the criteria to be fulfilled for eligibility must be legally, socially and ethically justifiable.[6] With regard to whether a person is deemed morally fit to be a parent, most discussion of eligibility has centred on groups who are not married or people who deviate from the traditional heterosexual relationship paradigm.[7]

Thus, some of the most common screening criteria are sexual orientation, marital status, consent of the spouse, number of existing offspring and physical disability. There has been considerable examination of the cost of infertility treatment and how this reinforces class divisions,[8] discrimination against single parents and discrimination against homosexual couples. The focus on the heterosexual couple reinforces the stereotype of the nuclear family. But, perhaps more tellingly, where reproductive technology is seen to be about reconstructing the heterosexual family unit there is also a tendency to equate being unmarried, single or a lesbian with promiscuity. The unmarried or single woman is seen as being unable to commit to one partner and therefore must, by necessity, have many sexual partners. The lesbian woman is seen as engaging in what is deemed to be inappropriate or unnatural sexual activity. The emphasis has been on preventing those who have 'dubious sexual attitudes' – in practice, only women – from gaining access to infertility treatment. Thus a woman's history of sexual activity can preclude her from access to reproductive technology, as was the case in *R v Ethical Committee of St Mary's Hospital (Manchester), ex parte Harriott.*[9]

The applicant in that case sought IVF treatment, but was removed from the waiting list after the hospital became aware of her background – she had been turned down as a suitable foster or adoptive parent, because she had a criminal record involving prostitution offences, and a 'poor understanding' of fostering. At St Mary's hospital, the criteria for offering treatment were that *couples*:

> ... must, in the ordinary course of events, satisfy the general criteria established by adoption societies in assessing suitability for adoption ... [and there] must be no medical, psychiatric or psychosexual problems which would indicate an increased probability of a couple not being able to provide satisfactory parenting to the offspring or endanger the mother's life or health if she became pregnant.[10]

The applicant sought judicial review of the refusal to treat her, but failed on the basis that she had been given an opportunity to make representations against the refusal, so that there was no procedural unfairness. Schiemann J said that, even if the court were to accept Harriott's proposition that the consultant's decision was amenable to judicial review, 'it could not be suggested that no reasonable consultant could have come to a decision to refuse treatment to the applicant'. He commented further that while the court was prepared to accept, *obiter*, that a blanket policy to refuse treatment to 'anyone who was a Jew or coloured' might be illegal, in this case the hospital's criteria were regarded as acceptable.[11] The judgment tacitly assumes that a reasonable decision by a consultant on who should be given IVF treatment cannot be challenged.

Apart from the fact that promiscuous women are deemed unsuitable parents because of their perceived reckless and unstable lifestyle and family context, promiscuity in turn is seen as the cause of some women's infertility (like abortion). It has widely been thought that factors leading to the increase in female infertility include, among other things such as environmental pollution, workplace hazards, and nutritional deficiencies, the use of contraceptives, such as the IUD, and increases in the incidence of venereal disease.[12] This in turn has developed into a 'blaming the victim mentality', whereby, if you are deemed to have caused your infertility through inappropriate sexual behaviour, you should not then be entitled to infertility treatment.

Reliable contraception removed the threat of unwanted pregnancy and heralded changes in sexual behaviour. Women could still find, however, that when they wished to conceive they were unable to do so.

> More or less effective contraception permits heterosexual activity without the hazards of reproduction. But even more significantly, forms of artificial reproduction such as artificial insemination by donor and in vitro fertilisation permit reproduction without the hazards of heterosexual activity.[13]

Despite some changes in contemporary thinking, infertility is still seen, socially, as a stigma.[14] As infertility can result from the use of some contraceptives, botched abortions and contracting STDs, it may be perceived as a type of punishment justly administered to those women who transgress accepted gender norms for sexual and reproductive activity. Since contraception prevents pregnancy, its use may be seen as an excuse, or grounds for promiscuity. If as a woman, however, you have engaged in sexual activity outside the bounds of heterosexual marriage and you have been exposed to the 'hazards' of such activity – that is, exposure to STDs – or have experienced complications with contraception, then you cannot expect help with infertility treatment.

Women's Access to Reproductive Technology in the United Kingdom

The legislation regulating the practice of infertility treatment in the United Kingdom is the Human Fertilisation and Embryology Act 1990, which came about as a result of the Warnock Report.[15] Before 1984, discussion of reproductive technology took place away from the public domain. Dame Mary Warnock and the Committee of Inquiry into Human Fertilisation and Embryology were charged that year with examining the 'social, ethical and legal implications' of the new reproductive technologies, although they spent much of their time discussing how to assimilate the existence of in vitro embryos into British law – that is, they contemplated the legal status of the human embryo. The Committee decided by a majority (three of the 16 members voted against) that a 14-day limit should be placed on research using human embryos. Each research project should be licensed and monitored by a statutory body and any failure to comply with the conditions of the licence would result in its withdrawal and, possibly, in criminal proceedings being taken out against the licensee.[16] Their recommendations came into effect in 1990 in the shape of the Human Fertilisation and Embryology Act. The statutory body, the Human Fertilisation and Embryology Authority, was set up a year later.

Immediately after the Warnock Report, and before the legislation was enacted, the Medical Research Council and the Royal College of Obstetricians and Gynaecologists set up the Voluntary Licensing Authority (VLA) in 1985. The VLA, which became the Interim Licensing Authority (ILA) in 1989, drew up a Code of Practice to guide research and medical procedures in the treatment of infertility. They granted licences to, and inspected, centres offering IVF treatment, monitored treatments given, and assessed research proposals involving embryos.[17]

> Centres offering IVF treatment were required by the ILA guidelines to have an ethical committee to scrutinise their treatment and research programmes, and their objectives included the protection of the *interests of patients and of any children resulting* from the use of assisted reproduction.[18]

While *research* that is undertaken in assisted conception units is still monitored by an ethics committee and licensed by the Human Fertilisation and Embryology Authority under the Act, the *treatment services* offered by those units are subject to a different kind of scrutiny. As no category of prospective parent is specifically excluded by statute, clinics have been free to develop their own guidelines about what kind of people should, or should not, be offered treatment, subject only to the requirements of the non-statutory Code of Practice issued by the Human Fertilisation and Embryology Authority.[19] The result, unsurprisingly, is that some clinics are more liberal than others (some are constrained by local authorities[20]) but they all abide by the principle that they will not treat just anybody. Why?

While the Human Fertilisation and Embryology Act 1990 does not directly preclude specific groups of women from gaining access to infertility treatment, it does:

- provide for licences to be issued to treatment centres which, in turn, set ethical guidelines that may differ from one centre to the next
- set a requirement to 'screen patients' – that is, check the patient's medical

history to see whether they have any problems that may preclude them from becoming recipients of infertility treatment[21]

- provide that 'a woman shall not be provided with treatment service unless account has been taken of the *welfare of any child* who may be born as a result of that treatment (including the need of that child for a father), and of any other child who may be affected by the birth'.[22]

This last point, embodied in section 13(5), is effectively the central tenet of the Act today. One of the strongest arguments against the use of artificial reproductive techniques is based on consideration of the interests of children. This, to some extent, helps put the issue of eligibility into focus. Yet significant problems can be, and have been, shown in relation to this point. Pertinent questions are:

- How can the welfare of something that does not, and may never, exist be taken account of?
- How can the future circumstances into which that child may be born be fully known and assessed years in advance?
- Is the existence of a father at a child's conception any guarantee that there will be one at the birth or indeed for the rest of the child's life?[23]

The manner in which section 13(5) came into being is quite telling in relation to the context in which it is seen fit to give fertility treatment to prospective parents. While the Warnock Report makes a brief reference to the interests of the child, the Human Fertilisation and Embryology Bill published in November 1989 made no mention of the welfare of the child. It was only during the committee stages of the Bill that the clause came into being. In February 1990, during a House of Lords Committee on the Bill, Lady Saltoun of Abernethy expressed concern about the availability of fertility treatment:

> [T]here have been cases where IVF treatment has been given to unmarried women, or unmarried couples. Whether it is in this country or not I am not certain. But surely, therefore, some prohibition of this should appear on the face of the Bill. It should not appear in regulations, which can be altered ... but it should appear on the face of the Bill, where an Act of Parliament will be required to change it.[24]

Her concern led her to table an amendment to the Bill, which sought to outlaw 'placing an embryo in an unmarried woman'. The vote went 61 against and 60 for. However the Lord Chancellor, Lord Mackay accepted the spirit of the amendment saying 'it would be clearly unfortunate if this Bill was seen in any way to be conflicting with the importance we attach to family values'.[25]

At the report stage of the Bill, he tabled his own amendment which became part of the Act. The emphasis shifted from prohibiting access to treatment to unmarried women to taking account of the *welfare of the child*. But the sentiment and the effect were just the same as Lady Saltoun had intended. The government's hope was that unsuitable candidates for treatment would be dissuaded from continuing with treatment:

With the child and welfare amendments we have just discussed there is a likelihood that through counselling and discussion with those responsible for licensed treatment they may be dissuaded from having children once they have fully considered the implications of the environment into which their child would be born or its future welfare.

Because human and family circumstances can vary so widely there are advantages as well as problems in not trying to draw sharp dividing lines. The second amendment will help the clinician in exercising his responsibility by requiring the authority to include welfare of children in the code of practice to be drawn up under Clause 24.[26]

The Warnock Report and the Human Fertilisation and Embryology Act clearly defined the best interests of the child in heterosexist terms. It preferred married couples in a stable union. Thus it said that:

... as a general rule it is better for children to be born into a two-parent family, with both father and mother, although we recognise that it is impossible to predict with any certainty how lasting such a relationship will be.[27]

Anxieties about the unregulated use of reproductive technology and the assertion of a heterosexual ideology are clear within the discourses and practices of assisted reproduction. Section 13(5) of the Human Fertilisation and Embryology Act gives an explicit moral role to clinicians – the doctor (normally figured as male) is constructed as the normalizing agent, deciding who is a suitable mother:[26] '[Section 13(5)] is the first time doctors have been directed, by statute, to consider the prospective patient's fitness to care for a child when deciding whether to offer treatment.'[29] The doctor is able to limit treatment to those people (women) who society considers to be worthy of parenthood. Yet Thomson contends that the doctor's role goes beyond limiting treatment to the worthy; it acts to define gender.[30] Section 13(5) embodies dominant contemporary gender definitions, but it does so through indirectly regulating reproductive behaviour rather than being directly prohibitive. The legislation aims to prohibit those in non-heterosexual and unmarried relationships from receiving treatment. That is, it aims to assert and reinforce appropriate heterosexual gender behaviour (specifically in women) but does so through the principle of the 'welfare of the child' which gives the doctor a free rein to 'guide' individuals as he sees fit.

The clause embodies fears that gender relations may be realigned by unrestricted access to the technologies of assisted reproduction. The principle of the 'welfare of the child' was substituted for the 'status of the woman' as the appropriate criterion for access. However, as Douglas states, 'this is much vaguer and less objectionable than overtly discriminating against certain women on the basis of marital status or sexual orientation'.[31] The concept of the 'welfare of the child' signifies a great deal more than an objective assessment of the well-being of any child born as a result of treatment services. It asserts a subjective assessment of what forms of sexual and social relations and parenting are acceptable. It is on this basis that access to IVF is effectively unchallengeable.

The need to avoid direct discrimination is affirmed by the Code of Practice, which further suggests the motivating intent behind section 13(5). The Code provides that '[I]n deciding where or not to offer treatment services ... [c]entres should avoid adopting any policy or criteria which may *appear* arbitrary or discriminatory'.[32] The concept of 'welfare' thus forms an acceptable means of *indirectly discriminating* against women deemed unsuitable parents. To explicitly screen access to such treatment via the 'status of the woman' would be seen as direct discrimination. But, even under the welfare of the child principle, the primary concern remains the provision of services to unsuitable women: thus, status is still paramount and the legislation acts to reassert traditional gender roles.

The only available means of protesting against a decision taken by a hospital to deny a patient infertility treatment is through judicial review, as was unsuccessfully attempted in *R* v *Ethical Committee of St Mary's Hospital (Manchester), ex parte Harriott*.[33] The decision in that case, however, illustrates the difficulties of such a route, and the author is not aware of any such actions being successful or, indeed, whether any such actions have taken place. The discussion above explains perhaps why this is the case. The 'welfare of the child' principle seems universally accepted – few people would actively wish to do something contrary to the welfare of any child. Thus it is very difficult to assert that the 'welfare of the child' principle acts either to directly or indirectly discriminate against the interest of prospective parents – specifically women.

Women's Access to Reproductive Technology in Australia

Every state in Australia and the Australian Capital Territory (ACT) and Northern Territory (NT) has legislation on the status of children born as the result of the use of donor gametes or as a result of donor insemination (DI), rather than artificial insemination by donor (AID). The first legislation in the world 'relating to the regulation of certain procedures for the alleviation of infertility, or to assist conception' was the Australian State of Victoria's Infertility (Medical Procedures) Act 1984 which was based on the recommendations of the Waller Committee.[34]

The Victorian Infertility (Medical Procedures) Act 1984 only applied to legally married couples. Marriage was not defined to include a *de facto* relationship, and therefore only legally married couples could have access to artificial reproductive technology (ART). However, in the case of *MW and Others* v. *Royal Women's Hospital and Others*[35] the Human Rights and Equal Opportunity Commission found that the denial of ART services to three women in heterosexual *de facto* relationships was contrary to the Sex Discrimination Act (Commonwealth) 1984.[36] The Sex Discrimination Act, which prohibits discrimination in the provision of goods and services on the basis of marital status, thus conflicted with the state legislation which limited access to IVF to legally married couples. Accordingly, section 8 of the Victorian Infertility Treatment Act 1995 now includes *de facto* couples.

In a similar case, *Pearce* v. *The South Australian Health Commission*,[37] the South Australian Supreme Court found the Reproductive Technology Act 1988 (SA) to be in direct conflict with the Sex Discrimination Act (Commonwealth) 1984 when a woman, who was separated from her husband, was denied access to IVF treatment. The South Australian Act provided that licences to practise ART were subject to a condition preventing the application of procedures except for the benefit of married couples, defined to include two people living together as husband and wife who are not married and who have cohabited for five years (either continuously or over a six-year period). The provisions of the South Australian Act were held to be invalid in so far as they conflicted with the Sex Discrimination Act, because of the operation of section 109 of the Commonwealth Constitution. That section provides that, when a law of a state is inconsistent with a law of the Commonwealth, the latter shall prevail and the former shall, to the extent of the inconsistency, be invalid. It was suggested subsequently that the Sex Discrimination Act should be amended to allow for discrimination on grounds of marital status and the most recent attempt to do so was the Sex Discrimination Amendment (No. 1) Bill introduced in 2001.

As a result of these cases, it appears that provisions which seek to legislate against access to ART on the basis of marital status are likely to be vulnerable to a challenge, pending any amendment of the Commonwealth Sex Discrimination Act, or any granting of an exception under that Act in relation to ART. It is likely that this would apply to other relationship criteria apart from marriage – that is, any requirement that the woman be in a relationship of any sort (be it a heterosexual or a homosexual *de facto* relationship).

The Anti-Discrimination Act (NSW) 1977 also renders it unlawful to discriminate in the provision of goods and services based on marital status and homosexuality. There is, however, a general exception if the discrimination is done in compliance with other legislation; thus, under this Act, a medical practitioner could lawfully deny access to ART on the basis of marital status provided that the application of that criteria was mandated under NSW legislation. However, the issue regarding the Sex Discrimination Act (Commonwealth) discussed above would remain. In the case of *JM* v. *QFG, GK and the State of Qld*[38] the Queensland Anti-Discrimination Tribunal awarded a lesbian woman compensation for the humiliation and offence suffered when a clinic refused her donor insemination services because of her sexuality.[39]

This legislation and the associated case law suggests that, like the United Kingdom, control of infertility treatment in Australia is also underpinned by the principle of the 'welfare of the child'. The Chairman of the Family Law Council of Australia, Justice Fogarty stated that the welfare and interests of the child should be the paramount consideration in control of AID, IVF, embryo transfer and related procedures, and the issues arising from them: 'we are not convinced that this is presently the case,' he said.[40] The most recent review into a state's legislation addressing the regulation of artificial reproductive technology – the review by the NSW Government into The Human Tissue Act 1983 – has reiterated that perspective. In its discussion paper, *Important Questions for the Community: Assisted Reproductive Technologies, 1998*, the government suggests that eligibility factors other than marital status need to be considered, including:

- if the couple already have children (either from existing or prior relationships), but have subsequently become infertile (eg through age or illness);
- if one member of the couple has a terminal illness;
- if *the woman has an infectious disease* and there is the possibility of its transmission to the foetus conceived through ART;

- if one or both members of the couple suffer a debilitating mental or physical illness or disability which the practitioner feels will affect their ability to parent.[41]

The Victorian, South Australian and Western Australian legislation does not deal with these issues specifically; instead, they leave it to the medical practitioner's discretion whether or not to take these factors into consideration when providing IVF treatment. However, the South Australian Code of Practice requires that treatment cannot be provided except where there is a referral by a medical practitioner stating that neither spouse is suffering from any illness, disease or disability that would interfere with their ability to *care for a child*. Both spouses must also sign a statutory declaration that neither is subject to a term of imprisonment, or has been found guilty of an offence involving violence, or a sexual offence involving a child or has had a child permanently removed from his or her custody (other than by adoption). A licensee may also refuse to give treatment if he or she is of the opinion, after assessment by a child protection services unit, that there is a reasonable likelihood of the couple not properly caring for, or nurturing, a child throughout childhood. The South Australian Code of Practice states that a licensee must, in deciding whether or not to give infertility treatment, or to accept the donation of reproductive material from any person for use in infertility treatment, treat *the welfare of any child* that may be born in consequence of the treatment as the paramount consideration. The South Australian Health Minister, Dean Brown, has called on the federal government to exempt state reproductive programmes from the Commonwealth Sex Discrimination Act, so that they can refuse treatment to single women, and impose an upper age limit – for women, not men.

The Western Australian Act does state that a couple's cause of infertility cannot be age. The Victorian Act, however, includes the following provision:

> It is Parliament's intention that the following principles be given effect in administering this Act, carrying out functions under this Act, and in the carrying out of activities regulated by this Act:
>
> a) the welfare and interests of any person born or to be born as a result of a treatment procedure are paramount;
> b) human life should be preserved and protected;
> c) the interests of the family should be considered;
> d) infertile couples should be assisted in fulfilling their desire to have children.[42]

These principles are listed in descending order of importance and must be applied in that order. The factor of specific interest for this essay is whether the welfare of the child principle acts to prevent women with an infectious disease from receiving ART.

The Victorian Act provides that, before a woman undergoes a treatment procedure, a doctor must be satisfied, on reasonable grounds, that she is unlikely to become pregnant from an ovum produced by her and sperm produced by her husband or *de facto* partner other than by a treatment procedure; or a doctor who has specialist qualifications in human genetics must be satisfied that, if the woman became pregnant from an ovum produced by her and sperm produced by her husband or partner, a genetic abnormality or a disease may be transmitted to a person born as a result of the pregnancy. The inclusion of the transmission of 'a disease' as a reason for treatment procedures would appear to encompass the situation where a fertile couple may seek treatment using a donor procedure because *the husband* has an infectious disease, such as hepatitis C or HIV which may be passed on to the mother and/or the foetus if it were conceived using his sperm. In South Australia and Western Australia, licence conditions prevent the application of ART to a couple unless they are, or appear to be, infertile or there is a risk that a genetic defect would be transmitted to the child if conceived naturally.

Thus, part of the acceptance of ART in contemporary society is that it can be used to *eliminate disease* – not potentially pass it on. Persons might carry a genetic disease, which they do not wish to pass on to their child. The use of ART, donated gametes, or pre-implantation embryo biopsy, to determine whether the embryo has inherited the defective gene, may be used for such a purpose. All donors of gametes (semen and eggs) must be tested and shown to be free of infection with HIV.[43]

Concerns have been expressed that prohibiting unmarried women's access to AID and IVF treatment may inadvertently lead to the perpetuation of genetic diseases that society might otherwise wish to eliminate.[44] This is based on the realization that, since AID can be self-administered, the effect of limiting some women's access to ART may force those who would otherwise obtain the treatment from a licensed clinic to bypass the formal system introduced by legislation – namely, that the donor's semen be screened for diseases which can be passed on to the recipient.

Thus women's access to infertility treatment is premised on a discourse of eliminating disease, for it is assumed that no good mother would willingly pass on a disease to a potential child. Therefore why would a woman who knew she was HIV positive choose to try for a child when there is the risk of transmission? The bulk of Australian legislation, however, is premised on the basis of preventing the transmission of diseases from men to women and then preventing further transmission to the potential foetus. Apart from the more recent NSW review, the legislation does not fully address the issue of the disease-carrying mother. Yet this notwithstanding, women are not exempt from the discourse of disease accompanying such reproductive technology nor from its implications for notions of acceptable gender behaviour.

A Suitable Parent: Old Moral Prejudices Disguised as New Ethical Dilemmas

HIV has always carried a considerable social stigma in Western society. In the field of infertility, HIV attracts 'marked but inconsistent' discrimination.[45] We are constantly presented with two major concerns associated with the impregnation of an HIV positive woman:

1   The risk of transmission of HIV to the child *in utero* or during birth. Reported rates vary, but in Europe they are between 14 and 18 per cent. Evidence

suggests, however, that very few foetuses are infected *in utero*; most are infected either during passage through the birth canal or through breastfeeding. These risks have been markedly reduced by recent changes in obstetric practice (for example, caesarian section and bottlefeeding), and the lowest achievable rate of transmission now stands at between 2 and 4 per cent.[46]

2   The fact that the infected parent has a shortened life span. The principle of the 'welfare of the child' largely reflects society's perception that the need of the child for a father be given due consideration (this is most explicitly stated in the Human Fertilisation and Embryology Act). In the context of HIV, this appears to be extended to the child's need for a mother, since any resulting child may be brought up without the infected parent for a significant proportion of its life.

If these are valid objections, then one would expect the same criteria to be applied to different diseases with similar characteristics, but they are not. The low rate of HIV transmission compares very favourably to the rates of transmission of 50 per cent for genetic conditions inherited in an autosomal dominant or sex-linked manner, or 25 per cent for autosomal recessive. It is very similar to the 1 to 2 per cent risk run by the offspring of insulin-dependent diabetics of developing the condition themselves. Similarly for hepatitis B, the transmission rate in the absence of immunoglobulins or immunization is, at worst, 95 per cent and, even with their use, remains in the region of 5 per cent.[47] Yet it is inconceivable that women with either of these conditions would not be supported in their attempts to conceive a child through ART.

With regard to the second point, equal consideration for the presence of both parents seems to be a fallacy. With regard to a couple in which the male partner is HIV positive, the greatest concern centres on the risk of transmission to the woman during her attempts to conceive. In this case, the importance of the presence of the male partner during child-rearing takes a back seat. Indeed, if the couple opt to use donor sperm, the child's need of a father is largely overlooked. This approach is congruent with society's general approach to fertility practice, as there is no upper age limit for the male partner in IVF. Apparently, society is prepared to tolerate men fathering children at an age when they potentially might not be present for the majority of the child's life. The emphasis is more on enabling men to father children, rather than on encouraging them to take fuller responsibility for their overall welfare and upbringing.[48]

Therefore, some questions remain: is our reaction to giving an HIV positive woman access to infertility treatment based on the origins of HIV or on a prejudice about HIV and the people who contract this infection? Patient eligibility criteria, such as those discussed in the previous sections (for example, the age of mother) are often passed off as clinical decisions, but mostly they are purely ethical and moral decisions. Questions about the 'welfare of the child' are inevitably questions about who constitutes a 'suitable couple', which in reality comes down to the question of who constitutes a 'suitable mother'. Old moral prejudices about appropriate gendered behaviour and HIV are masqueraded as 'new ethical issues' in reproductive technology. This becomes apparent when the law on access to fertility treatment is tested, as highlighted in the following case study from the United Kingdom.

The BBC TV series *Making Babies* presented the case of a request for treatment from a woman who was HIV positive. Fertility specialist Professor Robert Winston, head of the Hammersmith hospital's IVF unit, decided to treat the woman after she was refused treatment at another hospital. The woman, known only as Sheila, was in her 30s, was in good health and had been HIV positive for ten years. She was a former heroin addict who, it is believed, caught the virus from a former boyfriend. She had been off drugs for eight years and had been in a 'totally supportive relationship' for five years. She was unable to conceive naturally because of damaged fallopian tubes. Professor Winston indicated that, initially, he had been reluctant to offer treatment because of the mother's potentially shorter lifespan and the risk of infecting the child. He subsequently changed his mind, and although Professor Winston had approval from the chairman of the hospital's ethics committee to proceed with Sheila's treatment, he did not have the full support of other members of the IVF team. Professor Winston eventually managed to persuade his colleagues, and Sheila underwent her first round of treatment in 1995 but failed to conceive.

Responses to the case described illustrate the metamorphosis of 'old prejudices' relating to women, infertility and STDs into a contemporary context. Apart from a few voices of support,[49] the decision to treat Sheila was largely met with public and political outrage.[50] Richard Nicholson, editor of the *Bulletin of Medical Ethics* argued that the decision was not in the *best interests of the child* and that it essentially indulged patient desires over the principle of 'clinical need'. Glenda Cooper, writing for *The Independent*,[51] appeared to support this view when she pointed out that the patient was a 'paying customer'. Her article implied that if you can afford to pay for services then essentially you can get what you want, irrespective of significant moral issues. The British Medical Association did not support Professor Winston because of the danger of the potential child being orphaned.[52] Tony Rutherford, director of the Assisted Conception Unit at Leeds General Infirmary also indicated that he considered the risk of infection to the child too high. Tory MP John Marshall, a member of the House of Commons Health Select Committee said the Professor should 'hold his head in shame'. He added:

> I don't believe it is right that unmarried mothers should be encouraged to have children because that will store up future problems, and I don't believe it is right that women who have been infected with the HIV virus should be encouraged to have children because the babies themselves could be infected.[53]

Angela Lambert in an article entitled 'Is this Doctor in Danger of Playing God?',[54] interviewed Professor Winston and largely presented the argument that he was an arrogant man who thought he could 'play God'. She cites as her evidence his argument that the origins of medicine were deeply socialist:

> He believes you are there to help people in distress, even if the distress is their own doing. Here perhaps is a clue to his reasons for treating Sheila, whose past history of heroin-addiction and present HIV status are certainly her own doing. ... Perhaps Nature, which so far has resisted all attempts to implant a foetus in Sheila's womb, will have her own way in the end. This would be seen by some as the decision of a higher authority that even Professor Winston cannot overrule.

All this clearly indicates how, in modern-day society, people continue to believe that individuals are punished for 'bad' things they have done in their life. Clearly, Lambert sees Sheila as being punished with infertility because of her past 'wrongdoings' or, indeed, that her infertility has come about as a direct result of those wrongdoings. She tries to imply that Professor Winston also thinks that this is the case but, being the arrogant man that he is, he can circumvent God's will. At a superficial level it can be pointed out that Professor Winston makes no such claim but, more to the point, Sheila's infertility is completely unrelated to both her former drug addiction and her HIV status: there is no cause and effect between the two. Further, to make the gross overgeneralization that both her former drug addiction and her HIV status are her 'own doing' shows a complete disregard for Sheila's personal circumstances and reflects the deeply held social stigma surrounding HIV infection and those who are infected.

This public perception of HIV has had effects on the management of those infected, those at risk of becoming infected and indeed the perceived risk of infection in general. This culminates in the legal regulation of women with this disease in an indirect manner, via the exploitation of the 'welfare of the child' clause in the Human Fertilisation and Embryology Act. This conservative interpretation of the 'welfare of child' clause is really a method for screening out women deemed unsuitable because their HIV positive status signifies something degenerative about their sexual behaviour, and hence acts to regulate the sexual activity of women.

Thus, I would suggest that debate on access to fertility treatment actually centres around two separate, but interrelated discourses. First and foremost is the discourse on what constitutes a fit mother. If an 'unfit mother' is described as someone who may die very early on in the child's life, then all women are at risk of being unfit mothers – we all run the risk, from one cause or another, of premature death. But we know that what constitutes the 'fit/unfit mother' is much more than this. A comparison of two highly publicized British cases clearly illustrates how our 'ethical responses' to issues in reproductive technology have nothing to do with the technologies themselves and everything to do with the women requesting the treatments.

In October 1996 Mandy Allwood lost all of the eight babies that she had conceived as a result of using fertility drugs. Around the same time, the young widow Diane Blood was refused permission to use her dead husband's sperm for her own insemination treatment. The media frenzy that accompanied both cases was characterized by claims that science was running ahead of ethics but, as Tizzard points out, there was nothing scientifically new about either of the cases since the technology relating to each case had been in use for some time.[55] Rather, the issue at hand was the status of the women themselves.

Mandy Allwood sold her story to a tabloid newspaper and employed the services of a publicist. This was not considered admirable behaviour for any self-sacrificing woman intending to give birth to eight foetuses. Her private life came under public scrutiny: the fact that she was unmarried, her partner had 'another family' and her reproductive history were all analysed by the public. She was deemed unfit to carry on with the pregnancy as it was clearly a money-making media stunt. Like Mary Beth Whitehead[56] before her, Mandy Allwood made the mistake of seeking commercial remuneration for what is considered to be the most altruistic and self-sacrificing of acts – motherhood. Diane Blood was also assessed according to her personal qualities. However, she was largely thought of as a good, self-effacing, God-fearing woman who suffered grief at the loss of her husband and who desperately wanted a child. The Human Fertilisation and Embryology Authority's refusal to comply with her wishes was seen as cruel and unfair.

An examination of the facts of the two cases, however, suggests that, technically, the public should have been more supportive of Mandy Allwood. The existence of a partner (read father) is seen as an important criterion for fertility treatment: Mandy Allwood had a partner whereas Diane Blood did not. It is also generally considered that fertility treatment should be reserved for those who have a medical problem which makes conception difficult or impossible: Mandy Allwood had such a difficulty whereas Diane Blood did not. The treatment Mandy Allwood had received was within the bounds of legislation, yet the harvesting of Mr Blood's sperm without his written consent was, in fact, illegal. Nonetheless, public responses to the two women were in deep contrast: Diane Blood was perceived to deserve the reproductive technology on offer and Mandy Allwood was not. These two cases highlight how responses to modern-day issues in reproductive technology have nothing to do with the technologies themselves and more to do with public perceptions of appropriate gendered behaviour.

Second, there is the discourse of what constitutes an acceptable disease. Perceptions of legitimacy in relation to screening on genetic bases are negotiated through two key discourses: one of risk and the other of voluntarism. '[T]he language of risk is a loaded one. As a diagnostic discourse, it resolutely individualizes the character of disability and thus sidesteps an interrogation of the social attitudes, conditions and inequalities that shape the experiences of disabled people'.[57] Part of the stigma surrounding HIV is that it is perceived to be the result of someone's degenerate sexual activity – something they have brought upon themselves. This is no different from early conceptions of the relationship between other STDs and women's infertility. Yet, if an HIV positive woman were not infertile, it would be she who chose whether or not to become pregnant. Many of those who are concerned at the thought of unlimited access to infertility treatment generally accept that no legal or social control can regulate natural reproduction amongst fertile people who are 'unsuitable'. However, they feel that this should not prevent society from vetting 'unsuitable' parents and precluding them from participating in artificial reproduction. But, as Liu points out, '[t]his argument, if successful, would create the theoretical and conceptual anomaly of reproductive control over those who are infertile whilst ignoring parents who conceive naturally'.[58]

The movement to control women's pregnancy-related behaviour,[59] and the apparent priority given to the future upbringing of a child and to the production of normal babies, reinforces the messages being sent by the development of reproductive technologies and their regulation.[60] That is, it acts to reinforce the role of medico-legal discourse and practice in regulating appropriate gender behaviour not only by its definition of disease, but also by its determination of those who may be granted access to its developing technologies.

Conclusion

Michelle Stanworth notes how reproductive technology 'crystallise[s] issues at the heart of contemporary controversies over sexuality, parenthood, reproduction and the family'.[61] Thus, concerns about the 'status of women' seeking assisted reproduction are similar to those that converged around the women targeted by the Contagious Diseases Acts of 1864, 1866 and 1869.

The notion of 'fitness for parenting' is becoming increasingly prevalent in discourses surrounding access to reproductive technology, yet our perception of 'suitable' parents is an ambiguous and amorphous social and psychological concept. The idea of reproductive freedom appears to be seriously threatened when eligibility for infertility treatment to enable an individual to have children is on the agenda. While society might agree that the allocation of resources should be closely scrutinized if prejudice is not to dominate decision-making, it is apparent that, to date, little seems to have been done to evaluate the bases on which scarce resources are morally to be located.

The growing technological separation of reproduction and sex, and the reshaping of moral questions associated with reproduction as new ethical dilemmas (for example, discussion of the welfare of the child in place of the status of the woman seeking assistance), means that an array of arguments may be produced to limit the availability of resources to groups whose rights to reproduce are already regarded as unimportant. It is clear that the law both can be, and indeed is, used as a mechanism to support this state of affairs – that is, the direct and indirect intervention in, and regulation of, women's private sexual and reproductive practices.

Acknowledgements

Special thanks to Juliet Tizzard of Progress Educational Trust for her early help on this essay.

Notes

1   Weeks, J. (1989), *Sex, Politics and Society: The Regulation of Sexuality since 1800*, London: Longman, p. 11.
2   Foucault, M. (1980), *Power/Knowledge. Selected Interviews and Other Writings. 1972–77*, ed. Colin Gordon, Brighton: The Harvester Press.
3   Weeks, *Sex, Politics and Society, op cit.*, n. 1, p. 11.
4   Millns, S. (1995), 'Making Social Judgements That Go Beyond the Purely Medical: The Reproductive Revolution and Access to Fertility Treatment', in Millns, S. and Bridgeman, J. (eds), *Law and Body Politics: Regulating the Female Body*, Aldershot: Dartmouth, p. 81.
5   Liu, A. (1991), *Artificial Reproduction and Reproductive Rights*, Aldershot: Dartmouth, p. 55.
6   Douglas, G. (1991), *Law, Fertility and Reproduction*, London: Sweet and Maxwell, p. 119.

7   Liu, *Artificial Reproduction, op. cit.*, n. 5, p. 55.
8   See Steinberg, D. (1997), 'A Most Selective Practice: The Eugenic Logics of IVF', *Women's Studies International Forum*, **20**(1), pp. 33–48.
9   [1988] 1 FLR 512.
10 Ibid., at p. 516.
11 Douglas, *Law, Fertility and Reproduction, op. cit.*, n. 6, p. 120.
12 See Houghton, D. and Houghton, P. (1987), *Coping With Childlessness*, London: Unwin Paperbacks, p. 19.
13 Overall, C. (1987), *Ethics and Human Reproduction: A Feminist Analysis*, Boston: Allen and Unwin, p. 172.
14 See Pfeffer, N. (1993), *The Stork and the Syringe: A Political History of Reproductive Medicine*, Cambridge: Polity Press.
15 Warnock, M. (Chairman), *Report of the Committee of Inquiry into Human Fertilisation and Embryology*, (1984) Cmnd 9314, London: HMSO (hereafter Warnock Report). See also Cusine, D. (1989), 'Legal Issues in Human Reproduction', in McLean, S. (ed.), *Legal Issues in Human Reproduction*, Aldershot: Gower, p. 18.
16 Tizzard, J. (1998), 'Reproductive Technology: New Ethical Dilemmas and Old Moral Prejudices', in Lee, E. (ed.), *Abortion Law and Politics Today*, London: Macmillan Press, pp. 185–88.
17 Douglas, *Law, Fertility and Reproduction, op. cit.*, n. 6, p. 113.
18 Ibid., p. 121 (emphasis added).
19 Tizzard, 'Reproductive Technology', *op. cit.*, n. 16, p. 190; and see below.
20 In the United Kingdom there appears to be no uniformity of practice. St Mary's hospital's IVF unit offers treatment to couples who have been living together for at least three years, whilst the IVF unit at King's College hospital has no policy regarding the patient's relationships, although where the relationship, or lack of it, may present a problem, the case will be considered on an individual basis.
21 Human Fertilisation and Embryology Act 1990, s. 13(5).
22 Ibid.
23 Tizzard, 'Reproductive Technology', *op. cit.*, n. 16, p. 191. The point was expressly acknowledged by Warnock – see below.
24 House of Lords, *Official Report*, 6 February 1990, cols 788–9.
25 Ibid., col. 800.
26 House of Lords, *Official Report*, 6 March 1990, col. 1098.
27 Warnock Report, *op. cit.*, n. 15, para 2.1.
28 Thomson, M., (1996) at p. 109, 'Legislating for the Monstrous; Access to Reproductive Services and the Monstrous Feminine', *Women's Access to Healthcare: Law, Society and Culture*, Working Paper No. 4, Liverpool: Feminist Legal Research Unit, University of Liverpool.
29 Douglas, G. (1993), 'Assisted Reproduction and the Welfare of the Child', *Current Legal Problems*, **53**. Cited in Thomson, 'Legislating for the Monstrous', *op. cit.*, p. 124, n. 28.
30 Thomson, 'Legislating for the Monstrous', *op. cit.*, n. 28.
31 Douglas, 'Assisted Reproduction', *op. cit.*, n. 29, p. 58.
32 HFE Authority (1998), *Code of Practice* (4th edn), London: HMSO, para. 3.3. An earlier section is cited in Thomson, 'Legislating for the Monstrous', *op. cit.*, p. 130.
33 [1988] 1 FLR 512.
34 As with the United Kingdom, legislation in Australia has been preceded by government reports and inquiries in nearly all states and at the federal level. See, for example, the Victorian Committee to Consider the Ethical and Legal Issues Arising from In Vitro Fertilisation (August 1984), the Special Committee Appointed by the Queensland

Government to Inquire into the Laws Relating to Artificial Insemination, In Vitro Fertilisation and Other Related Matters (March 1984), Family Law Council (July 1985), Committee of Inquiry to Investigate Artificial Conception and Related Matters in Tasmania (June 1985).

35 H96/26, 96, 33 and 96/48, A. Kohl, 12 March 1997.

36 NSW Government Health Department Discussion Paper (1998), *Important Questions for the Community: Assisted Reproductive Technologies*, p. 3.2. At <http://www.health. nsw.gov.au/health-public-affairs/art/important.html>.

37 SA Supreme Court SCGRG 1114 of 1996; S5801, 10 September 1996. See also *McBain* v *State of Victoria* [2000] FCA 1009. A similar criterion applies in Western Australia.

38 [1997] QSC 206.

39 *The Law Handbook: The Easy to Use Practical Guide to the Law in NSW* (6th edn), 1997. Sydney: Redfern Centre Publishing, p. 1007.

40 Kirby, M. (1989), 'Medical Technology and New Frontiers of Family Law', in McLean, *Legal Issues*, *op. cit.*, n. 15, pp. 7–8.

41 NSW, *op. cit.*, n. 36, p. 3.3.

42 Infertility Treatment Act 1995, s. 5, replacing Infertility (Medical Procedures) Act 1984.

43 Interim Licensing Authority (1989), *Guidelines for both Clinical and Research Applications of Human In Vitro Fertilisation*, para 13(h)(i). Human Fertilisation and Embryology Authority, (2001) Code of Practice, Annex C, London: HFEA.

44 Liu, *Artificial Reproduction*, *op. cit.*, n. 5, p. 63.

45 Johnson, M. (1997), 'Letting Prejudice Take Over', in *Progress in Reproduction* (news journal of the Progress Educational Trust), **1**(1), March, p. 6.

46 Ibid., pp. 6–7.

47 Ibid.

48 This attitude is reflected in the positive public and media reaction to the development of new reproductive technologies that would enable HIV positive men to father children without the risk of transmission of the disease. See 'Parenthood Hope for Men with HIV', *Sunday Telegraph*, 2 May 1996: sperm-washing procedure offers 'new hope'.

49 The group Positively Women (support and information service for women with HIV) supported and welcomed the decision by Professor Winston. Sam Abdalla, director of the IVF unit at the private Lister Hospital in London also supported the decision.

50 Quinn, S. (1996), 'Fertility Treatment for HIV Woman Sparks Controversy', *The Guardian*, 13 May.

51 Cooper, G. (1996), 'Aids "Fertility" Row', *The Independent*, 14 May.

52 Quinn, S. (1996), 'Fertility Treatment for HIV Woman Sparks Controversy', *The Guardian*, 13 May.

53 Hope, J. and Brooke, C. (1996), 'The HIV Woman and Storm in a Test-tube', *Daily Mail*, 14 May.

54 Ibid.

55 Tizzard, 'Reproductive Technology', *op. cit.*, n. 16, p. 196.

56 *In the Matter of Baby M* (1988) 537 A 2d 1227 (NJ Sup. Ct), an (in)famous surrogacy case.

57 Steinberg, 'A Most Selective Practice' *op. cit*, n. 8, p. 43.

58 Liu, *Artificial Reproduction*, *op. cit.*, n. 5, p. 55.

59 This is largely evidenced in the United States but is also apparent in the United Kingdom and Australia.

60 McLean, S. (1989), 'Women, Rights and Reproduction', in McLean, *Legal Issues*, *op. cit.*, n. 15, p. 226.

61 Stanworth, M. (ed.) (1987), *Reproductive Technologies: Gender, Motherhood and Medicine*, London: Polity Press, p. 18.

Chapter 4

Psychologizing Abortion: Women's 'Mental Health' and the Regulation of Abortion in Britain

Ellie Lee

Introduction

This chapter discusses the place of 'mental health' in the regulation of abortion in Britain. I aim first to explain why law and policy on abortion was framed in Britain through reference to the effects of pregnancy on a woman's mind. I also hope that I can make a convincing argument as to why we might consider such law and policy problematic for women.

Throughout, I hope to illustrate one central point about the term 'mental health'. My contention is that 'mental health', in the context of abortion law and policy, cannot be understood as an objective, definable phenomenon. 'Mental health' is rather a code for a set of ideas, dominant at the time when the Abortion Act was passed, and arguably still highly influential, about women, pregnancy, doctors and the role of the law. To put it another way, 'mental health' is a shorthand term which expressed perceptions held by those who introduced law and policy about a set of interrelated social questions.

Legislation or policy on abortion which makes reference to women's mental health does not therefore do so on 'objective' or asocial grounds. On the contrary, regulation of abortion on 'mental health' grounds is as much driven by ideology and politics as is its regulation on any other ground – for example, that of protecting foetal rights. I hope, through this chapter, to make it clear that it is important not to accept the appearance of neutrality, present where regulation is framed in terms of 'health', and instead to ask questions about what such framing of law and policy represents for those whose access to abortion is regulated on this basis.

To develop my argument, I shall focus on two aspects of abortion law and policy, the 1967 Abortion Act (as amended) and the 1974 Lane Report. There are, of course, many other aspects to the regulation of abortion: there were a further 16 abortion bills introduced into the British parliament between 1967 and 1992.[1] However, the 1967 Abortion Act and the Lane Report do constitute particularly significant components of the development of the regulation of abortion in Britain.

Unlike other abortion bills which were unsuccessful, the 1967 Act (and the 1990 reform to the Act) was endorsed by the government of the day. The Labour government allocated extra parliamentary time for the discussion of abortion in

1966–67. This was important in that it meant sufficient parliamentary time was made available for debate, and there was therefore a good chance that the new legislation would be passed. In contrast, numerous other abortion bills introduced in the past 30 years failed to get very far, because insufficient time had been allocated for debate. The Lane Report was similarly officially endorsed, since it was the result of the work of a committee set up by the Conservative government of the time. The Lane Committee's approach to investigating the Abortion Act in practice, and its findings set out in the Lane Report, can therefore be taken as representative of the official attitude to abortion. Together, therefore, the 1967 Abortion Act (as amended) and the Lane Report merit analysis because of their status and significance in the development of the contemporary framework for abortion regulation.

The 1967 Abortion Act

Abortion in Britain still remains formally illegal. The procedure is regulated by sections 58 and 59 of the 1861 Offences Against the Person Act[2] which set a maximum penalty of life imprisonment for attempting to procure an abortion and criminalize anyone, including the woman herself, who attempted to procure an abortion. From 1968 onwards (when the 1967 Abortion Act came into force), the 1861 Act had to be read in conjunction with the 1967 Act. A defence was provided against the offences defined in the prior legislation because, in the 1967 Act, doctors were empowered to carry out legal abortion on the grounds specified in the clauses of the Abortion Act.[3]

Neither doctors nor women were frequently prosecuted under the 1861 Act. Even before 1967, the number of prosecutions for illegal abortion was very small. In 1919, for example, 60 people were tried for procuring abortion and 42 convicted. This stands against a pre-1967 illegal abortion rate estimated at between tens of thousands to 100 000 abortions annually.[4] Although figures vary widely and are accepted to be inaccurate because of the absence of proper records, it seems clear nonetheless that, before legalization, abortion was common and generally accepted in the popular mind, if not in the law, as a method of birth control. However, the fact that abortion remained illegal, with exceptions permitted, is significant because of the way in which this formulation of the law constructed abortion. The assumption behind the 1967 Abortion Act was that abortion was *prima facie* wrong and was to be prohibited unless there were mitigating circumstances – namely, those specified in the Act – and provided two doctors agreed that one of these circumstances applied to the woman in question.

Since 1967 only one amendment has been made to abortion law, through section 37 of the 1990 Human Fertilisation and Embryology Act. The terms of the Abortion Act 1967 (as amended in 1990) are as follows:

Section 1(1): Subject to the provisions of this section, a person shall not be guilty of an offence under the law relating to abortion when a pregnancy is terminated by a registered medical practitioner if two registered medical practitioners are of the opinion formed in good faith –

(a) that the pregnancy has not exceeded its twenty-fourth week and that the continuance of the pregnancy would involve risk, greater than if the pregnancy were terminated, of injury to the physical or mental health of the pregnant woman or any existing children of her family; or

(b) that the termination is necessary to prevent grave permanent injury to the physical or mental health of the pregnant woman; or

(c) that the continuance of the pregnancy would involve risk to the life of the pregnant woman, greater than if the pregnancy were terminated; or

(d) that there is substantial risk that if the child were born it would suffer from such physical or mental abnormalities as to be seriously handicapped.

1(2)   In determining whether the continuance of a pregnancy would involve such risk of injury to health as is mentioned in paragraph a) or b) of subsection (1) of this section, account may be taken of the pregnant woman's actual or reasonably forseeable environment.

According to the British philosopher Janet Radcliffe-Richards,[5] the key feature of this law was that its moral basis was unclear. British law was not based on principles regarding the appropriateness, or inappropriateness, of legal abortion: legal abortion was not deemed 'right' or 'wrong'. This absence of abortion as a matter related to legal principle can be illustrated clearly through a comparison with US abortion law.

The 1973 *Roe* v. *Wade* ruling by the US Supreme Court deemed first-trimester abortion a constitutionally protected privacy right.[6] In its ruling, the Court said that the right to privacy '… is broad enough to encompass a woman's decision whether or not to terminate her pregnancy'.[7] While the Court took it for granted that a doctor would be consulted, the law ultimately left decision-making during the first trimester to the woman. A principle was thus established in law of a woman's right to decide on abortion. Although, clearly, this legal principle has been undermined in the United States, in particular by restrictions on abortion passed at the level of individual states,[8] abortion in federal US law nonetheless remains constructed as a question of a woman's right.

In Britain no such principle underpinned abortion law. The woman was given no right to abortion but, it should noted, neither was the foetus ascribed any legal protection in abortion law until the 24th week of pregnancy. Throughout pregnancy, the right to decide whether or not a woman could legally end a pregnancy was deemed to rest in the hands of two doctors, who could agree to the request for abortion on medical grounds. It was the judgement of two doctors which was therefore primary in deciding whether a woman's request for abortion complied with the terms of the Abortion Act.

Consequently, feminist scholars have pointed out that British abortion law *medicalizes* abortion.[9] Legal scholar Sally Sheldon, on the basis of her study of the parliamentary debate about the 1967 Abortion Act and the 1990 Human Fertilisation and Embryology Act, has defined 'medicalization' as '… the pre-eminence of a medical discourse or narrative, and the marginalisation of other understandings or knowledges'.[10] In this chapter I draw on this concept of 'medicalization', as developed by Sheldon and others,[11] to draw attention to the key feature of the regulation of abortion in Britain. I explain that, in Britain, the regulation of abortion rests on a construction of abortion not as a woman's right, when she is faced with unwanted pregnancy, but as legally permissible only on *medical* grounds as an alternative to continuing a pregnancy. Drawing primarily on the work of Sally Sheldon and Mary Boyle, I will first discuss this defining aspect of British law, and indicate why abortion law in Britain came to be formulated in these terms.

The Doctor and the Woman

Mary Boyle has pointed out that, under the terms of the Abortion Act, '[a] woman may decide that she wants an abortion, but it is doctors who decide whether she may have it'.[12] She and Sally Sheldon have discussed how this framing of the law came into being. They ask how it came to be the case that, while it is the woman who will have the abortion, it is doctors who decide whether or not she is allowed to. In order to supply some answers to this question, Sheldon and Boyle have carried out thorough analyses of the parliamentary debate on abortion. Some of their key points are outlined below.

Boyle suggests that the claim that the abortion decision was a medical decision was sometimes simply asserted. For instance, parliamentarians argued in support of the new law using references to medicine: 'It seems to me a very big decision, and must always be a medical decision'; '… obviously the decision must be a medical one'; '… it must always be a medical decision'.[13] In these comments, no justification for the claim that abortion decisions required the exercise of medical judgement was given. It was simply taken for granted that decision-making should lie with doctors.

Other parliamentarians suggested that abortion should *only* be legal for 'medical reasons'. For example, it was argued that '… the main basis of the Bill is medical. Good ethics in medicine and surgery demand that an operation should not be done unless it is justifiable or indicated for medical reasons.'[14] The effect of this argument was to draw a line between 'good' medical reasons for abortion and 'bad' social, or what were often called 'trivial', reasons. This kind of appeal to medical justification for abortion had the clear effect of delegitimizing reasons for abortion that were not 'medical'. It also means that 'abortion on demand' – that is, abortion where the woman is not required to specify the reason for her abortion request – was ruled out.

Sheldon also analyses the construction of medical authority in this debate. She points out that parliamentarians used very different terminology when they talked about doctors from when they referred to women seeking abortion. The latter were talked about as being in great distress, in need of pity, sympathy, and assistance from others: in sum, as 'victims'.[15] In thus characterizing the woman involved, reformers frequently made reference to the plight of those who sought backstreet abortions. Sheldon quotes one MP who, talking in support of reform, described women who seek abortion as the 'distracted multi-child mother, often the wife of a drunken husband' and the woman who 'returns to a distant town there to lie in terror and blood and without medical attention'. Another talked of 'mothers with large families' suffering from the 'burdens of large families', and another of the 'woman in total misery'.[16]

While the concern expressed about the effect of illegal, backstreet abortion was genuine, the woman was in effect disparaged as a victim of desperate circumstances. As Greenwood and Young have pointed out, this woman was '... not only on the fringe, but literally physically inadequate'.[17] Abortion law reformers emphasized the desperation, poverty and instability of women who wanted abortion.[18]

In contrast with the image of the desperate woman, the doctor was depicted as a 'calm, responsible, rational and reassuring figure', as 'highly skilled and dedicated', as 'sensitive, sympathetic', as a member of a 'high and proud profession', and as displaying 'skill, judgement and knowledge'.[19] Unlike the worn-down, distraught woman, he was conceptualized to be in a position to make rational, considered decisions, and as such, was clearly the best candidate for the law to empower with the authority to make abortion decisions.

It should be noted that the contrast made between doctors and women was characteristic of the arguments put forward by supporters of reform. Indeed, it could be argued that the success of abortion law reform was predicated on the granting of decision-making power in abortion to those considered responsible and trustworthy – namely doctors – and the assurance that it would not be granted to those considered not so – namely women.[20]

Motherhood, Morality and Health

The second, related aspect of the medicalization of abortion was the construction of the negative effect of continuing pregnancy on the health of the woman, or her existing family, as legal grounds for terminating a pregnancy. This point can be illustrated by looking at the terms of the debate between opponents and reformers in 1966–67.

The way in which reformers and opponents of abortion law reform talked about women requesting abortion displayed both similarities and significant differences. Sheldon contends that these two 'camps' of opinion were fundamentally united, in that whether parliamentarians were for or against making abortion legal, they saw maternity as a state that women normally desired. Sheldon argues that: 'The image of the woman as mother is appropriated for the cause of both reformists and conservatives alike. It is not until the 1990 debates that (some) MPs feel able to challenge the inevitability of maternity for all women.'[21] The difference between opponents and supporters of reform was the way in which they constructed women who want abortion in relation to this norm.

For opponents, abortion was constructed as an abomination, which was antithetical to the desire any normal woman has to be a mother. It was construed as both immoral and 'unnatural'. For reformers, abortion was a 'necessary evil' which could help ensure that, when children are born, they are born to women who feel capable of mothering them effectively. On this basis, women could be justifiably exempted from maternity, and should be able to legally abort a pregnancy, if they were temporarily incapable of being 'good' mothers. By contending that their health would be placed 'at risk' through childbirth, abortion could then be justified on the grounds that women with poor health would make poor mothers. Hence, for reformers, access to abortion could help facilitate successful and effective motherhood by ensuring that women have children only in circumstances where they are healthy enough to mother them. The following brief extracts from the 1967 debate illustrate these differing positions.

Opponents of the Abortion Act saw the woman who sought abortion as '… a selfish, irrational child'.[22] Women who wanted abortion as the outcome of their pregnancy were said to be feckless, irresponsible and immature. By falling pregnant, but then requesting abortion, such women were said to demonstrate moral weakness by refusing to face up to their responsibility to the future child. This narrative constructed abortion-seeking women as outlandish and even as despicable. Comments made in parliament by the well-known opponent of legal abortion, Dame Jill Knight, illustrate this view:

> People must be helped to be responsible, not encouraged to be irresponsible … Does anyone think that the problem of the 15-year old mother can be solved by taking the easy way out? … here is the case of a perfectly healthy baby being sacrificed for the mother's convenience. … [23]

Women who sought to end pregnancy by abortion were characterized as whimsical and unthinking. Their motivation for abortion was construed as a desire to avoid responsibility by taking the easiest option available, rather than doing what was 'right'. It is striking that Knight used the example of a 15 year-old girl – a case where even those opposed to 'easy abortion' might accept that there are good grounds for ending the pregnancy. Although the idea of a child bearing a child is something few would actively support, this commentator could see, even in this situation, no 'good reason' for abortion. This carried the underlying implication that older women who sought abortion must be remarkably feckless and irresponsible to even consider such a course of action. Whereas Knight was contemptuous of women who seek abortion, other anti-abortionists, such as the Labour MP Kevin McNamara, expressed incomprehension that a woman could even consider abortion in the event of pregnancy:

> How can a woman's capacity to be a mother be measured before she has a child? Fecklessness, a bad background, being a bad manager, these are nothing to do with the love, that unidentifiable bond, no matter how strange or difficult the circumstances, which links a mother to her child and makes her cherish it.[24]

A longstanding argument in psychology and medicine, which has constructed women as having an 'unidentifiable bond' with their child or potential child, has been discussed in feminist writings.[25] Those who argue against abortion use this construction of women to delegitimize abortion as wrong for any woman, on the grounds that it goes against women's instinct to have babies. For opponents of the Act, women were fundamentally maternal and women who seek abortion were therefore feckless and irresponsible in their violation of this basic instinct.

Reformers, whilst agreeing that motherhood was the ideal and desirable end to pregnancy, '… represented the woman who would seek to terminate a pregnancy as a vulnerable, unstable (even suicidal) victim of her desperate social circumstances'.[26] According to David Owen, the then Labour MP for Plymouth, abortion was for the woman 'in total misery' who:

... could be precipitated into a depression deep and lasting. What happens to that woman when she gets depressed? She is incapable of looking after those children, so she retires into a shell of herself and loses all feeling, all drive and affection.[27]

In this comment, abortion was constructed as an adjunct to motherhood, not as being in opposition to it. The woman is already a mother and so has fulfilled her destiny to show care and affection to her offspring. However, bearing another child would diminish her ability to continue doing so, and hence abortion would be the best solution because it would enable her to continue being a good mother. Her grounds for abortion are therefore the 'depression' that would result from further childbearing. This approach is illustrated more clearly still in the following comment from Dr John Dunwoody (Labour MP for Falmouth and Camborne):

My belief is that in many cases today where we have over-large families the mother is so broken down physically and emotionally with the continual bearing of children that it becomes quite impossible for her to fulfil her real function, her worthwhile function as a mother. ...[28]

Here, abortion was seen as an option for a certain type of woman. She was already a mother, and so had fulfilled her 'real function'. She was also 'worn down' physically and emotionally, and so could not cope with another child. Sheldon suggests, therefore, that: 'Whilst the reformers believed that women seeking abortion had been wrongly stigmatised as criminals, they represented them as victims who needed help and guidance'.[29]

In summary, the law that emerged from this discussion had motherhood at its centre. Women were constructed as fundamentally maternal, and it was assumed that, normally, pregnancy should be carried to term. The woman who could legally terminate pregnancy was constructed as unable to effectively raise any additional children, and hence abortion was her best option. In 1967 a key theme for supporters of reform was whether the woman's health was good enough to allow her to bear and mother a child.

In the event, the reformers' arguments won the day, and, through the 1967 Act, doctors were empowered by law to take into account women's health in deciding whether or not a request for abortion was legal, on the grounds that this was relevant to the woman's ability to successfully mother a child. Under the law, a doctor can therefore allow an abortion if carrying the pregnancy to term constitutes a greater threat to the woman's physical or mental health than if the pregnancy were terminated. This construction suggests that abortion may represent some threat to health, but pregnancy carried to term may be a greater risk. In other words, women were construed in this debate as warranting legal abortion provided that they were physically or mentally unable to cope with bearing a child. Abortion was legalized only for those women too physically or mentally weak to cope with continuing their pregnancy to term.

Mental Health and Abortion Law

As I have argued, the 1967 Act medicalizes abortion. However, the construction of abortion as justifiable on 'medical grounds' is more complex than it might first appear. Following Kennedy, Boyle has argued that in general, and not just in abortion, what constitutes a 'medical decision', taken for 'medical reasons' is not self-evident.[30] Indeed, it is difficult to find a consistent and convincing definition of what such a decision constitutes. A decision taken by doctors is not adequate, since doctors make many decisions which are not medical. Perhaps the definition of a decision made by a doctor about health would be more convincing? Again, this is problematic, since what constitutes a decision about health is not at all straightforward. How, for instance, is the line to be drawn between interventions which are 'medical' and those which are 'non-medical'? For example, prescribing the contraceptive pill to a teenager to prevent acne and paying money to a body-piercing salon could both be described as activities which aim to improve the appearance of the individual concerned. Yet the decision to prescribe the pill would be deemed 'medical' since the pill is a 'treatment' paid for by the NHS. In the second case, the decision to purchase body-piercing would be deemed 'cosmetic' as this is a 'service' paid for by the individual. As Boyle suggests, what constitutes a 'medical decision' is not objective and descriptive, but is profoundly influenced by norms and values, and is subject to change and redefinition.[31]

In considering the definition of the abortion decision as a 'medical issue' in 1967, the exercise of value judgements, and the reworking of what is meant by 'health' was very apparent. If 'medical judgement' had been narrowly defined, it would have meant that the doctor was in a position to pass judgement about the likely effect of abortion on a narrow range of bodily processes – for example, the risk of perforating the uterus. However, in making an abortion decision, this is not what the doctor was said to be judging. Mary Boyle suggests that medical involvement in abortion decisions instead came to imply that the doctor should make value, rather than strictly medical, judgements about the foetus, the woman's wishes and about her social and personal circumstances.[32]

Sheldon also points out that the law rested on a broad definition of what the doctor was in a position to judge. Through the 1967 Act (section 1 (2) as set out on page 63) the doctor was empowered to take into account the 'woman's actual or reasonably foreseeable environment' in assessing her abortion request. As a result, '[t]he woman's whole lifestyle, her home, finances and relationships are opened up to the doctors' scrutiny. ... The power given to doctors far exceeds that which would accrue merely on the basis of a technical expertise.'[33] The Act thus relied on the construction of the doctor being in a position to make judgements that do not primarily rely on technical expertise. This broad conception of 'medical' expertise was in fact overtly argued for by the initiator of the 1967 Act, David Steel MP, who argued 'social conditions cannot and ought not to be separated from medical conditions. I hope that the Abortion Act by its very drafting has encouraged the concept of socio-medical care.'[34]

A further component in broadening the definition of what constituted a 'medical matter' was the place of a woman's psychological state, or 'mental health', in legal grounds for abortion. As I indicated earlier, the justification of abortion on the grounds that the continuation of pregnancy would bring about depression or other negative psychological states was made by reformers during the debate on the 1967 Act. However, the inclusion of the assessment and treatment of mental states as a medical matter, and therefore as justifiable grounds for abortion, is a move predicated on a noteworthy process through which health and illness had become redefined.

Boyle suggests that by the time of the 1967 debates the inclusion of 'mental health' as 'medical reason' for abortion was relatively unproblematic.[35] The construction of the problem of 'mental health' as a legitimate issue, deserving of medical attention, had already been established through a process which preceded the 1967 reforms. Boyle draws attention to two moments in legal history which, she contends, are significant in this respect. The first was the *Bourne* ruling. This ruling, made in 1938, acquitted a Dr Bourne, who had been charged with committing a criminal offence after performing an abortion on a 14-year-old girl who had become pregnant after being raped by soldiers. The significance of this ruling is discussed by Boyle as follows:

> In the early decades of this century, however, there was an increasing discussion about the lawfulness of abortion for mental rather than physical reasons. The acquittal of Dr Aleck Bourne, who was prosecuted in 1938 for carrying out an abortion on a 14-year-old 'decent' girl who had been raped, suggested to some that a woman's mental state was as important as her physical state in abortion decisions. The nineteenth and early twentieth centuries, however, lacked an accepted system of thought which allowed the incorporation of a wide range of behaviour and psychological experiences into the notion of health.[36]

While the *Bourne* ruling indicated the way in which physical and mental health would emerge as having equal status as grounds for medical intervention, Boyle contends, however, that this conflation only became systematic later, with the 1959 Mental Health Act. She writes that this Act '... sought to blur or abolish any distinction between physical ailments and psychological distress or disturbing behaviour'. Further she argues that:

> The second assumption was that doctors have the knowledge and skills to make impartial judgements about these matters and that they should be allowed to do so free from public or judicial interference. Finally it was assumed that the intervention of psychiatry was always therapeutic and in the best interests of the patient.[37]

By the time the 1967 Abortion Act was passed, therefore, a legal framework was already in place through which doctors were established as the best placed to make judgements about what interventions should be made on the grounds of 'mental health'. As a result, a situation existed where '... physical and mental health held identical status as medical reasons for abortion; it was simply that different factors needed to be taken into account in judging whether these reasons were present in a particular case'.[38]

The blurring of the distinction between physical and mental health was therefore central to the formation of the 1967 Abortion Act. This process is worthy of comment for two reasons. First, it can shed further light on the particular way in which the terms of the Abortion Act are framed. Physical and mental health are given equality in this legislation, as a direct result of a historical process through which the meaning of 'health' was broadened and redefined. Second, the construction of legal grounds for abortion in terms of 'mental health' has been important in the development of the practice of abortion since 1967.

Under the Act, a woman can terminate pregnancy if continuing the pregnancy represents a threat to her physical or mental health, or to that of her existing family. In the years since the passing of the Act, this has turned out to be by far the most commonly used criterion given by doctors to give women access to abortion: over 98 per cent of the abortions carried out in England and Wales are for this reason.[39] The relatively greater threat to physical health posed by childbirth, in comparison to early abortion, has allowed liberally-minded doctors to judge just about any first-trimester abortion legal.[40] The mental health effects of abortion, as compared to childbearing have, however, also been important in allowing legal abortion. The case made by doctors where they believe a woman should be able to have an abortion has often been that continuing pregnancy to term will be psychologically damaging for the woman, and that therefore abortion should be allowed. In this way, assessment of the mental health of the woman has become a significant feature of the operation of abortion law.

The implications of this practice can be read in two ways. On the one hand, the very broad definition of health – in particular, the elasticity of the concept of 'mental health' – has created a situation where liberally-minded doctors can judge almost any abortion carried out relatively early in pregnancy to be legal. As David Paintin, a gynaecologist active in providing abortion both before and after the passing of the 1967 legislation has argued, '... the Act can be interpreted so that abortion can be provided virtually on request ...'.[41] He suggests that, even when the Act came into force in 1968, there proved to be a significant minority of doctors who were willing to interpret the Act as '...allowing them to provide abortion to women stressed by unwanted pregnancies'.[42]

Since that time, Paintin contends, doctors have increasingly come to use the WHO definition of health – that health is '... a state of complete physical and social wellbeing and not merely the absence of disease or infirmity' – and, as a result, doctors can certify '... that there is a risk of injury to mental health if they can identify factors in the woman's life that would stress her mental well-being if the pregnancy were to continue'.[43] Since '... such factors are present in the lives of all women who are motivated enough to consult a doctor about abortion' any woman can qualify for an abortion on this ground.[44]

Boyle has pointed out, on the other hand, what this means about the construction of women when the UK abortion law is applied in practice:

> ... the vast majority of abortions – over 90 per cent – are performed because the woman herself is said to be suffering from or vulnerable to mental disorder, usually neurotic or depressive disorder (ONS). Thus abortion legislation which relies on health grounds produces weak and vulnerable women.[45]

The psychologizing of abortion has thus generated what appears to be a contradictory and complex situation. The request for abortion can be, and is currently, deemed legal in the vast majority of cases. In practice, it is therefore relatively easy for women to gain permission for legal abortion (although accessing the service on the NHS, without having to resort to paying privately is another matter).[46] At the same time, abortion regulations produce 'weak and vulnerable women', through the citing of their risk of mental ill-health from continuing a pregnancy as grounds for legal abortion.

The Lane Report

In 1969, the first full year after the enactment of the Abortion Act in April 1968, 50 000 legal abortions were notified in England and Wales. This number doubled over the next two years, to reach a total of between 100 000 and 130 000 abortions for the next 12 years.[47] From the perspective of supporters of abortion law reform, the enactment of the 1967 Act was a great step forward, which led to a huge increase in the numbers of safe, legal abortions being performed. However, significant problems still existed, notably the great disparities between access to NHS abortion in different parts of the country due to obstructions created by doctors with a moral or religious objection to abortion. The problem was particularly apparent in Birmingham, and this led to the foundation of a non-profit referral agency by members of the Abortion Law Reform Association (ALRA). The agency later established abortion clinics of its own, and was named the Birmingham Pregnancy Advisory Service, later to become the British Pregnancy Advisory Service (BPAS).[48]

While significant difficulties still existed for women seeking abortion following the implementation of the Act, opponents of abortion, angered by the provision for legal abortion *per se*, believed that the terms of the Act were being flouted in practice, and that a larger number of women were being granted access to legal abortion than the Act should have made possible. In response to complaints about legalized abortion, and on the initiative of opponents of law reform, in 1971 the Conservative government set up a Committee of Inquiry into the Abortion Act under the chairmanship of the Honorable Mrs Justice Elizabeth Lane, the only woman High Court judge at that time. Doctors, psychiatrists, lawyers, social workers, health administrators and teachers sat on the Committee and spent three years investigating all aspects of abortion services.[49]

Despite the fact that the Committee had been established in response to opponents of reform, Madeleine Simms argues that it '… came to very positive conclusions about the effects of the Abortion Act'.[50] The resulting Lane Report argued that:

> By facilitating a greatly increased number of abortions the Act has relieved a vast amount of individual suffering. … We are unanimous in supporting the Act and its provisions. We have no doubt that the gains facilitated by the Act have much outweighed any disadvantages for which it has been criticised.[51]

This endorsement of the Abortion Act is significant since it can be taken as a measure of the official attitude taken by government towards abortion. The provision of legal abortion had been established, and accepted by the (Conservative) administration as a 'significant gain'. The Lane Report can therefore be taken, on the one hand, as a 'great blow' to the opponents of the Abortion Act.[52] On the other hand, as Simms has argued, the Lane Committee's conclusions were 'carefully moderate'.[53] The Report ensured that the emphasis of supporters of reform, who construed abortion as a procedure justified for 'victims' of unfortunate circumstances presided over by medical professionals, was continued.

In this respect, the way in which the Lane Report framed the 'gain' of legal abortion is significant. Abortion is justified where it alleviates 'individual suffering'. As Mary Boyle points out, abortion was construed by the Lane Committee as '... a form of therapy ... necessary in the face of women's psychological and physical suffering ...', rather than as a social and political issue connected to women's rights and equality.[54] The Lane Report therefore reinforced the medicalization of abortion, established through the 1967 Act.

Abortion on Demand?

I contend, however, that, as well as perpetuating the medicalization of abortion, the Lane Report also psychologized abortion in a specific, additional way. In the Lane Report, as I detail below, the decision whether or not to have an abortion was presented as psychologically difficult. Justification for allowing doctors to have continuing control over abortion decision-making was thereby maintained, but also recast through its claims regarding 'abortion counselling'. In order to illustrate this point, I first discuss the Lane Report's consideration of the case for 'abortion on demand', suggesting that, in rejecting this case, the Lane Report further psychologized abortion by construing the decision whether to have an abortion as too psychologically difficult for a woman to make without professional assistance. I shall also discuss the extension of this construction of abortion in the case it made for 'abortion counselling'.

One particularly interesting section in the Lane Report was entitled 'Who Should Decide?'. It was divided into subsections: 'The Patient or the Doctor?'; 'Individual Doctors or Panels or Referees?'; and 'Which Doctors?'.[55] Significantly it posed, for the first time, the question of who should have decision-making power in abortion since, in the parliamentary debates on the 1967 Abortion Act, this issue was totally neglected – it was simply assumed that the medical profession would have total control over decision-making. Now, four years later, the Lane Report indicated that this was an issue to be debated, conceding that there was an argument that the most appropriate approach would be to give the woman concerned the sole decision-making right. The Report stated:

> In principle there are two possible ways of reaching a decision as to whether an abortion should be performed: either it remains as at present a matter for medical discretion or it could be made a matter for the woman herself to decide. ... The latter case is often described as abortion on demand but there is also a situation which could be described as abortion on request. By abortion on demand we mean a situation where the woman asserts a right to abortion regardless of the doctor's professional opinion; on the other hand

abortion on request would involve a right thereto without regard to any statutory criteria but subject to a doctor's professional approval and willingness to perform the operation.[56]

The Lane Committee therefore recognized that abortion 'as a matter for the woman herself to decide' was a principle that should be taken into account as an approach to abortion decision-making. The Report noted that this viewpoint was contrary to the conditions of the Act and therefore, strictly speaking, outside the remit of the Committee's inquiry. However, the Committee decided that it still wanted to comment on this question since, as the Report pointed out, the exercise of medical discretion is a 'frequent cause of complaint that the Act is working unfairly'. It also argued that '... every woman requesting abortion should have her case carefully considered'.[57]

The notion that 'every woman should have her case considered' and the recognition that the exercise of medical power can be discriminatory and inequitable indicated a significant shift from the terms of the discussion in 1967. The absolute control of doctors in abortion decision-making was called into question, and the need for abortion as a solution to unwanted pregnancy was acknowledged as valid. However, the Committee's recommendations were striking in their ultimate denial of the case for women's autonomy in decision-making: 'Nevertheless we should have recommended against abortion solely at the request of the woman even if the matter had been fully open to us.'[58] The justification for this denial of women's autonomy in decision-making was as follows:

> The concept of medical care is, or is becoming that a patient should be treated as a whole person viewed in the light of personal physical and mental health and social conditions, and not merely as one suffering from a particular disease or condition requiring amelioration or cure. Given this wider view, in our opinion, it is in the interests of the patient as an individual that the abortion decision should be taken by doctors ... some women would find the burden of making their own decision, unsupported, a heavy one and in such cases the operation might well be followed by emotional turmoil and feelings of guilt.[59]

It was therefore maintained that it was the doctor's role to ensure the psychological well-being of women who wanted an abortion. The best way in which doctors could do this would be by holding a position of power in decision-making, thereby necessitating that the woman had to discuss her decision with her doctor. The logic is that in the same way that a patient could not mend a broken leg unaided, so a woman could not decide to abort a foetus without the intervention of her doctor. To do so would put her mental health at risk on account of the turmoil and guilt that she would allegedly experience as a result of abortion. In the Lane Committee's findings, this approach was described as 'holistic medicine'. The mind, as well as the body, was seen as a site for the exercise of medical judgement, and the role of the medical profession was defined as ensuring the woman's psychological well-being. This psychologizing construction thus justified the continuing role of doctors in abortion decision-making.

Counselling

The Lane Report was also significant in that it suggested that ways should be found to develop this 'holistic care' – in particular, through counselling. The Committee saw the role of the counsellor in the abortion process as an extension of what doctors should be doing in their consultations with women who wanted abortions. A section of the Lane Report, Section K, was dedicated specifically to counselling and contained a statement of the importance of this intervention: 'In our view … every woman seeking abortion should have the opportunity to obtain adequate counselling before an abortion decision is taken.'[60]

The argument put forward was that the woman *needed* to be counselled before she decided to abort a pregnancy. This recommendation is significant, in that it construed that the decision to end a pregnancy required counselling, unlike the decision to continue with the pregnancy. The Report detailed the purpose of counselling as follows:

> What is meant by counselling? … We see counselling as providing opportunities for discussion, information, explanation and advice. A woman considering abortion should be able to discuss and explore her difficulties and anxieties in an informal and unhurried manner … She should become more fully aware of the implications of the continuation, or alternatively the termination, of her pregnancy and helped to arrive at a wise and independent decision as to what her real wishes are. Further, when her personal and social circumstances are discussed, it may be possible to identify problems which would be appropriately dealt with by others, e.g. a psychiatrist or a social work agency.[61]

First, abortion was assumed to bring about 'difficulties and anxieties', which the woman should discuss with the counsellor. Second, she was seen as needing help to become fully aware of the implications of having a baby or ending the pregnancy: it was suggested that she must be 'helped' to find out what her real wishes were. This constructed the woman seeking abortion needing a counsellor in order to be able to think through her decision properly. Third, the possibility of further intervention by helpful professionals was suggested on the grounds that, in the course of discussing the woman's thoughts about abortion, more problems in her life might emerge.

It is important to note that the approach to abortion outlined by the Lane Committee formed the basis for guidelines for the provision of abortion services in the United Kingdom from 1974 onwards. They included the Guideline for Health Authorities published in July 1977, which used the Lane Committee's recommendations as the basis for directions given to NHS hospitals providing abortions. This Guideline says: 'The Department [DHSS] fully accepts the need for counselling and also recognises that it is already undertaken in the majority of cases where abortion is under consideration.'[62]

The Lane Report was therefore significant for two reasons. First, it offered strong support for the provision of legal abortion. The increasing number of women who accessed legal abortion, following the implementation of the Act, was therefore rendered acceptable. Second, as I have illustrated through my discussion of the Lane

Committee's findings on the role of medical professionals in abortion decision-making, the medicalization of abortion as established through the 1967 Act was endorsed. It was, however, also extended through the claim that abortion decision-making was psychologically difficult.

Conclusions

In this chapter I have argued that abortion has been psychologized in British law and policy. On the basis that abortion can be legal on health grounds, women's 'mental health' has been placed at the centre of the regulation of abortion. As I have explained, the fact that the law allows for abortion on these grounds has in practice enabled British women to access abortion, in early pregnancy at least, relatively easily. While not denying this practical advantage of British law, I would suggest nevertheless that it poses significant problems for women.

There are a number of important problems posed by construing abortion as legal on the grounds of health in general, but mental health in particular. First, there are practical problems that should be set against the practical advantages set out in this chapter. There are, of course, doctors who do not interpret the Act liberally and would therefore not define 'mental health' in a broad way. Because the exercise of doctors' discretion is at the heart of the Act, while the majority of doctors do interpret the Act liberally at the present time, some still do not, and this means that some women are penalized.

Also, however, there are very significant political problems posed by the mental health clause. It would be wrong to imagine that the inclusion of the term 'mental health' in the Abortion Act can be understood in separation from ideas about women, pregnancy and the medical profession. In fact, as I have illustrated in this chapter, 'mental health' is a subjective, not objective, term. It does not represent an objective, definable phenomenon which can be measured and assessed. Rather, the term 'mental health' can only be understood properly as shorthand for a set of ideas about women and motherhood, about the role and position of medical professionals and about the role of the law. My argument is that, when understood in this way, the placing of women's 'mental health' as the centre of the regulation of abortion has a number of problematic consequences.

First, the construction of abortion as legally justified to alleviate the suffering of individual women has had the effect of construing the abortion-seeking woman as a victim who deserves sympathy but also professional assistance in making the abortion decision. In this construction, women's ability to make reasoned choices, and to exercise control over their emotions, is called into question. Rather, the woman is construed emotionally frail – a person who, in the face of the psychological problems associated with choosing and living with abortion, needs the assistance of a counsellor, social worker or other professional. Whilst it may be that some women value the opportunity to talk to a counsellor about their decision to have an abortion, it is important to recognize the limitations and problems associated with this construction of the abortion-seeking woman.

Second, abortion construed as justified on mental health grounds has acted to minimize alternative arguments about abortion, which may serve women better. To suggest that abortion is about alleviating the suffering of the individual woman – a form of therapy – marginalizes other arguments about abortion and why women need it, most notably those which justify abortion in relation to women's social position, and in relation to the limitations of contraception. Women may be better served by a different kind of abortion law which posits abortion as a back-up to failed contraception, necessary if women are to exercise control over their lives and live them in the way they see fit.

Notes

1 Moore, S. (1992), 'Looking for Trouble: Unwanted Pain of an Unwanted Pregnancy', *The Guardian*, 8 October, p. 32.
2 Offences Against the Person Act 1861, s. 58: 'Every woman being with child, who, with intent to procure her own miscarriage shall unlawfully administer to herself any poison or other noxious thing, or shall unlawfully use any instrument or other means whatsoever with the like intent, and whosoever, with intent to procure the miscarriage of any woman, whether she be or be not with child, shall unlawfully administer to her or cause to be taken by her any poison or other noxious thing, or shall unlawfully use any instrument or other means whatsoever with the like intent, shall be guilty of an offence and being convicted thereof shall be liable to imprisonment.'
    S. 59: 'Whosoever shall unlawfully supply or procure any poison or other noxious thing, or any instrument or thing whatsoever, knowing that the same is intended to be unlawfully used or employed with intent to procure the miscarriage of any woman, whether she be or be not with child, shall be guilty of an offence, and being convicted thereof shall be liable to imprisonment for a term not exceeding five years.'
    These sections contained no time limit and made no distinction between abortions at different stages in gestation.
3 Bridgeman, J. (1998), 'A Woman's Right to Choose?', in Lee, E. (ed.), *Abortion Law and Politics Today*, Basingstoke: Macmillan, pp. 76–77; Simms, M. (1985), 'Legal Abortion in Britain', in Homans, H. (ed.), *The Sexual Politics of Reproduction*, Aldershot and Vermont: Gower, p. 79.
4 Brooks, B. (1988), *Abortion in England: 1900–1967*, Beckenham: Croom-Helm.
5 Radcliffe-Richards, J. (1982), *The Sceptical Feminist: A Philosophical Enquiry*, London and New York: Routledge.
6 Dworkin, R. (1995), *Life's Dominion: An Argument about Abortion and Euthanasia*, London and New York: Harper Collins, pp. 102–17; Tribe, L.H. (1992), *Abortion: The Clash of Absolutes*, New York and London: W.W. Norton and Company Inc., p. 11; Cohen, J.L. (1997), 'Rethinking Privacy: Autonomy, Identity, and the Abortion Controversy', in Weintraub, J. and Kumar, K. (eds), *Public and Private in Thought and Practice: Perspectives on a Grand Dichotomy*, Chicago and London: The University of Chicago Press, pp. 137–39.
7 Kissling, F. and Shannon, D. (1998), 'Abortion Rights in the United States: Discourse and Dissension', in Lee, *Abortion Law and Politics Today*, *op. cit.*, n. 3, p. 145.
8 Many laws which restrict abortion have been passed by individual states in the United States. According to the latest report from the Alan Guttmacher Institute, 29 states require parental involvement in minors' abortion decisions; 22 states require state-directed counselling before an abortion, with 14 of those requiring a mandatory delay following the counselling; 14 states restrict private and/or public employee insurance coverage for abortion; 34 states restrict Medicaid-funded abortion except in cases of

rape, incest or when the woman's life is endangered; 29 states have passed laws banning 'partial birth abortion' (in 20 the laws have been blocked by state or federal courts); and 40 states restrict later abortions.

The Center for Reproductive Law and Policy (www.crlp.org) has documented a host of other attempts to restrict access to abortion, including the introduction of needless regulations for clinics, covering such 'vital' elements of treatment as doorway width and lawn care. If passed, other laws will introduce penalties for women whose behaviour during pregnancy may harm the foetus, compel women to inform the 'father' about an abortion, and force funding for anti-abortion groups. In addition to all this, there are vast swathes of the mid-western and southern states with few, if any, abortion providers, and at least 90 small cities have no provider at all.

9   Sheldon, S. (1997), *Beyond Control: Medical Power and Abortion Law*, London: Pluto Press.
10   Ibid., p. 3.
11   Franklin, S. (1991), 'Fetal Fascinations: New Dimensions to the Medical-Scientific Construction of Fetal Personhood', in Franklin, S., Lury, C. and Stacey, J., *Off-Centre: Feminism and Cultural Studies*, London and New York: Harper Collins, pp. 190–205; Fyfe, W. (1991), 'Abortion Acts: 1803 to 1967', in Franklin *et al.*, *Off-Centre*, ibid., pp. 163–67; Greenwood, V. and Young, J. (1976), *Abortion in Demand*, London: Pluto Press; Hadley, J. (1997), *Abortion: Between Freedom and Necessity*, London: Virago, p. 217; Latham, M. (1998), 'Reform and Revolution: The Campaigns for Abortion in Britain and France', in Lee, E., *Abortion Law and Politics Today*, *op. cit.*, n. 3, p. 131; Sheldon, *Beyond Control*, *op. cit.*, n. 9; Sheldon, S. (1998), 'The 1967 Abortion Act: A Critical Perspective', in Lee, *Abortion Law and Politics Today*, *op. cit.*, n. 3, p. 43.
12   Boyle, M. (1997), *Re-thinking Abortion. Psychology, Gender, Power and the Law*, London and New York: Routledge.
13   Ibid., p. 64.
14   Ibid.
15   Sheldon, *Beyond Control*, *op. cit.*, n. 9, pp. 38–39.
16   Ibid.
17   Ibid., p. 76.
18   Ibid., p. 39.
19   Ibid., p. 40.
20   Francome, C. (1984), *Abortion Freedom: A Worldwide Movement*, London: Allen & Unwin, p. 84; Latham, M. (1998), 'Reform and Revolution: The Campaigns for Abortion in Britain and France', in Lee, *Abortion Law and Politics Today*, *op. cit.*, n. 3; Paintin, D. (1998) 'A Medical View of Abortion in the 1960s', in ibid., pp. 16–17; Simms, M. (1985) 'Legal Abortion in Britain', in Homans, *Sexual Politics of Reproduction*, *op. cit.*, n. 3, p. 10.
21   Sheldon, *Beyond Control*, op. cit., n. 9, p. 40.
22   Ibid.
23   Ibid., p. 36.
24   Ibid., p. 40.
25   Sayers, J. (1982), *Biological Politics, Feminist and Anti-feminist Perspectives*, London and New York: Tavistock Publications, pp. 149–55; Stanworth, M. (1994), 'Reproductive Technologies and the Deconstruction of Motherhood', in *The Polity Reader in Gender Studies*, Cambridge: Polity Press, p. 230.
26   Sheldon, *Beyond Control*, *op. cit.*, n. 9, p. 35.
27   Ibid., p. 20.
28   Ibid., p. 21.
29   Ibid., p. 20.

30 Boyle, *Re-thinking Abortion*, *op. cit.*, n. 12, p. 66.
31 Ibid.
32 Ibid.
33 Sheldon, *Beyond Control*, *op. cit.*, n. 9, p. 25.
34 Ibid.
35 Boyle, *Re-thinking Abortion*, *op. cit.*, n. 12, p. 66.
36 Ibid., p. 17.
37 Ibid., p. 18.
38 Ibid., p. 65.
39 RCOG Clinical Effectiveness Group (2000), *The Care of Women Requesting Induced Abortion*, London: RCOG Press, p. 10.
40 David Paintin notes that abortion is allowed if the risk of abortion is less than that of continuing the pregnancy. He points out that the death rate from legal abortion has been less than one per 100 000 abortions since the early 1980s, and the risk of death if pregnancies continue is about seven per 100 000. Hence abortion can, if doctors are so inclined, be provided within the terms of the Act for all women who request it. See Paintin, 'A Medical View of Abortion', *op. cit.*, n. 20.
41 Ibid., p. 17.
42 Ibid., p. 18.
43 Ibid., p. 17.
44 Ibid.
45 Boyle, *Re-thinking Abortion*, *op. cit.*, n. 12, p. 72.
46 ALRA (Abortion Law Reform Association) (1997), *Report on NHS Abortion Services*, London: ALRA; ALRA (2000), *Improving Access to Abortion: A Guide*, London: ALRA; Stanworth, 'Reproductive Technologies', *op. cit.*, n. 25, p. 230; Sheldon, *Beyond Control*, *op. cit.*, n. 9, pp. 56–57.
47 Simms, 'Legal Abortion', *op. cit.*, n. 20, pp. 84–85.
48 Ibid., p. 86.
49 Ibid., p. 89.
50 Ibid.
51 Ibid.
52 Ibid., p. 90.
53 Ibid.
54 Boyle, *Re-thinking Abortion*, *op. cit.*, n. 12, p. 25.
55 Lane Committee (1974), *Report of the Committee on the Working of the Abortion Act*, London: HMSO, p. 64.
56 Ibid.
57 Ibid.
58 Ibid.
59 Ibid., pp. 64–65.
60 Ibid., p. 288.
61 Ibid., p. 292.
62 DHSS, (1977), *Health Services Development: Arrangements for Counselling of Patients Seeking Abortion*, Circular, London: HMSO.

Chapter 5

European Assisted Conception Regulation: The Centrality of the Embryo

Melanie Latham

There is a vast array of assisted conception treatment services now available, ranging from donor insemination (DI), and in vitro fertilization (IVF), to gamete and embryo donation, surrogate motherhood and genetic diagnosis. Large numbers of women make use of these treatment services[1] and, indeed, increasing numbers of women have been in the public eye disputing their access to such services, whether they be Diane Blood seeking to make use of posthumous insemination, or postmenopausal women seeking in vitro fertilization. There is no reason to expect that this will change in the foreseeable future. Women may seek assisted conception treatment for many reasons including, for example, being post-menopausal, and being single or lesbian, whether fertile or infertile. They may hope to use donated sperm, ova, embryos, or wombs, perhaps in combination with their own reproductive material, now possible through assisted conception. This is more difficult for men. Women may have the option of gestating the foetus even if they are infertile. Men can never have such an option. Single or homosexual women may only need to access donated ova if they are infertile, or donated sperm whether they are infertile or not. Their single or homosexual male counterparts would need a surrogate mother to provide them with a child. This means that women have access to a potentially greater number of treatment services offered by assisted conception.

The treatments involved also affect women to a larger extent because they are more invasive of the female body. Infertility testing of the woman is more invasive if the ovaries and uterus are to be examined. IVF treatment involves a woman endangering herself physically.[2] For example, Hormone Replacement Therapy – often used as part of the IVF treatment process – uses hormones to stimulate the ovaries into creating a larger number of ova than the usual one, so that they may be fertilized to create a usefully large number of embryos. The implantation of any resulting embryo is also necessarily invasive. Surrogate motherhood, in particular, necessitates the acceptance of impregnation, gestation and birth only for the gratification of another. The surrogate will, by definition, agree to donate her body, and sometimes her ova, whilst never expecting to benefit from the resulting child.[3]

Restriction via the medicalization and medical control of access is therefore gendered in the sense that assisted conception provision predominantly affects women and restriction therefore predominantly discriminates against them. In this chapter I intend to examine the effect of the regulation of assisted conception across Western Europe on women and their potential reproductive rights. This includes an examination of national regulation across Western Europe, the new Convention on Biomedicine published by the Council of Europe and European Union law.[4] Emphasis is laid on the centrality of the human embryo in this regulation and the restriction of treatments that has arisen as a consequence. The restriction of patient access to assisted conception treatments has resulted from protection of the human embryo and the child the embryo will become. This has most often been entrusted to medical gatekeepers.

The Centrality of the Embryo in Europe

The embryo has been accorded a special position in the jurisdictions of Western European countries in their regulation of assisted conception. Through their regulation of the use in treatments of the human embryo Western European states have demonstrated how far they accord an intrinsic moral worth to the embryo, and how far this is to be balanced with any countervailing rights belonging to men or women.

The majority of European countries share a stipulation that the fertilization of gametes and their formation into embryos must take place in a suitably staffed and equipped medical centre or by suitably qualified medical professionals. All have an, at least nominal, three-embryo transfer limit (except in countries where there is no regulation at all, such as Italy) in order to prevent multiple births and the selective reduction of foetuses. They all also prohibit sex selection (unless this is therapeutic according to clinical opinion), germ line gene therapy (the attempt to cure genetic diseases by altering the human genome in ways that would be passed from one generation to the next) and cloning.

A group of what I will term 'conservative' countries all emphasize the rights of the embryo through their restrictions. Ireland therefore prohibits embryo storage, donation and research, pre-implantation diagnosis (PID) which necessitates the destruction of an embryo and prenatal diagnosis (PND) which may lead to termination where a foetal disability is detected.[5] Germany prohibits PID (but provides PND).[6] Sweden limits the provision of PID to those with serious, progressive and hereditary diseases and limits embryo storage to one year.[7] Austria permits embryo storage only in exceptional cases.[8] Switzerland prohibits embryo donation between couples.[9] Germany, Switzerland and Ireland[10] all force clinicians to limit embryo creation to three, all of which must be transferred to the woman's body – thus creating hazards for the woman patient and thereby emphasizing embryo rights. Italy, although it has no statutory regulation, does nominally prohibit embryo donation and the commercial exploitation of embryos through its Code of Medical Deontology 1995.

Of the other West European countries examined here, Denmark,[11] France,[12] the United Kingdom[13] and Spain[14] have much more liberal regulations in relation to embryo status and have balanced the status or moral worth of the human embryo much more favourably towards the rights of infertile adult patients. Each of these countries allows embryo donation, storage and research, PID and PND, although each also has its particular anomalies. Whilst two out of these four permit embryo research for up to 14 days, in France, only therapeutic studies on the embryo may be carried out up to a maximum of seven days. In France, too, embryo donation may only be carried out in exceptional and strictly regulated circumstances, whereby a couple needs judicial authority to receive a donated embryo, and their family, educational and psychological backgrounds will be investigated. Anonymity between couples, and donor consent, must also be assured in the United Kingdom and Spain. Both the French and the Spanish, however, seem to be unsure of their positions on the destruction of embryos and appear to be storing them indefinitely. Only in the United Kingdom has the regulation of the Human Fertilisation and Embryology Act 1990 and its implementation clearly enabled the full gamut of embryo storage, donation and research, PID and PND and embryo destruction. Initially, Denmark stood with the more liberal countries on the issue of embryo donation, but since 1997 the practice has been prohibited.[15]

The Convention on Biomedicine

In the Council of Europe's Biomedicine Convention of December 1996,[16] the embryo was also considered to deserve special mention in order to appease, and reach some form of compromise between, those European states that gave initial approval to the Convention. Their deliberations led to conflict particularly on the question of embryo research as they had each reached quite different regulatory responses to the issues raised by the use of the human embryo in assisted conception.[17] (Only six of these states have as yet ratified the Convention – see below.)

The Council of Europe must be commended. While the European Convention on Human Rights has been an invaluable tool for both individuals and states in challenging the conflicting laws, policies or practices of contracting states, the Biomedicine Convention is an instrument with potentially far-reaching powers that individuals can use to protect their rights where these are infringed by the biotechnology industry or medicine. Many of the rights defended by the Convention have the potential to protect women patients.

In summary, the Biomedicine Convention requires that its signatories ensure the provision of the following basic standards in their own countries:

- equitable access to health care (Art. 3) – (within that signatory state)
- free and informed consent by patients before any medical intervention on their person (Art. 5)
- no discrimination on grounds of genetic heritage (Art. 11)
- human genome modification for diagnostic or therapeutic purposes only and no germ line genetic modification (Art. 13)
- no sex selection unless this is on the grounds of a threat of the transmission of a serious sex-related hereditary disease (Art. 14)
- no financial gain from the human body and its parts (Art. 21)
- a system of adequate compensation for undue damage after a medical intervention (Art. 24).

The potentially positive effect of the Biomedicine Convention for women patients is tempered, however, by several limitations. For example, much of the application of rights by signatory states is discretionary. Furthermore, individuals do not have the standing to petition the European Court of Human Rights themselves; instead, governments of parties to the Biomedicine Convention may petition the Court to offer an Advisory Opinion interpreting the legal ramifications of the Convention (Art. 29). This can be time-consuming and frequently costly. Unfortunately for individuals who have considered their rights to be breached and have sought a solution based on the Convention, on average less than 10 per cent of applications have been ruled admissible.[18] In addition, any person seeking a remedy must also attach a right afforded by the Biomedicine Convention to one already protected by the European Convention of Human Rights (Art. 29, note 165).

The Biomedicine Convention also establishes rights for the embryo by limiting research on the human embryo (Art. 18). An Advisory Opinion can now be sought on embryo research under Article 18 of the Biomedicine Convention by attaching it to the right to life protected by the European Convention of Human Rights (Art. 2). This might threaten women's rights by establishing embryo status yet further, notwithstanding the fact that anyone seeking to protect the embryo would be subject to these procedural restrictions.

Furthermore, the Biomedicine Convention is currently legally binding on only six states which have ratified it and for which it entered into force on 1 December 1999: namely, Denmark, Greece, San Marino, Slovakia, Slovenia and Spain. Thus any threat of establishing embryo status through use of the Convention is presently limited to citizens of those countries, until such time as a majority of its signatory states have ratified it.

In the United Kingdom the Human Rights Act 1998 incorporates the European Convention on Human Rights. Having come into force in October 2000, it now confers binding legal effect on those provisions of the European Convention on Human Rights which it seeks to incorporate, where previously they enjoyed only persuasive moral authority. In relation, however, to the protection of embryo rights by the Biomedicine Convention, the Human Rights Act offers no remedy for those seeking its protection.

Feminism and Embryo Status

Questions about whether human embryos should have special status due to their inherent humanness have grown out of the process of using embryos in assisted conception. They are frozen and stored for future use when surplus numbers of them have been fertilized, and may then be donated by their genetic parent to others. In order for progress to be made in understanding infertility and reproduction, research on embryos has also been carried out. Are embryos being stored, donated, used, tested and researched upon because they belong, as property does, to genetic parents or clinics, or whoever has responsibility for them? Or do they have special status as potential humans carrying genetic material – humans who might suffer as a result of the 'dangerous and experimental' techniques being carried out upon them? Philosopher John Harris has argued that personhood is only acquired sometime after birth: '[p]ersons are beings with the capacity for valuing their own existence. In the case of human beings, they become persons when the capacity to value their own lives develops and will cease to be persons when they have lost that capacity.'[19] The opposite stance is taken by religious groups, such as Roman Catholics: in relation to the question of embryo rights and protection, mainstream Roman Catholicism has emphasized that life is 'a gift from God' and is therefore sacred. Life is also seen to begin at conception when a unique individual with its own genetic patterns and soul is created.[20]

Feminists themselves have criticized the growth in the legal status of the embryo since the advent of assisted conception provision. Very few have wanted to see any increase in legal status for embryos donated, stored and, most especially, researched upon. Those feminists and infertile women in the United Kingdom who campaigned for women patients to receive the best treatment during debate on the Human Fertilisation and Embryology Bill in 1989–90 were in favour of research being carried out on embryos rather than on infertile women, and on embryos being donated and stored to improve the chances of a successful pregnancy. It was feared that increasing the rights of the embryo *in vitro* might in turn increase those of the embryo *in vivo* and jeopardize women's abortion rights. This was a very real threat: amendments were eventually made to section 1(1) of the Abortion Act 1967, shortening the time limit of 28 weeks to 24 weeks, provided that the woman's health or life were not seriously threatened nor the foetus seriously disabled.

Legal attempts at increasing rights of the foetus have also been seen in English case law – for example, in *Paton* v. *British Pregnancy Advisory Service* (1978)[21] the rights of husbands were assessed. Mr Paton tried to obtain an injunction in the High Court preventing his wife having what would otherwise have been a lawful termination. This was refused as the husband had no legal right to be consulted by his wife under the 1967 Act. The husband in this case then took the matter to the European Commission on Human Rights alleging a violation of his rights, under Articles 2 and 8 of the European Convention on Human Rights, to a family life and the child's right to be born. The court found against him on the grounds that, following the 1967 Act, abortion was allowed in the early stages of pregnancy and therefore the life and health of the woman superseded both the rights claimed by the husband. One question that Sir George Baker P at the High Court did not decide was whether, had the doctors approved the abortion in bad faith, a husband would be allowed an injunction to prevent an unlawful abortion. However, such a judgment would be unlikely to be given in time to prevent a woman from going ahead with an abortion before the cut-off date.[22]

In *C* v. *S* (1987),[23] a woman's boyfriend, after initially having his application for an injunction refused by the High Court following *Paton*, on the grounds that he had no standing, was then refused the right as the father of the unborn child to contest the abortion in the Court of Appeal. In this case, the rights of the putative father seem to have taken a back seat to questions of viability and lawfulness. Heilbron J deemed that a foetus of 18–21 weeks was not viable and that therefore an abortion carried out on such a foetus would not be unlawful. On this basis, the boyfriend in question had no grounds for an injunction. This was confirmed by the *Attorney General's Reference (No. 3 of 1994)*.[24] This considered the case of a man who had stabbed his pregnant girlfriend causing the subsequent death of her child after it was born, due to its prenatal injuries. In this case, Lord Taylor CJ held that the foetus was not a person in being but was part of its mother until it had a separate existence of its own. Therefore, the foetus could not be deemed to have been murdered – only the woman assaulted and damaged. Thus a foetus did not enjoy the rights of a person separate from its mother.

Certain modern techniques designed to ensure viable pregnancy have increasingly pitched the rights of embryos and of women against each other. Embryo research necessarily involves women endangering themselves through assisted conception treatments in order to create embryos. With advances in intra-uterine therapy, monitoring and surgery, which can be beneficial to the embryo, the rights of the mother may in future be diminished, especially if separate doctors are treating mother and embryo and wanting to fulfil their moral and legal duties to each.[25] This would also create problems for women carrying an 'abnormal' foetus; women needing treatment that might threaten the foetus; and for pregnant women generally who might have to protect their foetus by law.[26]

Medical Gatekeepers

Women are less likely to have access to reproductive rights where the embryo enjoys a special status which restricts what is done to it and therefore what treatments are provided. This is also the case where access to treatments is governed by the vagaries of clinical discretion. Such restriction of access could arguably be likely both in countries such as the United Kingdom, which has regulation but leaves access to be decided by the clinician in charge of the clinic, and countries which have no regulation at all but allow clinicians themselves to decide who they will treat, often on a private basis, as in Italy.

The power of clinicians to determine access is evident in statutory form both in the UK Human Fertilisation and Embryology Act 1990 and the French bioethics laws of 1994. Those who do not fit with accepted ideas of parenthood have found themselves refused treatment according to strict and often questionable criteria which dash any hopes they had for a family and nullify their past efforts.

Section 13(5) of the Human Fertilisation and Embryology Act 1990 requires that the welfare of the child be taken into account by clinicians when they are assessing suitability for all licensed treatment 'including the need of that child for a father'. In the parliamentary debates the original intention by interest groups to outlaw all single and lesbian mothers from DI failed and section 13(5) is a compromise. This has, however, been charitably interpreted by the Human Fertilisation and Embryology Authority (HFEA). In its Code of Practice (Part 3) it has, to some extent, alleviated any threat to single mothers-to-be by accepting that there might not be a husband or partner, and allowing centres to consider, in such a case, 'whether there is anyone else within the prospective mother's family and social circle who is willing and able to share the responsibility for meeting those needs and for bringing up, and maintaining and caring for the child'.[27] Nevertheless, the relevance of the need for a father at all is, of course, questionable.

Additionally, access is further limited by the Code of Practice's long and detailed guidance for AID centres to follow when taking account of the welfare of the child.

Some of these are unnecessary when the efforts willingly undertaken by infertility patients are taken into account. Centres must consider, for example, expressed commitment to bringing up a child, and form an opinion on the ability to meet its needs. Other guidance is certainly of a social nature, such as centres having to take into consideration whether patients have had children removed from their care or whether there is evidence of a previous or relevant conviction.[28] Who should make the final decision based on such criteria? Can such decisions be left to the medical personnel involved, even when assisted by an ethics committee? Even GPs and 'any individual, authority or agency' are to be asked their opinion as to the suitability of parents, and account taken of the fact that a patient has not consented to this.[29] Even those services not requiring a licence need to use criteria for their donors, for example, if the insemination following sperm donation is to take place in a licensed clinic. Donors of embryos must be having treatment themselves. Moreover, although the prospective parents under review have the opportunity to give their views and to counter objections, their 'assessors' include any person at the clinic who has come into contact with them, and confidential information from an outside source can also be discussed with the medical team involved.[30]

Access to IVF has been limited further by the attitude of the UK government to health service provision. Because local health authorities have limited resources, a low priority has been given to infertility on the grounds that is not life-threatening and the treatment can be extremely costly. In NHS clinics, therefore, criteria which restrict access have become even more stringent in order to limit spending. By way of example, the criteria at the NHS-funded IVF Unit at St Mary's Hospital in Manchester in 1984 and 1985 included that the couple be in a stable relationship, childless and resident within the area covered by the regional health authority, with a limit set on treatment cycles to three per couple.[31] The 1990 Act does not indicate how a review of a decision to refuse licensed treatment services to a woman or couple might be brought. (It is obligatory, however, to establish and use an ethics committee to oversee the management of individual cases.[32])

The French bioethics laws of 1994 offer a different spin on access, but France still imposes stringent rules, and these are also governed by clinical discretion. The laws exclude from access to treatment any patients who do not seek treatment as a heterosexual couple seeking to replicate a conventional nuclear family structure, but, if patients meet that standard, the methods of funding treatment ensure that poverty is no bar to access. French patients may only be treated within a *projet parental* (parental undertaking). All treatment must be given in the spirit of a particular couple's undertaking to be a parent. Under Article 8 of the statute on donation and assisted conception, assisted reproductive techniques or a created embryo can only be used to help a couple have a child or to prevent the transmission to that child of a particularly serious illness. The man and woman must not only be alive at the time of any treatment cycle, but also be of procreating age (premenopausal), married or cohabiting for more than two years. They also have to give their annual written, informed consent beforehand to embryo transfer or artificial insemination.

Also under Article 8, an embryo can only be created to satisfy that particular couple's use of a treatment cycle to achieve a conception, gestation and then a child. Each couple is entitled to four treatment cycles or five years of treatment. As a general rule, couples undergoing treatment may only use one donated gamete, rather than both. In exceptional circumstances an embryo can be donated to a couple undergoing treatment by another such couple who have tried assisted conception without success. Both members of the donating couple must give written consent to donation of what is in effect 'their' embryo, whether the original gametes were donated or not.

In addition to the introduction of the *projet parental* by the 1994 statutes, the final part of Article 8, which deals with counselling, also serves to make life more difficult for French patients trying to gain access to treatment. Under the 1990 Act in the United Kingdom, counselling has to be provided to all patients receiving treatment in a licensed clinic. Patients themselves, particularly in the United Kingdom, campaigned for this to be introduced in clinics so that the more difficult aspects of treatment, such as the low success rates, the invasive surgery and the psychological problems associated with 'failure', can be discussed. In France, the issue of counselling was not taken up until the parliamentary debate during the run-up to the passing of the 1994 statutes themselves. Unfortunately for patients, the French form of 'counselling' is a double-edged sword. While the principal purpose of these sessions is to inform the couple of the low success rates, the difficulties of treatment, the law and what treatments involve, their other purpose is to verify the couple's motivation and to inform them of the possibilities of adoption. A month-long waiting period must then follow, which can be extended by a doctor, before written confirmation that treatment is to be allowed. This form of 'counselling' in France may only serve to deter couples, rather than help them in their decision-making or even contribute to an informed consent – especially those who do not fit the ideal model of parents-to-be.

The United Kingdom and France are not alone in limiting access to reproductive services. All across Western Europe attitudes towards the protection of the embryo and the child have restricted patient access. Certain 'conservative' countries, such as Austria, Germany, Ireland, Switzerland and Sweden, have felt that only the bare minimum of treatments should be made available to meet the procreative needs of an infertile couple. In these five countries, therefore, treatments such as post-mortem insemination and surrogacy are either expressly forbidden or very unlikely. Of these, Ireland is particularly conservative, outlawing all forms of gamete donation (through professional guidelines from the Irish Medical Council, 1994, rather than statute *per se*). The Irish would presumably argue that their policy forbidding gamete donation protects potential offspring who could suffer harm either psychologically or as a result of genetic defects. The governments of Germany, Austria, Switzerland and Sweden would no doubt concur, as they only allow sperm donation without anonymity.[33] In fact, Sweden does not even permit sperm donation to be used with IVF treatment. In Sweden, therefore, there may be even more evidence of an attempt by the public, and therefore by those regulating assisted procreation, to protect the welfare of the child, as they also have other laws on child welfare such as that prohibiting any physical punishment of a child.

France and Denmark have shown themselves to be more sympathetic to the needs of the infertile adult. Gamete donation and non-commercial surrogacy are therefore permitted in both countries. In Denmark a sperm donor is not provided with anonymity, however, and there are restrictions on donation in France (with a sperm donor being required to have already had children and to obtain the consent of his partner). Regulators in the United Kingdom and Spain seem to have tried to strike more of a balance between the rights of the child and those of the infertile adult seeking treatment. In these countries gamete donation with anonymity and storage are therefore provided, as is non-commercial surrogacy: a child born by artificial means cannot be an heir to the donor. Moreover, they are the only two countries to expressly permit post-mortem insemination (provided, of course, that the deceased donor has consented to such use being made of his gametes).

Four countries have little or no statutory regulation of assisted procreation – Belgium,[34] Italy,[35] Holland and Portugal.[36] In these countries treatments are regulated by certain regulatory bodies, self-regulation by clinics or regulations published by ethical committees. Gamete donation and non-commercial surrogacy are available in Italy and Holland, whilst gamete donation is available in Portugal and Belgium.[37] Through their lack of regulation, therefore, these countries are not expressing a wish to protect the interests of the child. The exception to this is perhaps Holland which is introducing a legal right for a child born from a donate gamete to have identifying information on the donor. However, these countries without regulation, whilst neither protecting the interests of the child nor emphasizing the duties of the parents, are *not* conversely establishing the rights of the adult or parent, as patients might be at the mercy of unregulated clinics and professionals. Ireland, too, can be added to this list of countries with no statutory legislation as provision there is regulated through professional guidelines from the Irish Medical Council, 1994, not by statute.

As might be expected, those countries which have conservative rules on gamete donation and anonymity in the interests of the child, have strict rules governing access. In Germany assisted conception is only available to married couples.[38] Their counterparts in Austria, Sweden and Switzerland must be heterosexual and in a stable relationship. These conservative countries are joined by Denmark[39] and France on this issue. Only the United Kingdom and Spain – the two 'liberal' countries – allow access to treatment to single women. Such access is, however, subject to clinical discretion and is open to interpretation in relation to sexual status, marital status or age. Although these countries superficially appear to be more liberal, relative to the more conservative countries, their regulations have only assigned more power to their respective medical professions rather than to the infertile patients themselves.

In countries with no detailed national rules governing access – Holland, Portugal, Ireland, Belgium and Italy – patients are even more at the mercy of medical discretion. Under the Irish Medical Council guidelines of 1994, a couple seeking treatment must be married. In Belgium, too, assisted conception is unfortunately only available to married couples under the Belgian Code of Conduct for the Medical Profession. Conversely, certain people in these countries – namely, the Dutch, Portuguese and Italians – may have more chance of finding a sympathetic clinician than in countries which have regulated access. This is possibly ironic, if one reason why countries have not regulated assisted procreation is that their strong cultural attachment to religion has resulted in an inability to reach a consensus on the relevant moral issues.

Procreative Tourism

The restriction of access has led to a growth in 'procreative tourism' whereby a woman who is unable to find the treatments she desires in her own country attempts to travel abroad for treatment.[40] This might be because treatment is prohibited in her own country, or only available in another country, or also because a treatment provided elsewhere is more successful or available from a better qualified or more experienced medical professional (although this latter reason is not dealt with here). German couples who are carriers of genetic diseases thus travel to Belgium for assisted conception treatment using pre-implantation diagnosis (PID) which is prohibited in their own country on the ethical and moral grounds that PID treatment involves testing an embryo for genetic disease and destroying it if it carries that disease. In the United Kingdom Diane Blood recently attempted to travel abroad for post-mortem insemination, having transgressed the rules of consent embedded in the 1990 Act. At her request, sperm had been removed from her husband while he was in a coma two days before his death. Although, in this particular case, there was no infertility and the sperm was not from a donated source outside the couple, the regulations of the 1990 Act and the HFEA still applied as soon as the sperm was stored. The HFEA initially ruled that treatment could not be carried out as there was no firm evidence that informed consent by Mrs Blood's husband to post-mortem insemination had been obtained under section 4(1) of the Act. The Authority also refused to allow release of the sperm for treatment to take place elsewhere in Europe. Mrs Blood then sought judicial review of this decision arguing that Mr Blood had intimated his consent. In October 1996 the High Court agreed with the HFEA.[41] At the Court of Appeal in February 1997, however, Mrs Blood was accorded the right to take the sperm abroad under European Community law, under Articles 49 and 50 EC, and receive medical treatment in another member state.[42]

British women are not alone in wanting to have access to the posthumous use of their dead husbands' sperm. In France, too, there have been cases of women who, like Diane Blood, have wanted to use sperm after the death of their partners, and several couples have wished to be able to keep sperm in storage for use in case of the husband's premature death. In the *Parpalaix* case,[43] the refusal of the donor insemination centre, CECOS, to hand over the sperm of a dead husband to his widow was deemed unlawful by the court. Under contract law (Article 6 of the Civil Code), the contract between CECOS and the Parpalaix couple obliged CECOS to hand back the sperm as the couple had not been made aware of CECOS objections to posthumous insemination.

The French have now, in fact, replaced the *Parpalaix* ruling by yet more restrictions. Under Article 10 of the French statute on respect of the human body of 1994, the consent necessary for each insemination and for each embryo transfer is now revoked after the end of a marriage or stable relationship, including after the death of one of the partners of the couple undergoing assisted conception treatments using a donor (unless, of course, treatment has already begun with that donated gamete). This is because treatment can only be given to a couple initiating a *projet parental* or parental undertaking together – in other words, setting out to be a parent-couple of any resulting child. Accordingly, it would appear that a French Diane Blood would not be able to gain access to the stored semen of her dead husband or partner, whether or not it could be proved that he had given his consent to post-mortem insemination, because he could not be there in person to consent to the insemination or embryo transfer taking place. Nor could a French Mr Blood use a surrogate to gestate an embryo that had been created from his dead wife's ova, or had been donated to the couple.

European Community Law and Reproductive Rights

One interesting point about the *Blood* case is that Diane Blood successfully invoked rights provided under EC law to enable her to have treatment that she was prohibited from having in her own country, the United Kingdom. Would Mme Parpalaix also have been able to go abroad for her posthumous treatment had she chosen to use European law? As mentioned earlier, such seeking of treatment abroad has been labelled 'procreative tourism'. Procreative tourism in Europe, though frowned upon by national and supranational governments, may actually be to the patient's benefit, and the only way for women patients to make use of their basic reproductive rights without the interference of government. Is this a way of increasing women's rights? Or does the lack of regulation in the more liberal countries that some women might visit for treatment pose risks for those women? Might women be endangered from a lack of testing of donated gametes or embryos, a lack of keeping records of donors' details or treatment information, or a lack of regulation of storage facilities? What of ensuring that the medical professionals administering treatment are suitably qualified?

What reproductive rights does European Union law provide? Diane Blood sought to have insemination treatment at an assisted conception clinic in another EU member state. Such treatment would normally come under the heading of 'services' for the purposes of EC law. Services are defined under Article 50 EC. These include, 'activities of an industrial character, of a commercial character, of craftsmen, and of the professions'. Thus medical treatment given by a medical professional could be classed as a service under Article 50. If a member state does not provide a certain medical service, and a citizen must seek treatment in another member state, the member state cannot prevent that citizen from travelling abroad. Further, that state must also pay for the treatment on their national health scheme.[44] This applies unless the member state has prohibited the treatment on ethical grounds, following the case of *Pierik No. 2* in which the European Court of Justice considered the issue of the public funding of a treatment prohibited on ethical grounds.[45] As a result, a German who is a carrier of genetic disease and feels it expedient to have PID treatment to select out embryos who might be carriers of that genetic disease cannot be prevented by her government from travelling to another country that has not prohibited PID as Germany has. The German citizen would have to pay for the PID treatment abroad, however, as Germany has restricted PID on ethical grounds.

Article 49 EC also provides that services are subordinate to the fundamental freedoms of the Treaty of Rome – namely, the free movement of goods, capital and persons. These are central tenets of EC law formulated in order to create and protect an internal market. If a case involving medical treatment comes closer to a definition of one of the other freedoms, particularly under the heading of establishment, then the service provider will be subject to the restrictions of that state if they are providing services there, in the sense that they are established there. They must respect the regulations and guidelines of the member state in which they are established.[46] But a person providing services contrary to the regulations of that member state must only furnish proof that they are providing that treatment on a temporary basis whilst resident in that country. Are there any restrictions on a member state's ability to restrict the internal market and competition across Europe by preventing a practitioner from establishing himself in that state in order to offer treatment prohibited by that state, and by preventing their own citizens from receiving that service in their own country? Under Article 46 EC, a member state is only able to limit treatment given in its own country on grounds of 'public policy, public security or public health', as long as these are clear, objective and proportionate,[47] whether or not they apply equally to their own and foreign citizens (are 'indistinctly applicable'). The member state could also argue, however, that it is not just protecting 'consumers' of services, but that the regulations are necessary, and therefore proportionate, in order to preserve '(moral and legal) principles underpinning family and kinship relations, the protection of human dignity and liberty and autonomy over one's body and body parts ...' or the protection of 'human life'.[48] Thus a country such as Ireland may well be able to restrict the delivery of services such as PID or abortion on its own soil on such grounds.

Diane Blood and other women in similar predicaments are now able to take advantage of jurisprudence on services that has been logically extended to recipients of services, since a service provider must not be restricted in his free movement through prohibition on the travelling of his customers – in this case, patients.

Article 50 EC also stipulates that '[s]ervices shall be considered to be "services" within the meaning of this Treaty where they are normally provided for remuneration' for which there must be an economic link between the service provider and the recipient.[49] This only governs treatment provided on a private basis, not treatment paid for by publicly funded national health schemes. This raises questions about the fairness of allowing those wealthy enough to pay for treatment access to the treatment that they want (or perhaps need, in the case of carriers of genetic disease), while effectively barring from treatment those on low incomes who cannot afford to travel abroad and pay. The spectre of the less well-off woman beholden to state regulation of her reproduction looms once more.[50]

Procreative tourism such as that enabled, and arguably encouraged, by European Union law may yet lead to legal complications in private international law. Nielsen, for example, has pointed out the dangers of cross-border assisted conception treatment in relation to parental rights.[51] This applies particularly where there are contradictions between the parental rights offered by one country which prohibits treatment and that of another country which allows those treatment services. Complications arise where a citizen of the former seeks treatment abroad in the latter, but then returns to their former country accompanied by their resulting offspring. Further problems can arise, for example, where one country prohibits donor anonymity, whilst the other does not. Can paternity of the anonymous donor be established in the country to which the patient returns and which does not allow anonymous donation but insists on the establishment of paternity, particularly if the child is resident in that country?[52] This can not only create legal problems for the person who has taken advantage of their freedom to seek treatment abroad, it can also create unexpected problems for their children. If the child develops a genetic disease, they will find it difficult to gain any relevant information on the donor in the country which insists on donor anonymity. In response to these problems, Nielsen proposes harmonization by European states of their different regulations.[53]

Conclusions

Is it possible to reach any sort of consensus about harmonization between the differing cultural solutions to assisted conception regulation found across Western Europe? First, there is the 'non-regulation camp' which has not sought to regulate treatments in statutory form. This camp contains Holland, Italy, Belgium, Portugal and also Ireland (although Ireland's lack of regulation has been classified here as being conservative in aim rather than non-committal). Second, there is the quasi-liberal camp of France and Denmark which protects the embryo and child to a large extent with restrictions on research and donation. This puts them somewhere between conservative and liberal. Third, we have the 'permissive-liberal camp' which currently also has only two members – the United Kingdom and Spain. Their regulations are very similar, if differing slightly in certain respects. In contrast to other European states, through their regulatory systems they have apparently chosen to favour the interests of the child much more than the interests of the man or woman seeking treatment. However, patient access is still governed by medical discretion. Finally, there is the 'conservative' camp which includes Ireland, Germany, Austria, Switzerland in relation to the protection of the embryo, and Sweden on issues of parental responsibility and access to treatment. Here, governments and societies have demonstrated their wish to: protect the interests of the child, born and unborn; limit medical discretion as well as patient access to treatment; and to emphasize their recognition of the moral worth of the human embryo. Can there be any meeting point among these different camps?

In fact, would harmonization be in the best interests of women patients? We have seen how far European women's reproductive rights to assisted conception have been limited both by national governments and, potentially, by the Convention on Biomedicine. These limitations have been caused by the central position that the human embryo is beginning to occupy in ethical debates, and by the restrictive criteria imposed by states and their medical gatekeepers. Women seeking assisted conception treatment have been forced to shop around as procreative tourists for treatments to which they are denied access in their own countries. Their ability to buy such medical services abroad is protected by European Community law. Certainly, women might be at risk if they obtain treatments in countries which are not sufficiently regulated, but is that not preferable to women being at risk from any harmonization or compromise reached between the various European states which might further entrench embryo rights?

Perhaps a middle way between these two extremes is preferable? At a minimum, Western European states could ensure that there was some recognition of bioethical rights by abiding by international conventions such as the Council of Europe's Convention on Human Rights (ECHR) and the Convention on Biomedicine.

Although it currently has only six signatories, the Convention on Biomedicine 1996 assures dignity, autonomy, privacy and non-discrimination in relation particularly to bioethical practices such as assisted conception treatment. Other international legislation which could assure a minimum level of bioethical or reproductive rights for Western European women might, of course, come from the European Union. The EU has already accorded recognition to the ECHR in the Amsterdam Treaty; it has issued directives relating to biotechnological inventions; and there could be mutual recognition under European law of the quality control of health professionals and services involved in the provision of assisted conception. This might lead to mutually recognized or agreed codes of conduct on such things as genetic counselling, for example. These would be in addition to the rights already provided under EC law, as the EU Treaty also provides equal access to services and health care.

Such measures might be particularly beneficial to women patients. They might be preferable to a harmonization process which poses political risks and might be impossible to attain. Additionally, women would benefit from a minimum standard of care as they gain access to the many assisted conception treatments now on offer across Europe.

Notes

1   In 1998–89, 27 151 patients received IVF treatment; 4338 received treatment involving donor insemination or GIFT (gamete intra-fallopian transfer): Human Fertilisation and Embryology Authority (2000), *Annual Report*, pp. 17–18.
2   See, for example, Lee, R.G. and Morgan, D. (2001), *Human Fertilisation and Embryology: Regulating the Reproductive Revolution*, London: Blackstone, pp. 142–43. See also <http://www.rcog.org.uk/guidelines/management.html> on ovarian hyperstimulation syndrome.
3   However, the Human Fertilisation and Embryology Act 1990, s. 27 deems the birth mother to be the legal mother of the child, until such time as a s. 30 parental order is issued. Moreover, a surrogacy 'contract' is legally unenforceable: Surrogacy Arrangements Act 1985, s.1A.
4   The countries surveyed here are the United Kingdom, France, Spain, Portugal, Italy, Germany, Austria, Sweden, Denmark, Belgium, Holland and Ireland.
5   Through professional guidelines from the Irish Medical Council, 1994, rather than by statute.
6   Das Embryonenschutzgesetz (1990).
7   The Swedish In Vitro Fertilisation Act (1988), Guidelines on the use of Prenatal Diagnosis (1995).
8   Fortpflanzungsmedizin-Gezetz, BGBI. No. 275/1992.
9   Code pénal Suisse du 21 décembre 1937 (1 January 1995).
10   Status of Children Act 1987. Irish Medical Council (1994), *A Guide to Ethical Conduct and Behaviour and to Fitness to Practice* (4th edn), Irish Medical Council: Dublin.
11   Act No. 275 of June 24 1992; Bekendtgorelse no. 392 of 17 May 1994.
12   'Loi no. 94-653 relative au respect du corps humain'; 'Loi no. 94-564 relative au don et à l'utilisation des éléments et produits du corps humain, à l'assistance médicale à la procréation et au diagnostic prénatal'.
13   Human Fertilisation and Embryology Act 1990.

14   Assisted Reproductive Techniques Act, Law No. 35/1988 of 22 November 1988.
15   This is under s.7 or Order no. 728 of 17 September 1997 on artificial fertilization made in pursuance of Law no. 460.
16   Convention for the Protection of Human Rights and Dignity of the Human Being with Regard to the Application of Biology and Medicine 1996.
17   At a meeting to discuss the status of the embryo at the Council of Europe in December 1996 (the Council of Europe Third Symposium on Bioethics, 'Medically-assisted Procreation and the Protection of the Human Embryo', Strasbourg, 15–18 December 1996), for example, differences in opinion between the assembled representatives were so vast that many feared that consensus on such matters as embryo research could never possibly be reached.
18   Jacobs, F.G. and White, R.C.A. (1996), *The European Convention on Human Rights*, Oxford: Clarendon Press, p. 8.
19   Harris, J. (1987), *The Value of Life*, London: Routledge & Kegan Paul, p. 25.
20   Cf. Papal Encyclical, *Evangelum vitae*, March 1995.
21   *Paton* v. *British Pregnancy Advisory Service* [1978] 2 All ER 987; *Paton* v. *UK* 3 EHRR 410 (1980).
22   Fox, M. (1998), 'Abortion Decision-Making: Taking Men's Needs Seriously', in E. Lee (ed.), *Abortion Law and Politics Today*, New York: Macmillan.
23   [1987] All ER 1230.
24   [1996] 2 All ER 10.
25   Mason, J.K. and McCall Smith, R.A. (1999), *Law and Medical Ethics*, London: Butterworths, p. 156.
26   Daniels, C. (1993), *At Women's Expense: State Power and the Politics of Fetal Rights*, Cambridge, Mass: Harvard University Press.
27   HFEA Code of Practice 1995, 3.19.a.
28   Ibid., 3.26.
29   Ibid., 3.43.
30   Ibid., 3.28.
31   In January 1985 those on the waiting list were told that: 'The Unit reserves the right to remove a couple's names from the waiting list and to decline treatment at any subsequent stage should any further information (of a medical or social nature) indicate the need to do so.' Entry on to the list now necessitated a three-year history of infertility, childlessness was defined as having no children by the present relationship or by adoption, and patients accepted on to the waiting list had to satisfy the general criteria established by adoption societies in assessing suitability for adoption. (Report of the Health Service Commissioner, case no. W.376/86-87, 'Administration of a waiting list for infertility treatment', HMSO, London, 1988.)
32   Mason, J.K. and McCall Smith, R.A. (1999), *Law and Medical Ethics*, London: Butterworths, p. 72. One obvious avenue of redress for women or couples refused treatment is to seek judicial review of a clinic's decision to refuse treatment. Given the relative liberality within the private sector in relation to access to treatment, disaffected patients are much more likely to have been refused treatment by the NHS. Their prospects of success in the courts are slim. First, the courts have consistently declined to force health providers to re-order their general priorities for treatment: see *R* v. *Secretary of State for Social Services, ex p. Hincks* (1980) 1 BMLR 93; *R* v. *Central Birmingham H.A. ex p. Walker* (1987) 3 BMLR 32. Second, so far, attempts by individuals to upset clinics' judgements as to their suitability for treatment have been unsuccessful. In *R.* v. *St. Mary's Ethical Committee ex p. Harriott* 1 FLR 512, Schiemann J explicitly endorsed an NHS clinic's freedom to take into account the potential parenting skills of the couple and to rely on evidence of past conduct to judge those skills as wanting. A significant

amendment to the HFEA Code of Practice in December 1995 was the emphasis on the age of the patient and their 'likely future ability to look after or provide for a child's needs' (HFEA Code of Practice para. 3.17 (d)). In an unreported case in 1994 (*R.* v. *Sheffield Health Authority, ex p. Seale*) Auld J upheld an age bar of 37 preventing older women from being afforded IVF. Only a judgement no reasonable clinic could possibly arrive at in rationing its resources would be struck down.

33 It remains unclear whether a sperm donor, as the genetic father, may be faced with a paternity claim in Germany and therefore forced to support the child: Giesen, D. (1997), 'Artificial Reproduction Revisited: Status Problems and the Welfare of the Child', in C. Bridge (ed.), *Family Law: Towards the New Millennium*, London: Butterworths, p. 245.

34 In Belgium the recommendations of the Warnock Committee (1984), *Report of the Committee of Inquiry into Human Fertilisation and Embryology*, Cmnd 9314, London: HMSO, have been accepted by the Committee of Medical Ethics of the National Scientific Research Fund. Each research protocol requires approval by the university and/or hospital ethical committee.

35 The National Ethics Committee of Italy has published reports discussing bioethics: Comitato Nazionale per la Bioetica, 'Parere del C.N.B. Sulle Techniche di Procreazione Assistita (1994); and Comitato Nazionale per la Bioetica, 'La Fecondazione Assistita' (1995); these sit alongside Italy's Code of Medical Deontology (1995) and its Civil Code, although no statutory regulation as yet governs assisted conception.

36 What regulation there is in Portugal is covered by the Penal Code and Law of June 1984; Decree-law 319/86; and Ministerial Decision 28/95.

37 In Belgium gamete donation is anonymous: see Giesen, 'Artificial Reproduction Revisited', *op. cit.*, n. 33.

38 Ibid.

39 S.3 Law No. 460, 10 June 1997.

40 Nielsen, N. (1996) 'Procreative Tourism, Genetic Testing and the Law', in N. Lowe and G. Douglas (eds), *Families across Frontiers*, Kluwer: The Hague.

41 *R* v. *Human Fertilization and Embryology Authority ex p. Blood* [1997] 1 FCR 170.

42 Following a further ruling in the Court of Appeal that the removal of sperm from a comatose man without his consent was unlawful under the terms of the 1990 Act in this case, it is now unlawful to use sperm without written consent, unless fresh sperm is used.

43 Consorts Parpalaix c/ le CECOS et autre, 1 August 1984, *Gazette du Palais*, 16–18 September 1984, p. 11.

44 Regulation 1408/71/EEC (OJ Sp. Ed. 1971 II, 416).

45 Tamara Hervey points out that it was submissions to the Court from the European Commission that suggest that member states are, 'permitted to refuse authorization for treatments "seriously contrary to the ethical rules prevailing" in its jurisdiction', on the grounds that member states retain competence to regulate public morality'. (See Hervey, T. (1998), 'Buy Baby: The European Union and Regulation of Human Reproduction', *Oxford Journal of Legal Studies*, **18**, p. 207.

46 For a discussion of the ramifications of European law determining how far member states are able to set guidelines, and thus the possibility that nation states will lose sovereignty over such important social policy, see ibid.

47 Article 39 (3) EC; Case 36/75 *Rutili* [1975] ECR 1219, para. 32.

48 Hervey, 'The European Union', *op. cit.*, n. 45.

49 Case C-159/90 *SPUC* v. *Grogan* [1991] ECR I-4685.

50 As it did in relation to contraception and abortion services before these were decriminalized and remunerated by the state. See Latham, M. (2002), *Regulating Reproduction: A Century of Conflict in Britain and France*, Manchester: Manchester University Press.

51 Nielsen, 'Procreative Tourism', *op. cit.*, n. 40.
52 Act on International Paternity Questions, s. 2.
53 Nielsen, L. (1998), 'From Bioethics to Biolaw' in C. Mazzoni (ed.), *A Legal Framework for Bioethics*, Kluwer: The Hague.

Chapter 6

The Angel in the House: Altruism, Competence and the Pregnant Woman

Anne Morris

In 1998 the UK Court of Appeal held that a caesarean section carried out on a competent woman against her express wishes was unlawful.[1] In so far as this recognizes that a woman who is pregnant does not, simply by virtue of her condition, lose her right to determine what shall be done to her body, the decision might seem to conclude in a legal, if not ethical, sense a controversial chapter in medico-legal debate.[2] Arguably, however, the focus has simply shifted from an overt consideration of the 'rights' of the pregnant woman versus the 'rights' of the foetus to the more subtle question of how a woman refusing treatment which would save her baby could possibly be categorized as competent.

Although cases where caesarean sections have been carried out on unwilling women have – rightly – attracted a good deal of attention and criticism, they are extreme examples of how women are treated during pregnancy and labour. This chapter reflects on this and considers in particular whether the concept of competence or capacity is peculiarly susceptible to manipulation where the patient is a woman, using the pregnant patient as the paradigm. It has been argued that 'the application and assessment of competence by both professionals and courts exhibit gender bias that would trouble even those who look primarily to formal equality to decide whether a given doctrine or area of the law disadvantages women'.[3] That this is especially so in pregnancy may be deduced from an observation that 'pregnancy and mental illness frighten doctors, and, for different reasons, both sets of patients are at risk of losing basic human rights'.[4]

Pregnancy might seem an odd focus for the arguments about the competence of female 'patients', since pregnancy is not an illness.[5] A woman may be pregnant for some time before she is either aware of it or seeks medical advice. However, once medical advice is sought (or otherwise provided) she becomes a patient under the care and, potentially, the control of others. Most instructions during pregnancy are complied with, if only because they do not impose any great inconveniences. Few women are so attached to particular cheeses or cleaning out cat-litter trays[6] that they would make an issue out of it. Of course, different considerations apply to injunctions which are either difficult to obey (in relation to addictive drugs, including tobacco and alcohol) or interfere with personal choices (for example, in relation to the kind of lifestyle, including paid employment, suitable for pregnant women).[7] At this point, the notion of how a pregnant woman *should* behave begins to colour the judgments of those around her.

The purpose of this chapter is not to debate 'natural' versus 'technological' childbirth, but it is relevant to note that pregnancy and childbirth were, for many years, managed by people other than doctors – namely, women and their midwives. The increasing control of pregnancy by health professionals – especially doctors – has been well-documented.[8] Professionals have taken over what was a private matter:

> All births, like all machines, carried in them the potential for pathology, the potential for breaking down. Technology that controlled and dominated the forces of birth, just as one dominated and controlled the forces of a machine, replaced midwives' attendance at birth … men assumed control of the right to designate births normal and abnormal and rose to dominate the social organization around childbirth.[9]

Clear evidence of this can be seen in the 'hospitalization' of pregnancy and childbirth. In 1927, 15 per cent of births occurred in hospital. This rose to 54 per cent by 1946,[10] and, in 1992, it was reported that the rate of hospital births had remained constant at around 98 per cent for the preceding ten years.[11] Equally significant is the increase in the rate of caesarean sections. The rate levelled off at just over 10 per cent of deliveries in the early 1980s, but rose from 11.3 per cent in 1989–90 to 15.5 per cent in 1994–95, and to 20 per cent by 2000.[12]

It is not only in the place of birth and method of delivery that pregnancy has become the preserve of the medical profession. Pregnant women are routinely subjected to all manner of examinations and tests and, however benign these may be, there is a sense in which this invasion of the intimate relationship between woman and foetus creates, for the latter, a separate identity. Once observed on the monitor, there is proof for external observers of the separate 'other' whereas, previously, it was the 'quickening' of the foetus *within* her that would represent their inseparability for the woman.[13] Certainly, this 'separation' of the woman and the foetus is integral to the maternal versus foetal rights debate – an opposition which many women, not only feminists, find at odds with the experience of pregnancy.

The Perfect Mother?

Questions of competence in pregnancy highlight the problem of the 'unreasonable' (pregnant) woman. There are two reported cases[14] in the UK in which doctors have been authorized to perform caesarean sections on unwilling, competent women and it is possible (though ultimately not very helpful[15]) to reduce the debate to one of competing rights: the woman's right to choose what will happen to her body versus the foetus's right to life. Such arguments have something in common with those used by pro-lifers in the abortion debate[16] while, in contrast, the treatment of women labelled *in*competent raises issues that are arguably analogous to those which arise in the force-feeding of anorexics.

The first English case concerning a competent woman was *Re S*,[17] in which a woman in labour declined surgery on the basis of her religious beliefs. The operation was authorized in an emergency court hearing although, by the time the operation was carried out, the foetus had died.[18] Given that the judge was told that death was imminent it is not surprising that there is little principle contained in the very short judgment but, nevertheless, much has been written about the shaky legal foundations of the declaration.[19] More recently, another S[20] was 36 weeks pregnant when diagnosed as suffering from pre-eclampsia, a serious complication of pregnancy which, if untreated, can endanger the life of both the woman and the foetus. S understood the risks but declined the recommended treatment which included an early induced delivery. Her continued refusal led to her detention in hospital under the Mental Health Act 1983 and the High Court granted an *ex parte* declaration authorizing doctors to treat her without her consent. A caesarean section was performed, to which S acquiesced rather than struggle. S (who initially lost custody of her baby) applied for judicial review and appealed against the declaration authorizing the operation. The reasons S gave, at the time, for refusing intervention are set out in the report. She wrote in lucid terms that she understood what she was being told, that she appreciated the risks connected with pre-eclampsia and that she held strong views about nature being allowed to take its course: 'I see death as a natural and inevitable end point to certain conditions. ... It is not a belief attached to the fact of my being pregnant, but would apply equally to any condition arising.' The evidence was that S satisfied a test of competence based on ability to comprehend and retain treatment information and to weigh it in the balance as part of the process of arriving at the decision.[21] The Court of Appeal (Judge LJ) concluded that 'while pregnancy increases the personal responsibilities of a woman it does not diminish her entitlement to decide whether or not to undergo medical treatment.... Her right is not reduced or diminished merely because her decision to exercise it may appear morally repugnant.'[22] The Court upheld a woman's right to refuse treatment thereby endangering the life or health of the foetus, stating:

> ... how can a forced invasion of a competent adult's body against her will even for the most laudable of motives (the preservation of life) be ordered without irremediably damaging the principle of self-determination? ... the autonomy of each individual requires continuing protection, even, perhaps particularly, where the motive for interfering with it is readily understandable, and indeed to many would appear commendable.[23]

Whilst this clearly reiterates that all competent adults, including pregnant women, are free to accept or reject medical treatment, it must be understood in the context of *Re MB*,[24] which predated it, and in which a similarly clear statement of law was made:

> A competent woman ... may for religious reasons, other reasons, for rational or irrational reasons or for no reason at all, choose not to have medical intervention, even though the consequence may be the death or serious handicap of the child she bears, or her own death.[25]

Crucially, however, MB was declared *in*competent (see below) and the treatment was authorized: freedom of choice is relevant only to those judged competent by others.

The resort to legal compulsion in the face of a medical dilemma in both 'S1' and 'S2' indicates the clear, and understandable, inclination of doctors, judges and others to preserve lives, including the life of a viable foetus.[26] Society has an interest in the preservation of life, and there are instances where a balance has to be struck between individual autonomy and state paternalism. Suicide, for example, is not a criminal offence but assisting a suicide is (however kind the motive). Becoming pregnant is – for consenting adults – a private matter, but the legal regulation of abortion indicates the limits which society is prepared to place on the idea of pregnancy as entirely within the private sphere. The 'problem' with pregnancy is clear – the desire by others to protect the foetus conflicts with the idea of the adult as an autonomous individual free to decline even life-saving treatment. At this point arises the temptation to assume that anyone prepared to 'sacrifice' the life of a viable foetus is either bad (and so should be overruled) or mad (and therefore cannot decide for herself).

The Function of Consent

The doctor–patient relationship has many facets, but consent to treatment remains the cornerstone. Patients cannot be required to accept treatment that they do not want no matter how painless, beneficial and risk-free it may be and no matter how dire the consequences of a refusal. This proposition is established as both an ethical principle and a legal rule, being founded on the principle of respect for the patient's autonomy or the patient's right to self-determination. The legal requirement for consent expresses respect for the patient's autonomy so that 'every human being of adult years and sound mind has a right to determine what shall be done with his own body; and a surgeon who performs an operation without his patient's consent commits an assault …'.[27] Note that this fundamental right applies only to those of sound mind – a restriction which emphasizes that only those judged competent may decide for themselves. Competence is the key to self-determination:

> … it is established that the principle of self-determination requires that respect must be given to the wishes of the patient, so that, if an adult patient of sound mind refuses, however unreasonably, to consent to treatment or care by which his life would or might be prolonged, the doctors responsible for his care must give effect to his wishes, even though they do not consider it to be in his best interests to do so …. *To this extent, the principle of the sanctity of human life must yield to the principle of self-determination.*[28]
>
> *If the patient is capable of making a decision* on whether to permit treatment and decides not to permit it his choice must be obeyed, even if on any objective view it is contrary to his best interests. A doctor has no right to proceed in the face of objection, even if it is plain to all, including the patient, that adverse consequences and even death will or may ensue.[29]

Competence, however, is not the only factor involved in establishing consent, since there are other requirements to be met, if the consent is to be legally effective.

First, consent must be voluntary and uncoerced. In particular, a patient's apparent consent or refusal may be nullified by the undue influence of a third party, which overbears the patient's will. In *Re T*,[30] for example, a woman's refusal of blood transfusions was held to have been the result of pressure from her mother who was a Jehovah's Witness. The Court of Appeal upheld the declaration by the High Court that it was lawful to transfuse, on the basis that T had not been able to make a genuine decision, in part because of her debilitated medical condition, and in part because she had been subjected to the undue influence of her mother. It was observed that it was wholly acceptable that a patient should receive advice and assistance from others, particularly members of the family, in reaching a decision about whether to accept or reject treatment, and it does not matter how strong the persuasion is, as long as it does not overbear the independence of the patient's decision:

> The real question ... is: does the patient really mean what he says or is he merely saying it for a quiet life, to satisfy someone else or because the advice and persuasion to which he has been subjected is such that he can no longer think and decide for himself? ... [T]he relationship of the 'persuader' to the patient may be of crucial importance ....[31]

Intriguingly, the passage from which this is taken contains no recognition of what is potentially a much more influential and also inherently unequal relationship – that of the doctor to the patient. Even in a society in which individuals are better informed and expect greater choice, there is still a tendency to defer to medical opinion. It is not necessary consciously to adopt a passive 'doctor knows best' attitude in order to be influenced by the advice of a medical professional. There are situations in which the most articulate, informed and assertive patient will accept medical advice, either because they are genuinely convinced by the arguments, or simply because they lack the determination or ability to resist: 'psychologists and psychiatrists have recognised for many years that "a patient's competence can be so powerfully affected by the quality of the doctor patient relationship as to be almost wholly contingent upon it ..."'.[32] A pregnant woman is doubly susceptible not only because of the relationship's inherent inequality, but also because of wider expectations of how she should respond. Of course, any question of coercion or duress is, in practice, only likely to be an issue where the patient is *refusing* consent since, if the patient is agreeing to medically justified treatment recommended by the doctor, the normal presumption in favour of an adult patient's competence will apply.[33]

Apart from being uncoerced, if consent is to be 'real' (and thus protect the doctor from an action in battery) it must be informed, which in English law means that the patient must simply be 'informed in broad terms of the nature of the procedure which is intended'.[34] In the context of competence, the need for information (however general) underlines how easily power may be exercised, since the doctor controls access to the information which the patient needs to make an 'informed' decision. A competent patient is one who can appreciate the consequences of a treatment decision, but this assumes that she is given all the necessary facts in a way which she is capable of understanding.[35]

Finally, if consent (or refusal) is to be effective, the individual must be competent. Clearly, the question of how competence is to be assessed, and who should carry out that assessment is crucial. There are several tests[36] that could be employed to decide if someone is competent, but the danger is that, in practice, a patient is labelled incompetent *because* they do not accept what others regard as being in their interests.[37] They must be incompetent because no reasonable or rational or comprehending individual would reject the advice given. An incompetent patient thus comes under the 'control' of the medical profession. True, the final arbiter of whether what was done was lawful is the court but, in the vast majority of cases, a prior court declaration will not be thought necessary, and a subsequent appeal to the court is both unlikely and, in any event, a poor remedy for the most fundamental interference with a person's bodily integrity.

The courts in the UK have only comparatively recently had to consider what is the test of competence in the medical context.[38] The cases establish that the starting point – in theory – is not whether the patient makes a decision which most reasonable people would make, but whether in making a decision – which may seem most unreasonable – the patient was able to understand what was being proposed and what would be the likely consequences of the decision. On the basis that, in order for consent to be valid, the patient need only be given information in broad terms as to the nature of the intended procedure, it should follow that the patient need only *understand* in broad terms in order to have sufficient understanding to be considered fully competent to give or withhold consent. This would appear to be quite a low level of understanding[39] and thus to be highly protective of patient autonomy. The truth of this, however, may well depend on whether the patient agrees with the doctor, and on preconceptions of what individuals who really understood would and *should* do.

In *Re C (adult: refusal of treatment)*[40] C, a 68 year-old man who had been confined in Broadmoor for 30 years, was diagnosed as having gangrene in his foot. In the opinion of his medical advisers, his chances of survival with conservative treatment were no more than 15 per cent and they advised amputation. C was a paranoid schizophrenic who believed, amongst other delusions, that he had been a great doctor and had the ability to cure himself. He also believed that, having being born with four limbs, he should die with four limbs and that God did not want him to have his foot amputated. C refused a below-the-knee amputation, but did consent to conservative treatment, which, contrary to medical expectations, was successful. When the hospital refused to give an undertaking that it would not amputate in any future circumstances, C sought, and obtained, an injunction preventing amputation without his express written consent. It was held that the question to be asked was whether C's capacity was so reduced by his chronic mental illness that he did not sufficiently understand the nature, purpose and effects of the amputation. The decision-making process was analysed in three stages: first, comprehending and retaining treatment information; second, believing it; and, third, weighing it in the balance to arrive at a choice.[41] Although C's general capacity was impaired by schizophrenia, it had not been shown that he did not sufficiently understand the nature, purpose and effects of the treatment he refused, and there was no direct link between C's refusal of amputation and his persecutory delusions. Moreover, he was content to follow medical advice and to cooperate in treatment, as long as his rejection of amputation was respected. This decision makes it clear that neither mental illness, nor compulsory detention in a psychiatric hospital, *by themselves*, mean that an individual is incompetent to make decisions about medical treatment. Although that can be stated as a general principle, each case is judged on its own facts and in its particular context, and it seems that doctors and judges (amongst others) may be applying different standards to different categories.

In *Re C* it was held that there was no direct link between his mental illness and his decision about his physical problem (although believing oneself to be a medical expert might be thought to colour one's views). There are, it has been held, cases in which the *condition* from which the patient is suffering does affect his or, more often, her competence to make decisions about the treatment. This argument has been used in relation to anorexics (a condition principally, though not exclusively, confined to women[42]). In *Re KB*[43] a woman of 18, suffering from anorexia nervosa, was detained under section 3 of the Mental Health Act 1983.[44] The court was asked to declare that naso-gastric feeding, if necessary by force, was medical treatment within section 63 of the 1983 Act, which provides that the patient's consent is not required for any medical treatment given for the mental disorder from which she is suffering if the treatment is given by, or under the direction of, the responsible medical officer. It was held that, in the circumstances, naso-gastric feeding was treatment within section 63 since '... the mental disorder from which she suffers is ... an eating disorder and relieving symptoms is just as much part of treatment as relieving the underlying cause'.[45] Arguably, force-feeding an anorexic is not the most obvious way to 'relieve' the underlying cause of her determination to exercise *control* by conquering her hunger.[46] More important in the context of this chapter, however, was the finding that, *in any event*, K was *incompetent*. She was physically very weak, and was also said not to understand the true situation, apparently seeing death as a long-term or theoretical prospect (medical opinion was that she could be dead within three weeks), and she was aware that when she got close to death she was likely to be resuscitated under the emergency provisions of the Act. On the basis that the treatment she was refusing was related to her mental illness, and *not* to some unconnected physical condition as in *Re C*, it was held that it would be lawful to force-feed her.

The attempt to distinguish KB from C is an interesting example of principles being manipulated to suit circumstances. First, there is the basic proposition that a person who is mentally ill (even if detained) is not *thereby* incompetent. That person retains the right to accept or reject medical treatment which falls outside the special provisions of the Mental Health Act 1983. Only if a patient is incompetent, judged on the common law test set out in *Re C*,[47] can treatment outside the Act's provisions be given. This is why C could not be forced to have his foot amputated. It is a fundamental part of the protection afforded to the mentally ill that they are not labelled as incompetent just because of their mental illness. Apparently, however, a patient with anorexia nervosa is incompetent *because* she is anorexic (refusing food): the treatment refused (food) is said to be connected to the mental illness. But, in *Re C*, was his refusal not also connected to the fact that he was delusional? The question is not whether the treatment and the illness are connected but whether the patient *understands* the issues involved. Perhaps KB *did* understand that, if she became even weaker, she would be resuscitated and that only in those circumstances would she relinquish 'control'. If she truly did not understand that she might die, that would undoubtedly be a basis for doubting her ability to retain, believe and weigh the information.

Susie Orbach has likened anorexics to hunger strikers,[48] but the attitude to the political hunger striker is very different from that evidenced with the anorexic. In *Secretary of State for the Home Office* v. *Robb*[49] it was held that it was lawful for the authorities to respect the decision of a prisoner to refuse food. Those who favour the forcible treatment of anorexics might argue that the hunger-striker is making a conscious (competent) political decision, while the anorexic is not, although Robb himself was diagnosed as having a 'disordered personality' but was nevertheless held competent to refuse food. In *Robb*, Thorpe J 'consigned to the archives of legal history' the case which had been regarded as authority on the question of hunger strikers in prison. In *Leigh* v. *Gladstone*,[50] in which a suffragette unsuccessfully alleged assault after being force-fed in prison, it was held that it was the duty of the prison authorities to preserve the lives of prisoners in their custody. Suffragettes, of course, used the hunger strike as a way of protesting their imprisonment and of maintaining a semblance of autonomy while incarcerated – something that the state would not allow.

C, with his paranoid schizophrenia, and Robb, with his disordered personality, were competent, while an anorexic may not reject food because the very act of refusing to eat is labelled as a manifestation of her 'mental illness'. The cases involving anorexics are important in the context of this chapter because they raise issues which relate to the labelling of women as (medical/psychiatric) problems *as a result* of their refusal to do what they are supposed to do: 'anorexics ... do not conform to the "good" sick person's role. They are, according to one former sufferer, "suspicious, frigid, untruthful, uncommunicative and determined to hang onto their symptoms at all costs."'[51] Anorexics make us uncomfortable for many reasons, not least because we see them as behaving 'irrationally'. The same is true of pregnant women (mothers-to-be) who reject their stereotype.

This is startlingly illustrated in *Tameside and Glossop Acute Services Trust* v. *CH*[52] where the pregnant woman had suffered from paranoid schizophrenia for years although, of course, the mere presence of a mental disorder does *not* deprive that person of autonomy.[53] CH was 38 weeks pregnant and had been detained under section 3, Mental Health Act 1983. The obstetrician, Dr G, wished to induce labour (because of signs of intrauterine growth retardation) and deliver vaginally but feared that, *if* a caesarean became necessary, the patient would resist. The view of Dr G and Dr M, the psychiatrist, was that CH was incompetent because she failed the threefold test set out in *Re C*. The judge accepted that the evidence was 'overwhelming' that CH lacked capacity to consent to or refuse medical treatment in relation to the management of her pregnancy. On that basis, the doctor would have been able to proceed with the proposed treatment but there was concern that, as forcible restraint might prove necessary, the proper basis for a declaration authorizing such restraint was statutory – that is, within the 1983 Act. Wall J declared that the proposed treatment was treatment for her medical disorder within section 63, and thus consent was irrelevant.

The use of section 63 in this case raises many questions,[54] but in this context it is equally important to consider the finding of incompetence – a fact which is more or less *assumed* by the court. CH, however, realised she was pregnant, wanted the baby and indeed had told her solicitor that she had no objection to a caesarean section should one become necessary. The view of the solicitor was that, notwithstanding her mental illness, CH was well-oriented and clearly aware of the problems suffered by the foetus, but was concerned that the hospital were not doing enough to care for the child, and that it was *her* devotion and concern which were keeping the foetus going. She feared that an induction would result in the baby being born too early and preferred to hang on for as long as possible. She said that her only interests were in saving the baby.[55]

Dr G, on the other hand, testified that he had 'had problems with the defendant throughout the pregnancy' and that she had rarely allowed examination. She had agreed to be induced, but Dr G feared that she might change her mind. He testified:

> In her deluded way she is doing her the best to protect the baby. Her understanding is that the baby is premature and that if it is delivered small it will not survive. I cannot get through to her that if we leave it where it is it will die.[56]

Dr G did accept that death *in utero* was not a *physical* risk to the mother, that induction did carry risks to the baby, and that there were risks in the caesarean section (the statistics of which the judge did not feel the 'need' to repeat). Essentially, however, Dr G felt that CH had no understanding of (perhaps 'did not agree with'?) what he was telling her about the baby *and* was incapable of taking a decision. He would not have come to court if he could have been sure that CH would not change her mind (about the induction). Dr M, the psychiatrist, had been treating CH with mild tranquillizers which CH believed were damaging to the foetus, a view which the judge categorized as 'clearly delusional'.[57] Dr M described CH's antagonism to him as her way of protecting her child. He was of the view that to have a stillbirth would be damaging both in the short and long term. Drs G and M subsequently wrote that 'it is not unreasonable to assume that, if a patient who is actively psychotic experiences a perinatal death, she will blame attendants and that this will compromise her compliance with future care as well as producing a grief reaction'. They argued that caesarean section was the alternative to 'regular sexual assaults to insert prostoglandin pessaries, carry out vaginal examination, rupture the forewaters or apply a foetal scalp electrode. Maintaining an intravenous transfusion and monitoring in an uncooperative, potentially violent, patient would be difficult.'[58] It is tempting to suggest that restraining any woman and forcing invasive surgery on her would do little to encourage her trust in the medical profession.

The overwhelming impression left by the treatment of CH, as it appears from the judgment and subsequent discussions, is that the finding of incompetence was primarily based on her refusal to accept (believe) what she was being told. It is ironic, to say the least, that in so far as CH was delusional, this was because the anti-psychotic drugs which controlled her schizophrenia had been withheld in pregnancy, as being a risk to the *foetus*. The deterioration in her mental state which resulted was then used as the basis for finding that she was incompetent. It would be impertinent for a legal academic to second-guess those who were treating CH, but the suspicion remains that the decision as to competence was coloured by the fact that a mentally ill woman who refused to believe what she was told by doctors and thereby – according to those doctors – was endangering the foetus *must* be incompetent (although presumably she was assumed competent when she consented to the tests which led to the diagnosis of growth retardation). How does this compare with C and his gangrenous foot, when he refused to accept what the doctors told him about his chances of survival, on the basis that he knew better than they because he had been an internationally renowned doctor?[59] Remember that in *Re C* the medical advice turned out to be wrong – conservative treatment worked. In *CH*, she was not even given the opportunity to consent to treatment *were* it to become necessary.

Angels and Other Women

'The Angel in the House' is the title of a popular poem adopted as a paean to the idealized Victorian womanly woman.[60] This woman was, above all, identified by her relationships to others. She was guardian of the home (her natural habitat), demonstrating amongst her wifely virtues the sublime altruism of one whose desires are subordinated to the happiness of others. Whilst much has changed, at least superficially, women may not have entirely vanquished the Angel and what she represents. For centuries, women have been identified by, and with, their reproductive functions.[61] Their childbearing potential has been used not only to keep them within the 'private' world of the home and out of the 'public' sphere of work, politics and power but also to justify their being labelled, by men, as weak (as in weaker vessel), hysterical,[62] and generally as deviating from the (male) norm.

Pregnancy is an obvious setting for these female failings. It is remarkable how much of what has been written about how women feel, and should or should not behave, in pregnancy has been written by men. Consider this, written in a popular book about pregnancy: 'The final authority on any individual pregnancy is, of course, the doctor or midwife in charge of the pregnant woman.'[63] The author continues: 'all women tend to become emotionally unstable at times when their hormone levels are either changing or at their highest, such as puberty, pregnancy, the menopause and also immediately before the onset of each menstrual period.'[64] Not only does this imply that there are very few normal women at any given time, apart, presumably, from the pre-pubescent and postmenopausal, but women are also meddlesome, professing to know about pregnancy and childbirth:

> Why do women have to recount such [horrifying] stories to one another [about pregnancy and childbirth], especially when the majority of them are blatantly untrue? ... Probably more is done by wicked women with their malicious lying tongues to harm the confidence and happiness of pregnant women than by any other single factor.[65]

Pregnancy and childbirth, having been colonized by the (male) professionals, have also been deemed by them to put women in a different category from non-pregnant women. The remark by a judge that a pregnant woman is 'no longer just a woman, she is a woman ... with child'[66] was doubtless not meant in any sinister sense (although it defeated her claim), but it does illustrate the apparent inability to view pregnancy and childbirth as simply a part – and not necessarily the defining experience – of a woman's life. The idea that motherhood fulfils and makes a woman's life complete finds expression not only in media representations of radiant pregnant women and smiling, serene mothers, but also in the way in which pregnant women are treated. Not only do women cease to be 'just' women when pregnant, they are also assumed to become, if not incapable, then certainly unpredictable and irrational. This was bizarrely demonstrated in Australia where a planning decision was challenged in the Supreme Court on the ground that a member of the Tribunal was five months pregnant when making the decision. The grounds of appeal were that, when the presiding member heard the case and gave her decision, she 'suffered from the well known medical condition ("placidity") which detracts significantly from the mental competence of mothers-to-be'.[67]

Ussher notes that 'the notion of female psychology has been used to maintain the notion that women are weak and potentially volatile during reproductive "crises", of which pregnancy is the primary one'.[68] In the same passage, she refers to the opinion of one obstetrician who proclaimed: 'regression in the course of pregnancy is universal and normal, and pregnancy has aptly been called a "normal illness" ... just as the regression of the pregnant woman brings to the surface childhood fears, so we find the pregnant woman as suggestible as a child'.[69] The assumption that women lose whatever rational capacities they may have had (when not premenstrual) whilst pregnant and 'regress' has a clear and disturbing message for those seeking to establish that a pregnant woman is capable of making decisions about what shall be done to her (and her foetus). It is as though the usual presumption in favour of competence which applies to adults is displaced so that the child-woman-with-child must *prove* that she is rational, sensible and able to weigh up the information she is given, by coming to a decision which 'fits' the general assumptions about what 'real' women do.

At this point, it is important to note that pregnancy has not only physiological effects (which become increasingly apparent), and psychological effects (whose existence is more problematic, since some might well depend on what women *expect* and are *expected* to feel) but also what might be termed the *cultural burden* that women carry along with the foetus. Not only have women long been divided into madonna and whore, but also into good and bad mothers. What is a 'good' mother? First and foremost, she is altruistic to the point of self-sacrifice. She will *always* put her children (and partner) first:

> ... being a good mother – or, to put it less judgmentally, the kind of mother who produces successful, confident children – requires a degree of selflessness. Even – dare I breathe the words – an element of self-sacrifice. This self-denial need only be temporary ... but it is the willingness of the woman to contemplate such sacrifice that is significant.[70]

'Good' mothers are *self*-denying. Denial of *self* means not just denying oneself food and material possessions, in order to see children fed and clothed,[71] but also denying the value of one's own beliefs, desires and preferences. *Good* mothers put others before themselves. *Good* mothers sacrifice themselves for their children – and this would certainly encompass acceptance of the risks, pain and consequences of surgical childbirth. Writing about women who choose not to have children, Joan Smith comments that 'the degree of anger and contempt showered on childless women is so disproportionate as to suggest that the refusal of the category of mother automatically displaces them into that of whore'.[72] Similarly, I suggest that a pregnant woman who rejects the pervasive notion of altruism is automatically labelled not just bad but mad – at least in so far as this means that she cannot possibly be 'in her right mind' if she is willing to risk not only her health but also that of the foetus.

The fear that a pregnant woman who does not conform to what is expected will, *by definition*, risk being categorized as incompetent is shown not only in *CH*, but also in *Rochdale Healthcare (NHS) Trust* v. *C*.[73] C's obstetrician was of the opinion that, without a caesarean section, both C and the foetus would die. C had previously undergone a caesarean and said she would rather die than have another. The obstetrician considered that C understood the consequences of what she was saying, and was competent. Johnson J overrode this and authorized the operation. In a breathtakingly sweeping statement he held that a 'patient ... in the throes of labour with all that is involved in terms of pain and emotional stress' was not capable of making a valid decision 'about anything of even the most trivial kind'. C's refusal was based on her earlier experience, but this was treated as being so unreasonable (or unnatural?) that she could not possibly be competent. In fact, C herself finally consented to the procedure – presumably because, in the final reckoning, she valued her own life and that of the foetus above the pain and discomfort of the operation.[74] C is transformed thereby from an unreasonable woman, to a 'good' mother.

S2 and her predecessor, S1, refused voluntarily to make that choice and remain as examples of 'mad' or 'bad' mothers who put themselves (or their beliefs) above all else. They would not do what they were 'supposed' to do and thereby endangered not only their own lives (misguided, but permissible) but also the lives of their unborn children (unacceptable and unnatural). Even in subsequently upholding a right of self-determination for a competent woman the court left open, in S2, the possibility of condemning her decision as 'morally repugnant'.[75]

The idea that a competent pregnant woman has the *legal* right to refuse treatment is foreshadowed in *Re MB*. This is an interesting case because, while it upholds the rights of the competent individual, MB was found to be incompetent on the facts. It is worth reciting the background to that decision. MB, who already had one child, was first seen at antenatal clinic when she was 33 weeks pregnant. She refused to allow blood samples to be taken because she was afraid of needles. When she attended again, at 38 weeks, the foetus was found to be in a partial breech position. The evidence given was that this was potentially serious for the foetus, the risk being assessed at 50 per cent, although there was little physical danger to the mother. The risk of vaginal delivery was explained to MB who agreed to a caesarean section, although anaesthesia was not discussed by the obstetrician, N, who felt that this was a matter for the anaesthetist. N maintained that a footling breech should always be delivered by caesarean section although there was an alternative procedure (which N had performed) of vaginal delivery with epidural anaesthesia (also involving a needle, but significantly less invasive) which could end in an emergency caesarean section. It is not apparent that this was discussed with MB, since the report simply states that N explained to her the risks of a vaginal delivery. MB signed a consent form for the caesarean section but refused to provide blood samples. Anaesthesia by mask was then suggested, to which MB agreed, even though the risks of the procedure were explained. Later, she retracted her consent and refused to discuss matters with anyone. She then went into labour. She agreed to a caesarean section (on certain conditions such as not seeing the needle) but when she got to the operating table, she again refused anaesthesia. At this point, the hospital obtained a court order and MB instructed lawyers to appeal. The appeal was dismissed at 1.00 am. The following morning MB signed a consent form, cooperated fully and gave birth to a boy.

During this saga MB was seen by F, a psychiatrist, whose view was that MB understood and accepted why a caesarean was necessary. He did not think, however, that she understood the full implications of refusing the advice. He commented that 'she is a naive, not very bright, frightened young woman, but is not exhibiting a psychiatric disorder'.[76] On the other hand, she was suffering from 'the abnormal mental condition' of needle phobia, and it was this which caused such panic that 'she was not capable of making a decision at all, in the sense of being able to hold information in the balance and make a choice'.[77] Her abnormal fear was the basis for finding that she was incompetent.[78] It must be recalled that MB actually *wanted* a caesarean section, and presumably was delighted with her baby's safe arrival and relieved, in retrospect, that the surgery took place. In that sense, concerns over non-consensual treatment may be allayed, but the question still arises as to whether a non-pregnant patient would be similarly treated. There was here a possible alternative non-surgical procedure. MB *wanted* a caesarean section but she had been told that it was *necessary*. The vaginal delivery would not have been safer for the foetus but it may have been more tolerable for the woman, particularly since she would probably not have had to see the epidural needle, nor worry about post-operative procedures. What would have happened if MB were not so naive and had said that she would prefer to try for a vaginal delivery? Would she still have been incompetent? Was she given that choice? If not, why not?

There is another point of general principle in *MB*, which can be obscured by the facts. In treating an incompetent patient the doctor must do no more than is reasonably required in the best interests of the *patient*.[79] Butler-Sloss LJ comments that, whilst it may be desirable for the mother to be delivered of a live and healthy baby, all that doctors may do in respect of a *competent* woman is to attempt to persuade her. The mother may 'later regret the outcome but the alternative would be an unwarranted invasion of the right of the woman to make the decision'.[80] If the woman is incompetent this right to decide is irrelevant but, nevertheless, treatment must be in *her* interests. The medical opinion was that the breech presentation posed no *physical* risk to MB, but that a stillbirth or the birth of a handicapped child would 'very likely' be 'harmful' to her in the long term, whilst the imposition of surgery would not inflict permanent damage. Butler-Sloss LJ noted that medical interests are not limited to 'best medical interests'[81] and that it was in MB's best interests to deliver a healthy baby. If the medical opinion is that a caesarean section is most likely to produce a live birth, and if a live birth is in the interests of the woman (as presumably will almost always be the case), there is a clear temptation to find a woman refusing that operation to be incompetent.

Cases where pregnant women have been declared incompetent have featured refusals or potential refusals of intervention and doctors who are telling them that intervention is necessary for them and(or) their babies. Where the medical professional prevails there is no issue as to competence. Stefan argues '... questions of competence arise only as a function of a relationship between two or more people and ... this relationship is necessarily a hierarchical one, characterized by dominance and subordination, by power and powerlessness'.[82] This is especially so where gender is an element and where women are refusing to conform to stereotypical expectations. The role which control plays in this process is highlighted if the position is reversed and the woman *demands* intervention.[83] In the context of a debate in the *British Medical Journal*[84] as to whether women should be allowed to opt for caesarean sections where these were not otherwise indicated,[85] it became clear not only that it is impossible to state beyond doubt which method of delivery is safer, but that some doctors feared that acceding to women's wishes would make them mere 'technicians'.

Conclusions

Ussher argues that being a woman is synonymous with being a mother and that 'motherhood is an integral part of our identity as women'[86] and notes, significantly, that being a mother entails the loss of identity as an autonomous person: 'A woman begins to assume the identity of mother in the eyes of society almost as soon as she is visibly pregnant, ceasing to be a single unit long before the birth of her child.'[87] A pregnant woman is expected willingly and easily to relinquish her sense of 'individuation' and to accept the transition – to conform to what is expected – to be a 'good' mother. Those who do not conform are seen as dysfunctional. Whereas, after the birth, this may be termed postnatal depression, beforehand it may well be seen as evidence of an inability to make decisions, and thus pregnant women who deviate from the norm, are 'incompetent'. No one would suggest that assessment of competence is straightforward or reducible to formulae: it 'cannot be done by following a set of "cookbook" procedures'[88] nor is it suggested that pregnant women may not, on occasion, be genuinely unable to weigh up the choices,[89] but there are circumstances in which those who make such assessments should be especially aware of preconceptions derived from their acceptance of prevailing social constructions of gender. Situating women within the framework of 'mother' should not be an excuse to label 'deviant' women as mad or bad.[90] It is perfectly possible that a woman who refuses intervention which would save her and her baby is *competent* to make that decision – even though we may condemn her for it.[91] She should be judged as an individual not as a 'mother'. It has been said that 'unfortunately maternal autonomy is often assumed to mean doing what the woman requests at a particular moment … [i]t is far more complex that that. Doctors should assist the mother in the process of exercising her autonomy in the best interests of herself and her child.'[92]

A woman must be clear about the consequences of her decision, but what if her view of her best interests does not coincide with the doctor's? What price autonomy then? Of course, there is no simple answer to such an awful dilemma:

> Sometimes the best obstetric care will be declined, with disastrous consequences, and nothing goes harder with an obstetrician than to listen passively to a decelerating fetal heartbeat. But our duty is to respect a woman's autonomy and to obey the law. Doctors, midwives, and childbirth educators must advise fully and honestly, may persuade, but may never coerce.[93]

A woman who rejects medical advice when confronted with childbirth may have many reasons for doing so. The obstetrician sees her at one particular moment, as a snapshot problem, but she is part of her own complex and continuing story. We may fail to comprehend her decision, and we may find it 'morally repugnant'; but we should not, because of this, take from her one of the most fundamental of human rights – the right to bodily integrity. A woman who delivers a dead or handicapped baby might have bitter regrets that she did not accept advice, as might a woman who had (or did not have) an abortion or a woman who wishes she had children (or had not had them). Physically, only women can be mothers, but 'motherhood' is a sociological not a biological construct. There is, after all, more than one sort of Angel and not all are found in the kitchen or nursery. Angels used to be seen as strong and powerful: 'a mighty angel took up a stone like a great millstone, and cast it into the sea …'.[94] Women are carrying a millstone of passivity in the face of society's assumptions about how real women behave. Being a mother demands strength and a recognition of one's own worth and identity, just as much as it requires a willingness to care and nurture. As Breen noted in her study of mothers:

> … those who are most adjusted to childbearing are those who are less enslaved by the experience, have more differentiated, more open appraisals of themselves and other people, do not aspire to the perfect, selfless mother which they might have felt their own mother had not been but are able to call on a good mother image with much they can identify and do not experience themselves as passive, the cultural stereotype of femininity.[95]

Pregnant women have the right to be treated as competent adults unless, and until, there is evidence that they cannot weigh up the information they are given and are incapable of appreciating the consequences. Competence depends on an ability to understand, not on altruism.

Notes

1 *St George's Health Care NHS Trust* v. *S*; *R* v. *Collins and others ex parte S* [1998] 3 All ER 673.
2 See also *Re S* (*adult: refusal of medical treatment*) [1992] 4 All ER 671.
3 Stefan, S. (1993), 'Silencing the Different Voice: Competence, Feminist Theory and Law', *University of Miami Law Review*, **47**, p. 763. I am indebted to Kirsty Keywood for alerting me to this article.
4 Bewley, Susan, Director of Obstetrics, Guy's and St Thomas's Hospitals (1997), 'Bad medicine and bad law', *British Medical Journal*, **314**, p. 1184, following *Tameside and Glossop Acute Services Trust* v. *CH* [1996] 1 FLR 762.
5 Which is not to say that pregnancy is risk-free. See, for example, Drife, J. and Lewis, G. (1998), *Why Mothers Die: Report of the Confidential Enquiries into Maternal Deaths in the United Kingdom 1994–96*, London: HMSO.
6 Which carry risks of, respectively, listeriosis and toxoplasmosis.
7 See Morris, A. and Nott, S. (1995), 'The Law's Engagement with Pregnancy', in J. Bridgeman and S. Millns (eds), *Law and Body Politics*, Aldershot: Dartmouth. There has been more litigation and legislation in the United States: see, for example, D. Johnsen (1986), 'The Creation of Fetal Rights: Conflicts with Women's Constitutional Rights to Liberty, Privacy, and Equal Protection', *Yale Law Journal*, **95**, p. 599; idem (1990), 'Rethinking (M)otherhood: Feminist Theory and State Regulation of Pregnancy', *Harvard Law Review*, **103**, p. 1325. For a Canadian perspective, see Diduck, A. (1993), 'Legislating Ideologies of Motherhood', *Social and Legal Studies*, **2**, p. 461.

8   See Oakley, A. (1979), *Becoming a Mother*, Oxford: Martin Robertson; idem (1980), *Women Confined*, Oxford: Martin Robertson.
9   Arney, W.R. (1982), *Power and the Profession of Obstetrics*, Chicago: Chicago University Press, p. 8.
10 Beech, B. (1985), 'The Politics of Maternity: Childbirth Freedom vs Obstetric Control', in S. Edwards (ed.), *Gender, Sex and the Law*, London: Croom Helm.
11 *Winterton Report*, Health Committee Second Report, House of Commons, Maternity Services, 1992, vol. 1, para. 25.
12 Department of Health (1997), *NHS Maternity Statistics, England: 1989–1990 to 1994–95*. London: Dept of Health (Bulletin 1997/28). Also RCOG (2001) National Sentinel Caesarean Section Report, London: RCOG Press.
13 The high uptake of ultrasound screening 'has been attributed to expectant couples' overwhelming desire to "see the baby"': Baillie, C. and Hewison, J. (1999), *British Medical Journal*, **318**, p. 805.
14 There may be other unreported cases. In 1997 Caroline Spear accepted £7000 in settlement of a claim for assault where she had been subjected to a caesarean section without consent: *The Guardian* 2 June 1997, p. 5.
15 See Wells, C. (1998), 'On the Outside Looking in: Perspectives on Enforced Caesareans', in S. Sheldon and M. Thomson (eds), *Feminist Perspectives on Health Care Law*, London: Cavendish.
16 Although the current abortion debate is couched in terms of competing rights, this was not always so. In the nineteenth century, when the American Medical Association began a campaign to criminalize abortion, it was suggested that:

> '... women who sought abortions were either inadvertent "murderesses" who elected abortion based on ignorance of fetal development or rebellious women who had abandoned their maternal duties for "selfish and personal ends". The portrayal of women as simply ignorant or selfish, rather than hostile to the fetus, reflected an idealised conception as woman as committed and confined to the sphere of home and family.': (1990), Rethinking M(o)therhood: Feminist Theory and State Regulation of Pregnancy, *Harvard Law Review*, **103**, pp. 1333–34.

17 *Re S* [1992] 3 WLR 806.
18 Once the foetus had died, it is arguable that S was free to decline treatment intended to save *her* life: Stern, K. (1993), 'Court-Ordered Caesarean Sections: In Whose Interests?', *Modern Law Review*, **56**, p. 238.
19 See ibid.; Thomson, M. (1994), 'After Re S', *Medical Law Review*, **2**, p. 127.
20 *St George's Health Care NHS Trust* v. *S, R* v. *Collins and others ex parte S* [1998] 3 All ER 673.
21 See *Re C (adult: refusal of treatment)* [1994] 1 WLR 290; *Re MB* [1997] 8 Med LR 217, below.
22 [1998] 3 All ER 673 at p. 692.
23 Ibid. at p. 688.
24 *Re MB* [1997] 8 Med. LR 217.
25 Ibid., p. 224.
26 It may also reflect the fear of litigation should the woman and/or foetus die or be injured.
27 *Schloendorff* v. *Society of New York Hospital* (1914) 211 NY 125, 126, *per* Cardozo J. Technically, it is a battery, not an assault.
28 *Airedale NHS Trust* v. *Bland* [1993] 1 All ER 821 *per* Lord Goff at p. 866. See also Grisso, T. and Applebaum, P.S. (1998), *Assessing Competence to Consent to Treatment*, New York: Oxford University Press, pp.13–14.
29 *Airedale NHS Trust* v. *Bland* [1993] 1 All ER 821, *per* Lord Mustill at p. 889.
30 *Re T (Adult: Refusal of Medical Treatment* [1992] 4 All ER 649; [1992] 3 WLR 782.

31 [1992] 4 All ER 649, 662, *per* Lord Donaldson MR.

32 Stefan, 'Silencing the Different Voice', *op. cit.*, n. 3, p. 778.

33 But see Grisso and Applebaum, *Assessing Competence, op. cit.*, n. 28 at p. 66.

34 *Chatterton* v. *Gerson* [1981] 1 All ER 257, p. 265; *Sidaway* v. *Bethlem Royal Hospital Governors* [1984] 1 All ER 1018. The courts have drawn a distinction between a lack of information which concerns the *nature* of the procedure (which gives rise to an action in battery) and a lack of information about risks associated with the procedure (where the action must be based in negligence).

35 See Robertshaw, P. and Thacker, R. (1993), 'Consent, Autonomy and the Infantilised Patient', *Medical Law International*, **1**, p. 33.

36 A classic exposition is Roth, L. Meisel, A. and Lidz, C. (1977), *American Journal of Psychiatry*, **134**, pp. 279, 281. They list: evidencing a choice; reasonableness of outcome; rationality of choice; ability to understand; and actual understanding. See also Grisso and Applebaum, *Assessing Competence, op. cit.*, n. 28, p. 31.

37 See Jones, M.A. and Keywood, K. (1996), 'Assessing the Patient's Competence to Consent to Medical Treatment', *Medical Law International*, **2**, p. 107.

38 Being more used to issues which arose in relation to the disposition of property, wills and marriage: see, for example, *Re Park's Estate* [1953] 2 All ER 1411.

39 At least in relation to adults: compare *Gillick* v. *West Norfolk and Wisbech HA* [1986] AC 112. Even with adults, it appears that the greater the risk of refusing (or accepting) treatment, the higher will be the requirement of competence: Grisso and Applebaum, *Assessing Competence, op. cit.*, n. 28, p. 24.

40 [1994] 1 WLR 290; see Stern, K. (1994), 'Competence to refuse life-sustaining medical treatment', *Law Quarterly Review*, **110**, p. 541; Gordon, R. and Barlow, C. (1993), 'Competence and the right to die', *New Law Journal*, **143**, p. 1719; Roberts, E. (1994), 'Re C and the boundaries of autonomy', *Professional Negligence*, **10**, p. 98.

41 See also *Re MB* [1997] 8 Med. LR 217, where the test was given a somewhat different formulation.

42 It has been estimated that 95 per cent of anorexics in Britain are women: Wolf, N. (1990), *The Beauty Myth*, Vintage: London.

43 *Re KB (adult) (mental patient: medical treatment)* [1994] 2 FCR 1051. See also *Re W (a minor)(medical treatment)* [1992] 4 All ER 627, in which the Court of Appeal doubted that W, who was 16, had sufficient understanding to make treatment decisions because anorexia nervosa can destroy the ability to make an *informed choice*. The dispute between W and her carers seems to have been about control. The order did not specify a form of treatment, but denied W the right to say what should happen and where. W was not refusing all treatment but she did want to stay where she was and decide for herself when she would eat. Her consultant regarded her as competent, but her wishes were overridden by the court.

44 Anorexia is included – not uncontroversially – in the definition of mental illnesses: *International Classification of Diseases of the World Health Organisation* (ICD-10), Berne: World Health Organisation.

45 [1994] 2 FCR 1051, p. 1053.

46 Orbach, S. (1993), *Hunger Strike: The Anorectic's Struggle as a Metaphor for our Age*, Harmondsworth: Penguin; Bridgeman, J. (1995), 'They Gag Women, Don't They', in Bridgeman and Millns, *Law and Body Politics, op. cit.*, n. 7.

47 And see now also *Re MB* [1997] 8 Med LR 217.

48 See Orbach, *Hunger Strike, op. cit.*, n. 46; also Dresser, R. (1984), 'Article and Commentary on Anorexia Nervosa: Feeding the Hunger Artists', *Wisconsin Law Review*, p. 297. But see the reply: Frost, N. (1984), *Wisconsin Law Review*, p. 375.

49 [1995] 1 All ER 677.

50   (1909) 26 TLR 139.
51   Dresser, 'Article and Commentary', *op. cit.*, n. 48, p. 320.
52   *Tameside and Glossop Acute Services Trust* v. *CH* [1996] 1 FLR 762.
53   *Re C (adult refusal of treatment)* [1994] 1 All ER 819.
54   See, for example, Grubb, A. *Treatment without consent (pregnancy); adult. Tameside and Glossop Acute Services Trust* v. *CH* (1996), *Medical Law Review*, **4**(2), p. 193; Yeates, V. (1996), 'In Whose Interests?', *New Law Journal*, **146**, p. 1182.
55   In contrast, the psychiatrist treating her said that, for a great deal of the time she had been detained, she had been disturbed, overaroused and even paranoid. Were she not pregnant he would have prescribed her strong anti-psychotic drugs.
56   [1996] 1 FLR 762, at 765.
57   Although there is a view that 'minor' tranquillizers can cause neonatal sedation and withdrawal: see Bewley, *op. cit.*, n. 4, p. 1184.
58   Goldthorp, W. O. and McDade, G. (1997), *British Medical Journal*, **315**, p. 1017.
59   Or with *Re JT (Adult: Refusal of Medical Treatment)* [1998] 1 FLR 48 in which a woman of 25 with learning difficulties and 'extremely severe behavioural disturbance' was found competent to refuse life-saving dialysis? See Grubb, A. (1998), *Medical Law Review*, **6** p. 105.
60   Patmore, C. (1949), 'The Angel in the House', in *The Poems of Coventry Patmore*, London: Oxford University Press. The poem was first published in 1854. See Woolf, Virginia (1942), p. 150, 'Professions for Women', *The Death of the Moth*, London: Hogarth Press: '… every house had its Angel … she was intensely sympathetic. She was immensely charming. She was utterly unselfish… She sacrificed herself daily. If there was a chicken, she took the leg, if there was a draught, she sat in it.'
61   Friedan, B. (1963), *The Feminine Mystique*, Gollancz: London; Firestone, S. (1971), *The Dialectic of Sex*, London: Cape.
62   'Hyster' being derived from the Greek for womb as in hysterectomy.
63   Bourne, Gordon, FRCS, FRCG (1984), 'Preface to First Edition', *Pregnancy* (4th edn), Pan Books: London.
64   Ibid, p. 12.
65   Ibid, p. 16.
66   She could not, therefore, compare herself with a man: *Turley* v. *Allders Department Store* [1980] ICR 66, p. 70.
67   Naylor, B. (1989), 'Pregnant Tribunals', *Legal Service Bulletin*, **14**, p. 41, cited in Graycar, R. and Morgan, J. (1990), *The Hidden Gender of Law*, Annandale, NSW: Federation Press. The action was withdrawn. The applicant, incidentally, was a male solicitor.
68   Ussher, J. (1989), *The Psychology of the Female Body*, London: Routledge, p. 78.
69   Ibid., referring to Heiman, M. (1965), 'A Psychoanalytical View of Pregnancy', in Rovinsky, J. and Guttman, A. (eds.), *Medical and Surgical and Gynaecological Complications of Pregnancy* (2nd edn), Baltimore: The Williams and Watkins Co., pp. 450–81. Ann Oakley (1993), *Essays on Women Medicine and Health*, Edinburgh: Edinburgh University Press, p. 13, refers to the infantilization of women and notes: 'pregnant women are especially seen as being incapble of taking decisions on behalf of themselves and their fetuses.'
70   Daley, Janet, *Daily Telegraph*, 4 February 1997, quoted in Smith, Joan (1998), *Different for Girls: How Culture Creates Women*, London: Vintage, p. 109.
71   Research has shown that where a family is poor, the woman is often poorest and contributes to family welfare by 'doing without': Graham, H. (1992), 'Budgeting for Health: Mothers in Low-income Households' in Glendinning, C. and Millar, J. (eds), *Women and Poverty in Britain: The 1990s*, New York: Harvester Wheatsheaf.
72   Smith, *Different for Girls*, *op cit*, n. 70, p. 89.

73 *Rochdale Healthcare (NHS) Trust* v. *C* [1997] 1 FLR 275, heard by Johnson J during the course of the hearing in *W* (above) and which he described, wrongly, as being very similar.

74 Presumably this decision was, on the basis of the judicial reasoning, incompetent.

75 As Butler-Sloss LJ noted in *Re MB*, the ethical dilemma may remain but the court is not a court of morals: 38 BMLR 175, 189.

76 At p. 180.

77 At p. 181.

78 Also *Re L (Patient: Non-Consensual Treatment)* [1997] 2 FLR 837: the needle-phobic patient agreed to a caesarean and wanted the baby safely delivered, but could not consent: she was deemed incompetent.

79 *F* v. *West Berkshire Health Authority* [1989] 2 All ER 545.

80 *Re MB* 38 BMLR 175, p. 187.

81 Ibid., p. 188.

82 Stefan, 'Silencing the Different Voice', *op. cit.*, n. 3, p. 766.

83 Compare cases where it is sought to sterilize an incompetent woman, where risks associated with long-term use of the contraceptive pill are emphasized: *Re B (a minor) (Wardship: Sterilisation)* [1988] AC 199; *F* v. *West Berkshire Health Authority* [1989] 2. All ER 545, 550.

84 See Paterson-Brown, S., Olubusola, A. *et al.* (1998), 'Controversies in Management', *British Medical Journal*, **317**, pp. 462–65 and the responses thereto.

85 The 'elective' caesarean rate rose from 4.9 per cent (1985) to 6.8 per cent in 1994–95, but this usually means that it is a *planned* caesarean section – as advised by the obstetrician, rather than elected by the woman.

86 Ussher, *The Psychology of the Female Body, op. cit.*, n. 68, p. 80.

87 Ibid., p. 81.

88 Grisso and Applebaum, *Assessing Competence, op. cit.*, n. 28, p. 17.

89 See, for example, *Norfolk and Norwich Healthcare Trust* v. *W* [1996] 2 FLR 615: a woman who was not mentally ill but with a history of psychiatric treatment arrived at hospital in labour, denying she was pregnant. She was found incompetent and a caesarean section was authorized. The facts seem to suggest an inability even to evidence a choice: compare *State of Tennessee* v. *Northern* (1978) 563 SW 2d 197. This is distinguishable from *CH* in which CH appreciated her condition but disagreed with her doctors about how to proceed.

90 The laws on infanticide are an interesting example of how childbirth was used to 'excuse' certain crimes: Boland, F. (1998), *Anglo-American Insanity Defence Reform: The War between Law and Medicine*, Aldershot: Ashgate, p. 103.

91 As we might condemn the refusal of a parent to donate a life-saving kidney.

92 Stirrat, G.M. (Professor of Obstetrics, University of Bristol) letter in *British Medical Journal*, 28 August 1998.

93 Goldbeck-Wood, Sandra (1997), 'Women's authority in childbirth', *British Medical Journal*, **314**, p. 1143. In 1994 the Royal College of Obstetricians and Gynaecologists issued 'A consideration of the law and ethics in relation to court-ordered obstetric intervention'. Para. 5.12: '… it is inappropriate, and unlikely to be helpful or necessary, to invoke judicial intervention to overrule an informed and competent woman's refusal of medical treatment, even though her refusal might place her life and that of her fetus at risk.'

94 Revelation, 18:21.

95 Breen, D. (1975), *The Birth of a First Child*, London: Tavistock, p. 193.

Chapter 7

Care, Control or Coercion? Women in the Mental Health System in Ireland, England and Wales

Faye Boland and Judith M. Laing

Introduction

This chapter will examine and contrast the treatment of female psychiatric patients in Ireland and England and Wales. It will focus on the role of psychiatry in oppressing women and will highlight deficiencies in the treatment, standards and quality of care, and mental health facilities for women in both countries. Historically, the specific needs of women have not been recognized in the provision of services by either country's mental health care system. Fortunately, recent developments in England and Wales are beginning to acknowledge that women's needs do require particular attention, but the position in Ireland remains less enlightened in this respect.

We will outline particular areas of concern for women, stemming from the application of the mental health legislation in both countries and the regime that follows compulsory commitment. In this manner we will highlight inadequacies in the current treatment of women in the mental hospital systems of Ireland and England and Wales. It is crucial to do so as, despite the introduction of 'care in the community' and the move away from hospital to community-based care, recent statistics in England and Wales suggest that the number of patients subject to compulsory hospital admission is increasing.[1] A steady decline in the numbers of hospitalized psychiatric patients is evident in Ireland[2] but, as the majority of involuntary patients are detained in health board hospitals,[3] it is imperative that 'psychiatric hospitals [do] not become forgotten places'.[4]

Women in the Mental Health System

Historically, the treatment of women within society, and by the medical profession in particular, has been characterized by coercion and domination. This is especially evident in the sphere of mental health. As noted by one feminist writer in the context of mental health care in England and Wales: 'by the end of the [nineteenth] century, women had decisively taken the lead in the career of psychiatric patient, a lead which they have retained ever since, and in ever-increasing numbers.'[5]

117

Feminist literature criticizes the continued 'medicalization' of women's behaviour and the role of the profession in dominating and controlling women.[6] The psychiatric profession has long been criticized as being a weapon of social control for individuals who may be displaying unusual, disruptive or 'abnormal' behaviour.[7] The so-called 'anti-psychiatrists' such as Goffman, Laing, Scull and Szasz have challenged the benevolence of the medical profession, arguing that mental illness is a social construct and that a diagnosis of mental illness is based purely upon subjective evaluations and value-laden judgements. This is particularly marked in its application to female psychiatric patients and has meant that some women's problems, which may have economic, social or ethical explanations, tend to be erroneously regarded as psychiatric problems.[8] The response to an Irish government consultative document *Developing a Policy for Women's Health*[9] endorses this view. Respondents criticized the preoccupation of the Irish health services with treating mental illness and the absence of services to protect and promote mental health, commenting that the failure of the mental health and health services in general to offer women support in coping with crises arising in their lives and which threaten their mental health, lead to women's problems being medicalized. Medication in such circumstances can mask the underlying problems and can lead to an addiction to the prescribed drug.[10] The tendency to overprescribe medication is rooted in traditional misconceptions about women. It is argued that when they deviate from, or complain about, their traditional role as mother, wife or sex object, the logical conclusion is that they must be sick, and doctors will readily prescribe drugs as the cure, thereby ignoring the actual stresses and social factors which affect women's lives.[11]

Many writers have highlighted how these paternalistic and dominating attitudes and practices are reflected in the operation of the mental health legislation in England and Wales.[12] The broad definition of mental disorder, and wide interpretation of the criteria for admission under the mental health legislation in England and Wales, have led to women being overrepresented within the psychiatric population.[13] In Ireland the focus of concern has been on wrongful involuntary committals of women to psychiatric hospitals, often initiated by their husbands following or during the break-up of a stormy marriage.[14] This has been facilitated by wide detention criteria and lax commitment procedures under the Irish Mental Treatment Act 1945.[15] Coercion and domination by the medical profession is also evident in relation to the treatment criteria and regimes in both systems and will be further explored below.

The Treatment of Women under the Mental Health Act 1983

Compulsory psychiatric admission in England and Wales is currently governed by the Mental Health Act 1983 (the 1983 Act). This provides for compulsory civil admission to hospital for assessment under section 2; for treatment under section 3; and, in a matter 'of urgent necessity', an emergency admission under section 4.[16] In order to satisfy the admission criteria it must be established that the person concerned is suffering from a 'mental disorder' of a 'nature or degree' which 'warrants' (under section 2 or section 4) or makes it 'appropriate' (under section 3) for him or her to be detained as an inpatient. In addition, this detention must be 'necessary for the health and safety of the patient or for the protection of others'.

The patient may be detained in hospital, on the basis of two medical recommendations, under section 2 for assessment for a period of up to 28 days, and under section 3 for treatment for up to six months. Although an emergency admission under section 4 may be made on the basis of one medical recommendation for a period of up to 72 hours, there is no power to impose treatment during that time.

In relation to the criteria for admission, the 1983 Act stipulates that the patient must be suffering from a 'mental disorder'. Mental disorder is defined in section 1(1) as embracing 'mental illness, arrested or incomplete development of mind, psychopathic disorder and any other disorder or disability of mind'. Although the phrase 'any other disorder or disability of mind' appears to be broad, section 1(3) of the 1983 Act stipulates that a person may not be classified as mentally disordered 'by reason only of promiscuity or other immoral conduct, sexual deviancy or dependence on alcohol or drugs'. Further limits are imposed in the 1983 Act, as there is a requirement that persons with mental impairment and psychopathic disorder (the two minor categories of mental disorder) should be 'treatable' before they can be compulsorily admitted to hospital for a long period of time.[17] Applications for admission can be made by an approved social worker (ASW) or the person's nearest relative (NR – as defined in section 26 and, *inter alia*, includes the patient's spouse, parents and children), and must be supported by the necessary medical recommendations.

Despite the presence of the elaborate legal definition in the criteria for admission, the Code of Practice, which accompanies the 1983 Act, stipulates that, in practice, 'the identification of an individual who falls within these legal categories is a matter for clinical judgement'.[18] Thus, much discretion is left in the hands of the medical professionals involved regarding the interpretation of the relevant terms.[19] This has been described as the 'medical domination of the terminology of mental illness'[20] and means that the psychiatric profession has a good deal of control over the admissions process.

Psychiatrists also retain great discretion and power after admission during the compulsory treatment process. Once the patient is in hospital, various treatments may be given against that patient's will under Part IV of the Act. However, under sections 57–63, more prolonged and intrusive forms of treatment, such as neurosurgery, require the patient's consent, and a second medical opinion is required if electro-convulsive therapy (ECT) or medication for mental disorder (for a period longer than three months[21]) is given without the patient's consent. The second opinion procedure was introduced in the 1983 Act to curb the powers of the medical profession and bolster the rights of detained patients, by providing a system of peer review in relation to the administration of compulsory treatment.

Under the 1983 Act an individual may be detained for medical treatment, but the definition of treatment in the Act is extremely expansive. Indeed, it could cover almost any kind of medical nursing and 'care, habilitation or rehabilitation', provided that it is given for the mental disorder.[22] Thus, treatment can amount to little more than therapeutic containment. As noted by Hoggett, this definition is very broad and wide enough to include 'a carefully designed programme of behaviour modification' which is designed to meet the needs of a particular group of patients.[23] Another consequence of this broad definition is that, whilst the treatment must be given for a mental, and not a physical, disorder, the distinction is not always easy to draw. It has been observed that some physical conditions may often be the 'cause' of a mental disorder so, by treating the *cause*, there is also treatment for the mental disorder.[24] Moreover, it is also acceptable to treat the *consequences or symptoms* of the mental disorder in addition to the causes (that is, the underlying disorder). As a result, a range of physical treatments for women patients have been permitted, which, undoubtedly, go far beyond what parliament and the legislation must have intended.[25] This is demonstrated by cases such as *Re KB*,[26] *B* v. *Croydon Health Authority*[27] and *Re MB*[28] where a wide definition of medical treatment has been given under section 63 of the 1983 Act. Accordingly, enforced artificial feeding through a naso-gastric tube is regarded as treatment for anorexia nervosa[29] or other disorders with a tendency for self-harm,[30] and medical treatment also includes the performance of a caesarean section against the will of a female detained patient.[31] This is regarded as wholly unsatisfactory as 'it is only by stretching the logic and language of section 63 almost to breaking point that Caesareans can be viewed as treatment for mental disorder'.[32] It is also highly questionable whether physical treatments, such as forcible feeding, are actually in the best interests of the patients. As noted by one commentator: 'Force-feeding crushes the patient's will, destroying who the patient is. This is the antithesis of what a successful, therapeutic treatment must be.'[33] Consequently, it is likely to damage the clinical relationship and may exacerbate the sufferer's condition in the long term.

These cases demonstrate that, where women behave in an unacceptable and uncaring way by rejecting their maternal and traditionally 'feminine' instincts, they are at risk of being labelled mentally ill and may be subjected to such invasive physical treatments against their will. In the words of Fegan and Fennell, it shows us: '... that women are still at risk of having any behaviour which conflicts with 'accepted moral standards' attributed to an 'unstable psyche' by psychiatry and other powerful discourses, including law.'[34] This is totally unacceptable, particularly in light of the fact that such invasive interventions constitute 'serious intrusions' into the bodily integrity, autonomy and dignity of women and cannot always be justified on the basis that they are in the patient's best interests, as they have 'questionable therapeutic value'.[35] This is a clear example of the domination of female psychiatric patients and illustrates how the views and wishes of female patients are overridden in the compulsory treatment process.

The 1983 Act permits certain other forms of especially intrusive treatment, such as prolonged psychotropic medication, ECT or psychosurgery. However, as noted above, there are additional criteria that must be met under sections 57–63 of the 1983 Act before such treatment will be authorized. Most section 57 cases have involved referrals for psychosurgery. It is worrying to note that figures published by the Mental Health Act Commission reveal that women are disproportionately represented in the psychosurgery statistics,[36] although there is very little, if any, research to suggest why this is the case. The effectiveness of psychosurgery has been questioned,[37] as has its use as a means of controlling violent individuals.[38] The use of psychosurgery as a means of controlling behaviour brings the practice 'into the realms of using surgery as a mechanism for social control rather than for the *bona fide* treatment of illness'.[39]

Statistics from the Department of Health also reveal that women are disproportionately represented in the referrals for, and administration of, ECT.[40] The overrepresentation of women in the ECT statistics may be due to the fact that women are more prone to a diagnosis of depression or anxiety disorder,[41] and ECT (which involves passing an electric current over the brain) is regarded as an effective treatment for those particular disorders. Despite this fact, it must be recognized that ECT is an extremely controversial treatment which has damaging side effects such as confusion and severe long-term memory loss/disorder[42] and is potentially life-threatening.[43] Consequently, it is argued that it should never be given without the patient's consent. Concerns have also been expressed about the practice of administering ECT. During the last 20 years, the Royal College of Psychiatrists has published guidelines covering the appropriate personnel, training and facilities for the safe administration of ECT. However, a 1998 audit of ECT practices revealed that there have only been modest improvements in local practice throughout that time.[44] Some clinics were still using machines considered outdated in 1989 and only a third of clinics in the sample had clear policies to help guide junior doctors in administering ECT effectively. Research in the UK conducted in the early 1980s suggests that, where ECT is administered poorly, it is less effective and more likely to produce adverse side effects.[45]

Drug treatments are also regarded as an effective intervention for depression. Research suggests that women are also at a much greater risk of being prescribed sedatives and other psychotropic drugs.[46] It has been suggested that this may be due to the fact that 'male doctors are more likely to perceive a physical illness as a psychological one when a patient is a woman' and 'that this type of medication is more socially acceptable for women than for men'.[47] This overreliance on medication for female patients is also controversial. Prolonged and concurrent use of many psychotropic and anti-depressant drugs can lead to 'life diminishing and life threatening' conditions. For example, research conducted on behalf of MIND in the early 1990s revealed that many patients experienced adverse side effects from drug treatments, ranging from blurred vision, palpitations, drowsiness, memory loss, insomnia and muscle tension, to epilepsy, hallucinations and sexual dysfunction in severe cases.[48] The use of anti-psychotic drugs can lead to tardive dyskinesia, which is characterized by bizarre, uncontrollable movements of the tongue, face, mouth or jaw and may be accompanied by involuntary movements of the trunk and limbs. This condition is reversible in only one-third of the patients who suffer its consequences.[49] Onset of the disorder is masked by the drugs that cause it, so that the symptoms do not appear until the drug treatment is stopped and the disorder is so advanced that it cannot be cured.[50] Research suggests that female patients may be more susceptible to this condition.[51] Furthermore, certain side effects of neuroleptic drugs are sometimes misdiagnosed as agitation or psychosis, with the result that psychiatrists then increase the dosage of the very drugs that cause the disorders.[52]

The compulsory treatment procedures under the 1983 Act are inadequate, as they fail to accord sufficient respect to patient autonomy, with no reference to bodily integrity or dignity. The system of second medical opinions – that is, peer review – is not an adequate safeguard as, in practice, it is generally perceived to be nothing more than a 'sterile formality',[53] which rubber-stamps the first recommendation. Too much discretion is given to the medical professionals to authorize the compulsory treatment. Too little weight is given to the patient's *capacity* to consent to treatment, which is completely overlooked in the 1983 Act and is given only limited recognition in the accompanying Code of Practice.[54] With so little emphasis being placed on the patient's capacity to consent to the treatment, one might question how truly genuine and informed a given patient's consent will be. Indeed, as noted by some commentators who conducted research into patients' experiences of compulsory admission and treatment, 'genuine informed consent remains an empty promise for many patients'.[55] Consent is also problematic where a refusal to consent to treatment is a symptom of an underlying mental disorder – for example, in cases of anorexia where the disorder manifests itself in a refusal to eat food, and the proposed medical treatment is forcible feeding.

Gender issues are also largely ignored in the Code of Practice, as it contains only a few oblique references to the relevance of sex in the admissions and treatment process.[56] Unless and until the legislation gives greater recognition to the wishes of the patient and the relevance of gender to that decision, female patients will continue to be disadvantaged in the compulsory treatment process.

In addition to the concerns surrounding the administration of compulsory treatment in hospital, concerns also exist relating to the standards of care that are provided, the inappropriate conditions and the quality of services and treatment within the mental health facilities.[57] The Mental Health Act Commission (MHAC) is required to oversee the implementation of the 1983 Act and to investigate the standards of care for detained patients in mental institutions in England and Wales. The presence of the Commission is intended to provide a level of independent oversight, which is not found in the same form in Ireland. However, the Commission has proved to be deficient in several respects. Although it is required to carry out regular inspections and to produce a biennial report making observations and recommendations, its powers are generally ineffective as there is no duty imposed on the hospital managers to act on or implement the recommendations.[58] In this respect, the Commission's powers as a watchdog to improve standards of care and containment for detained patients are completely inadequate. Moreover, as it has no powers with respect to voluntary (informal) patients who comprise over 90 per cent of the mental hospital population, its effectiveness as an independent watchdog is also inhibited. Despite regular inspections by the MHAC, the range and quality of care and the treatment facilities for women within hospitals are inconsistent, inappropriate and insensitive to their needs. This is particularly evident in relation to female patients detained in secure conditions,[59] whose position was severely criticized in the Commission's biennial reports throughout the 1980s and 1990s. Little has been done to improve those services and standards in the supervening years, however.

The Commission's most recent report highlighted that conditions for female mental patients generally are still grossly inadequate.[60] In its reports it has repeatedly expressed concern about the appalling levels of security; the lack of privacy and dignity; and the shortage of single-sex wards for female patients. It has also criticized the high prescription rates of psychotropic drugs and the excessive application of ECT to female patients.[61] The Commission has also commented that the environments and many of the behaviour, rehabilitation and treatment programmes in secure hospitals are male-oriented and dominated and this clearly does not serve the best interests of female detainees. This has been borne out by other research into the experiences of female patients, particularly in the special hospital system in England and Wales.[62] Accordingly, the MHAC has stressed that there is an urgent need to provide separate facilities for women, which are adequately staffed by female carers who are sensitive to their particular needs. This has recently been reinforced by a Health Select Committee report into the provision of mental health services[63] which was highly condemnatory of the inappropriate conditions and the 'gender-blind' services for female patients in secure hospitals[64] and recommended that the only way forward is for women's secure services to become a completely separate service.

A study by MIND in 2000 into patients' views of conditions on psychiatric wards has cast further doubt on the quality and standards of care in psychiatric hospitals.[65] Questionnaires were sent out to psychiatric patients across England and Wales, and more than half the patients stated that the ward was an untherapeutic environment. Just under half felt that the ward conditions were bleak and depressing, and had a negative effect on their mental health. Of particular significance, however, is the fact that a third of patients found the atmosphere on wards unsafe and frightening; a small number of patients said that they had experienced sexual harassment on the ward, and almost half the respondents expressed the view that their dignity and privacy was not respected on the ward. The questionnaire also covered the issue of single-sex accommodation, and almost a third of respondents stated that they did not have access to such accommodation. The results are extremely worrying, particularly in the context of female patients who are obviously being denied their rights to privacy, dignity and access to single-sex wards, and who may feel unsafe, frightened and subjected to sexual abuse as a result. As noted by one of the patients who responded to the questionnaire, '[o]n the mixed ward, men were not supposed to go into women's sleeping area but they did all the time and the staff didn't try to stop them – the same with bathrooms'.[66]

The position of female patients detained under the 1983 Act has proved to be extremely unfavourable and disadvantageous. Experiences such as those outlined above indicate the need to place individual patients' needs and interests at the forefront of treatment delivery and service provision. As noted by the findings of the MIND survey, 'there is a need to ensure that the public policy framework matches up with the reality for service users at the sharp end – i.e. in hospital wards'.[67] However, the future may not be as bleak as might be imagined, as the government now seems to be taking a number of positive steps to remedy these deficiencies. In December 1998 it issued a Green Paper to modernize the National Health Service and provide a new strategy – 'a third way' for mental health.[68] The Labour government's 'safe, sound and supportive' mental health strategy proposes a new system – a 'new vision' for mental health services, which will provide security and support to the patients and the public alike. Included amongst the proposals are 24-hour crisis help lines and emergency outreach teams, more acute beds and support accommodation, specialist secure units and improved training and guidance.[69] Part of this strategy to provide safe services embraces the need for NHS Trusts to ensure that all patients are protected from physical, psychological or sexual harm while they are being treated in mental health facilities, and to recognize that the needs of male and female patients may be different. Consequently, the Department of Health has issued guidance on mixed-sex accommodation for mental health services, which outlines the practical steps that NHS staff should take to ensure the safety, privacy and dignity of patients.[70] The guidance suggests, *inter alia*, that staff should be sensitive to the needs of female patients and should ensure their safety by providing separate sleeping accommodation, toilets and washing facilities.[71] A specific officer should be appointed in each facility to deal with women's issues, and female patients should be able to choose their key worker and have access to a female member of staff at all times.[72] This is extremely encouraging and does address the concerns about the safety and privacy of female patients. Of greater note, however, is the fact that the guidance also states that the government is committed to phasing out mixed-sex hospital accommodation and that it hopes to eliminate mixed-sex accommodation in 95 per cent of health authority areas by 2002.[73] This objective has been reinforced by the National Director of Mental Health, Professor Louis Appleby, who identified this as one of his main objectives for reform of the mental health services.[74] This is an extremely welcome and important development that will significantly enhance the status of female patients. It can only be hoped that the government will succeed in meeting its objective and provide sufficient resources to do so. The early signs suggest that some mental health units have been slow to respond to the Department of Health Guidance[75], whilst others have complied with only the basic requirements, and have done so 'in a way that still does not afford women patients the safety and security that they should be able to expect'. For example, women-only washing and toilet facilities may be provided, but they are placed within wards in such a way that women have to pass male sleeping areas at night to reach them. This is wholly unsatisfactory and indicates that there is still much more that can be done to improve conditions in mental health units for female detained patients.

Fortunately, this new 'mental health' strategy has been backed by some financial investment,[76] and the government has also instituted a legislative review and reform of the 1983 Act, which forms an integral part of the new proposals.[77] The government appointed an Expert Committee to advise on, and make recommendations for, legislative change[78] and, on that basis, it published another Green Paper in November 1999,[79] followed by a White Paper in December 2000 with its own model for reform of the 1983 Act.[80]

The 1999 Green Paper outlined various options for change, some of which were based upon the 'Expert' Committee's proposals. The government received a significant number of responses to the Green Paper and has taken the proposals forward in the White Paper. First and foremost, the White Paper proposes a radical overhaul of the 1983 Act and recommends replacing the current system of admission under sections 2, 3 and 4 with a simplified procedure and a single point of entry. Accordingly, there should be a preliminary examination, followed by a full, formal structured assessment, on the recommendation of three professionals[81] and taking place either in the community or in hospital, before an individual can be made subject to compulsory care and treatment based on a preliminary care plan. This initial assessment and treatment period would be limited to a maximum period of 28 days, following which any further compulsory care and treatment (in hospital or in the community) would need to be authorized under a compulsory order by an independent judicial decision-making body – for example, a mental health tribunal.[82] This would represent a significant departure from the current process, removing the power to impose long-term compulsory treatment from the medical profession and placing it in the hands of an independent tribunal. The presence of the tribunal is designed to promote consistency and strengthen the rights of detained patients by subjecting the use of compulsory powers to independent scrutiny. This would undoubtedly eliminate some of the concerns expressed above about the extensive powers given to the medical professionals under the current system.

It is noteworthy that the compulsory order would enable compulsory treatment to take place in the community as well as in hospital. Hitherto, this has not been possible under the 1983 Act, although there are limited powers to provide a degree of supervision in the community under the guardianship provisions in section 7 of the Act and aftercare under supervision by virtue of the Mental Health (Patients in the Community) Act 1995. Not surprisingly, the possibility of compulsory treatment in the community is one of the most controversial aspects of the proposals. The White Paper also proposes a new and expanded definition of mental disorder, as well as amended criteria for the making of a compulsory order.[83] Notably, the amended criteria abandon the treatability requirement and, rather than focus on the patient's capacity, centre on the risk posed by the patient (to herself or others) in order to justify the imposition of the compulsory order. In light of the concerns expressed above about the breadth of the current definition of mental disorder and the need to give greater recognition to patient capacity, this is extremely unfortunate. Should the White Paper's proposals find their way on to the statute book in their current form, they are unlikely to strengthen the legal position of female detained patients.

The Green Paper also considered the compulsory treatment provisions under the 1983 Act. It adopted a broad approach to the use of compulsory treatment, proposing that 'treatment for mental disorder' should be undefined, although certain specific treatments would require special safeguards.[84] This approach has been confirmed in the White Paper.[85] The proposed treatments requiring statutory safeguards would include psychosurgery, which would require consent and a second opinion.[86] This effectively mirrors the current procedure under section 57 of the 1983 Act. Currently, when patients lack the capacity to provide valid consent to psychosurgery, the treatment cannot proceed. However, it is extremely worrying to note that the White Paper proposes that 'the requirement of' patient consent could be overridden in exceptional cases when the patient is unable to consent due to permanent or potentially long-standing incapacity. In such circumstances, the White Paper states that the case for psychosurgery should be referred to the High Court for approval if there is 'clear evidence that [the patient] might benefit' from the treatment.[87] Whilst it is acknowledged in the White Paper that such cases will be 'very rare', this provision is cause for concern as, arguably, it will provide less protection than the 1983 Act for patients who lack capacity to consent to compulsory treatment.

In relation to the administration of ECT, the 'Expert' Committee had recognized the existing controversy and recommended that it should also be subject to special statutory provisions.[88] But the government has adopted a different approach and remains to be convinced of this need. Despite the fact that ECT is an extremely invasive procedure, which has been used inappropriately in the past, the White

Paper states that it is accepted that ECT 'is a vital treatment that can save lives, particularly in cases of very severe depression'.[89] Consequently, the government proposes to preserve the status quo and, as now, clinical teams will be able to provide ECT to a patient without consent if a second medical opinion concurs.[90] This rejection of the 'Expert' Committee's firm recommendation is worrying in light of the concerns that have been expressed about the use of ECT, and which we outlined above. In 1999 the Department of Health published statistics on the use of ECT treatments, which reveal that, of the 700 patients formally detained whilst receiving ECT treatment between January and March 1999, 59 per cent did not consent to treatment.[91] It may be that the government's failure to provide for special safeguards would be counteracted by the creation of a new watchdog body – the Commission for Mental Health – which is intended to have stronger and wider powers than the current Mental Health Act Commission.[92] However, it must be noted that the current Commission has already expressed its concerns about the facilities for and use of ECT and emphasized that it is a matter to which it will be paying particular attention in future.[93]

Unfortunately, the government has also rejected the 'Expert' Committee's proposal for special statutory safeguards for depot medication (an injection which releases the drug slowly over several weeks as opposed to taking drugs orally in tablet or liquid form), force-feeding and prescribing above recommended levels.[94] The White Paper simply states that specific guidance on the use of these treatments will be included in the Code of Practice on the new legislation. Not only is it questionable whether this proposal has gone far enough, it also is worrying in light of the fact that the proposed concept of treatment has been phrased so broadly in the Green and White Papers. Concerns have already been expressed at the breadth of the concept of treatment under the 1983 Act,[95] which has been controversially interpreted to include physical intervention such as force-feeding and enforced caesareans, where it is considered to be treatment for the mental disorder.[96] The White Paper does nothing to remedy these deficiencies and, in this respect, the proposals are seriously flawed. The UK Psychiatric Pharmacy Group responded to the Green Paper and voiced its own concerns about the breadth of the concept of treatment, and the lack of appropriate safeguards in the context of the administration of certain types/quantities of medication.[97] It suggested that certain drug treatments should be subject to additional safeguards,[98] but the government has not taken heed of such expert advice and the White Paper fails to ensure that adequate safeguards, particularly against controversial compulsory treatments, are in place. In that respect, the White Paper is simply paying lip service to the rights of psychiatric patients. This is especially so in the case of female patients, who predominate in the psychosurgery, ECT, force-feeding and medication statistics.

The legislative reform and new mental health strategy will be complemented by the National Service Framework standards for mental health care,[99] which are designed to improve accessibility and quality, as well as raise the standard of care provision. The Framework establishes modern standards and service models for mental health in five key areas[100] and has been sent to all local/health authorities and NHS Trusts in England and Wales.[101] The government has also introduced a range of other initiatives, such as the Patient's Charter on mental health care, setting out patients' rights and the standards of service which the public can expect to receive across all areas of the National Health Service,[102] which is also designed to improve the quality of service provision. These measures may combat some of the concerns about the inappropriate and unequal treatment of women, provided that there is sufficient funding, regular monitoring of standards, sensitivity to gender issues and that the particular views, needs and specific interests of women are explicitly recognized in the process.[103]

The special needs of female psychiatric patients have yet to receive this degree of attention from the Irish government, despite a number of recent unpublished discussion documents[104] recognizing the special needs of disturbed mentally ill patients, patients with an intellectual disability and the mentally ill in the prison population.[105] Nor have the particular needs of women been recognized in proposals to reform the existing law. We will now examine the current mental health legislation in Ireland, which lags far behind the 1983 Act in England and Wales, in terms of protecting against coercion of involuntary detained women and will highlight the unsatisfactory treatment regimes and conditions in many Irish public psychiatric hospitals.

The Treatment of Women under the Mental Treatment Act 1945

Detention in Ireland is governed by the Mental Treatment Act 1945 (the 1945 Act), as amended. Under this Act, detained patients are divided into two categories: temporary patients who may, in theory, be detained for up to two years[106] or 12 months in the case of an addict;[107] and persons of unsound mind, who may be detained indefinitely.[108] In respect of a temporary patient reception order, an application will be made by a spouse or relative[109] to the person in charge of the hospital. This must be accompanied by a medical recommendation from a registered medical practitioner to the effect that, following examination, in his or her opinion the patient is suffering from a mental illness requiring not more than six months treatment for recovery and, on account of his or her mental state, is unsuitable for treatment as a voluntary patient or is an addict who is believed to require at least six months' preventive and curative treatment for recovery.[110] Alternatively, the relative will obtain a medical recommendation to the effect that the patient is a person of unsound mind who requires care and treatment and is unlikely to recover within six months.[111]

The 1945 Act provides no definition of mental illness/unsound mind, leaving 'the psychiatrist [or general practitioner] to apply his own subjective criteria as to who should and should not be confined'.[112] As under the 1983 Act, this deference to the medical viewpoint has led to the medicalization of abnormal female behaviour.[113]

As in England and Wales, the Irish mental health legislation's shortcomings in relation to treatment issues are of particular concern to women, as are standards of care in Irish psychiatric hospitals. Infringement of Irish psychiatric patients' rights to liberty, autonomy, bodily integrity, dignity and privacy under the current mental health regime has been well documented.[114] Carey *et al.*[115] have observed that the compulsory detention order has served 'the function of having the patient admitted to hospital, after which both patients and staff showed little concern for their legal status but concentrated on treatment issues. The indications were of a paternalistic approach by hospital staff and a benign indifference to civil rights issues.'

The paternalistic ethos of the 1945 Act was also recognised *In re Philip Clarke*[116] where O' Byrne J commented that:

> This Act as shown in the title, was primarily intended to provide for the prevention and treatment of mental disorders and the care of persons suffering therefrom [and] ... is of a paternal character, clearly intended for the care and custody of persons suspected to be suffering from mental infirmity and for the safety and well-being of the public generally.

The 1945 Act's failure to provide a definition of treatment and the comments of O'Byrne J suggest that the concept of treatment is broad enough to include custody, nursing care and treatment of the physical causes, consequences and symptoms of a mental disorder.

Once committed, the 1945 Act, as amended, provides 'a serious lack of legal protection for the involuntary patient'.[117] Hospital admission as a temporary patient allows staff to hold the patient for 12 hours pending the making of a reception order.[118] However, the 1945 Act provides no guidance on whether treatment can be given during this time.[119]

Wrongful detention of family members in Ireland, under the 1945 Act, has received widespread media coverage.[120] The victims of wrongful committal have reported that medication made them forgetful and blunted their determination to fight.[121] In addition, the fact that they were on medication has been used against them, to suggest their unreliability as regards child custody and management of property.[122] It is, therefore, alarming that the 1945 Act contains no requirement to obtain consent to treatment (whether personal or by proxy) from a patient who is the subject of a hospital reception order.[123] Rather, it has been 'widely assumed' that consent to treatment is not required of an involuntarily detained psychiatric patient[124] and that all forms of treatment can be given under the common law doctrine of urgent necessity.[125] An authority to enforce or impose treatment is suggested by the absence of a provision for observational hospitalization without treatment as exists in England and Wales[126] and by the title of the 1945 Act. This view is given added weight by the criteria for admission as a *temporary patient*,[127] which include unfitness for treatment as a voluntary patient[128] on account of his or her mental state. Furthermore, Hamilton CJ in *SC* v. *Smith & others*[129] has observed, in relation to detention of a person of unsound mind:

> Though the decision made by the registered medical practitioner to make a recommendation for a reception order may, and the decision of the medical superintendent to make a chargeable patient reception order will, result in the deprivation of the liberty of the person to whom they relate, such decisions ... are decisions entrusted to them by the Oireachtas [parliament] in its role of *providing treatment* for those in need, caring for society and its citizens, particularly those suffering from disability, and the protection of the common good. These decisions can only be made when it is established that the person to whom they relate is a person of unsound mind and is a proper person to be taken in charge of and detained *under care and treatment*.

It has been argued that, once an effective inability to consent to necessary hospital treatment exists, it logically follows that treatment for mental illness might be lawfully instituted and, indeed, continued without the patient's consent once admitted,[130] whether as a temporary patient or as a person of unsound mind. It has also been noted that to sanction detention without consent, without conferring a power to treat without consent, 'appears illogical to the point of being self-defeating'.[131] However, it does not always follow that the presence of mental disorder means that the patient is incompetent to make treatment decisions on his or her own behalf.[132] This practice has the potential for serious adverse effects on female detained patients who, in theory, may be subjected to ECT, invasive and irreversible[133] psychosurgery or medication having adverse side effects, against their will and without regard to the patient's own values.[134] In Ireland there is no statutory framework regulating treatment in the context of civil commitment.[135] The Irish position is in sharp contrast with the UK 1983 Act, which requires patient consent as well as a second medical opinion for psychosurgery (section 57) and either consent or a second medical opinion for ECT.

The Irish government's proposals for a new Mental Health Act, expounded in their White Paper in 1995, noted two known cases of persons referred to England for psychosurgery in the previous ten years. Both of these incidences occurred in 1993.[136] The White Paper was confident that the 1983 Mental Health Act's requirement, *inter alia*, of the patient's informed consent to this form of surgery were 'stringent safeguards'.[137] However, in relation to anorexics and patients who are administered ECT, it may be the case, as has occurred in England and Wales, that a patient's refusal to consent to treatment will be treated as a symptom of the disease, thereby warranting medical intervention. Regarding the administration of ECT, it has been noted that asking the patient for consent to ECT is pointless because 'the patient's refusal or inability to consent to treatment is itself a symptom of his illness'.[138] Even where the patient does consent to ECT, the disorders which it is used to treat, such as severe depression and catatonic and affective schizophrenia, may interfere with the patient's ability to give a valid consent.[139] (This is also a concern in relation to consent to psychosurgery.) The practice in many Irish psychiatric hospitals has been that, where responsible relatives are in agreement with doctors, treatment has gone ahead, but such agreement is usually informal.[140] Furthermore, evidence exists that proxy consent is not always sought for ECT and other drug treatments.[141]

In the absence of legislation governing ECT, the Royal College of Psychiatrists' guidelines are relevant to Irish psychiatrists.[142] However, the 1997 *Report of the Irish Inspector of Mental Hospitals* has revealed that, in one Irish psychiatric hospital, ECT was administered in beds, virtually in full view of other patients.[143] In another psychiatric hospital ECT was prescribed and administered on the instructions of a junior doctor within 24 hours of a patient's admission.[144] This hospital also lacked an exclusive recovery area for ECT patients.[145] The Inspectorate of Mental Hospitals' checklist relating to the establishment of satisfactory clinical and administrative practice in mental health services has recently been formalized into a Code of Practice, *Guidelines on Good Practice and Quality Assurance in Mental Health Services*. The Code sets down stringent requirements in relation to the administration of ECT,[146] requiring, *inter alia*, that adequate treatment facilities be provided. It also stipulates that ECT be administered to patients only with their fully informed written consent on an appropriate consent form with provision for the patient's signature, relative's signature, if appropriate, and a section indicating that the doctor has fully explained the procedure to the patient or relatives, if appropriate. Although this is a step in the right direction, the Code has no legislative force and, therefore, it remains to be seen whether it will provide adequate protection for female detained patients. In 1999, 1068 patients were administered ECT,[147] although the number of female detained patients embraced by this figure is unknown. In Ireland, anorexia is a problem that may affect as many as 1 per cent of adolescents and young adult females, and naso-gastric feeding may be enforced, although it is limited to situations where the disorder has reached a life-threatening stage.[148] As noted above force-feeding can damage a therapeutic relationship and may exacerbate the sufferer's condition. The possibility of enforced caesarean sections remains a live one, given the right to life of the unborn child recognized by the Irish Constitution.[149]

In light of the recent increase in the number of sudden deaths from psychotropic medication[150] it is alarming to note the Irish Inspector of Mental Hospital's observation in 1998 that drug-prescribing in some psychiatric hospitals is often arbitrary and made without regard to appropriate clinical diagnosis. The Inspector was struck by the number of patients, particularly long-stay patients, who were on numerous drugs simultaneously, often at high dosages, and by the fact that, in some cases, prescriptions had not been reviewed for some considerable time.[151] He also noted no entries by consultants in some case notes and felt that, in some services, the practice of consultants in regard to note-taking fell short of what would be considered good professional practice.[152] Thankfully, this situation has improved in many services since publication of the 1998 report.[153]

Privacy is lacking for women in Irish psychiatric hospitals, most of which have integrated wards,[154] and successive annual Inspector of Mental Hospital's Reports have criticized the absence of individual curtain screens in the dormitory areas of many public psychiatric hospitals.[155] However, the Inspector has failed to criticize the provision of integrated units and, in one particular instance, recommended one as 'the ideal arrangement' for a particular catchment area.[156] Unsatisfactory and unacceptable conditions in many public Irish psychiatric hospitals have also been highlighted.[157] In one hospital [l]eaking roofs, rotting external joinery, substandard interior decor and furnishings, compounded by a lack of patient activation, contributed to produce a most depressing picture'[158] in 1998. In the old building of the only high-security psychiatric hospital all the rooms had 'night pots' with the resultant practice of 'slopping out' in the mornings due to inadequate room sanitation.[159] Another recurring theme has been the lack of occupational therapists and rehabilitation services[160] and an inappropriate mix of patients in many public Irish psychiatric hospitals. In some hospitals, patients with a mental handicap, long-stay functional psychotics, older patients and newly admitted acute patients from the admission ward are all placed together, hampering appropriate therapy and management of patients.[161] The Inspector's Reports have also drawn attention to overcrowding,[162] reporting three beds in one hospital corridor in 1998,[163] and the following shocking account seems a relic of Dickensian times rather than reflective of a modern health care system:

> Much of the accommodation ... was provided in large institutional rooms that combined sleeping accommodation, dining space, day facilities and a nurses' station all in the one

area. For most of these patients there was little to stimulate or interest them; they had their final meal at 4.30 p.m. and some were in bed by 5 p.m. to accommodate the nursing roster. Concern was expressed at the fact that there were two patients in bed in the day area who were dying and this space was shared by fellow patients from the same ward.[164]

The Irish government's Mental Health Bill 1999 holds the promise of some improvement for women who are detained in psychiatric hospitals. However, treatment will be defined broadly[165] as including the administration of physical, psychological and other remedies relating to the care and rehabilitation of a patient under medical supervision, intended for the purposes of ameliorating a mental disorder. This will enable force-feeding to continue but may prevent enforced caesareans. Psychosurgery will require the patient's consent and authorization by a tribunal[166] which will have to be satisfied that psychosurgery is in the best interests of the patient's health.[167] Although the tribunal will comprise a barrister or solicitor with at least ten years' experience and a consultant psychiatrist,[168] it seems legitimate to question whether the tribunal is likely to 'rubber-stamp' the recommendation of the referring psychiatrist. Consent is defined in section 55, as consent in writing, obtained freely without threats or inducements, where the consultant psychiatrist responsible for the care and treatment of the patient has certified in a form, specified by the proposed Mental Health Commission, that the patient is capable of understanding the nature, purpose and likely effects of the proposed treatment and that he or she has given the patient adequate information, in a form and language that the patient can understand, on this. A decision to carry out psychosurgery shall not be given effect before the expiration of the time for bringing an appeal to the circuit court.[169] Although this will do much to clarify the current unsatisfactory state of the law, the ability of mentally handicapped and demented individuals ever being able to give valid consent has not been addressed.[170]

The Mental Health Bill proposes that administering, to a detained person, ECT or medicine for mental disorder after three months of medication will require consent (as defined in section 55 above) or approval from a second consultant psychiatrist in a form specified by the proposed Mental Health Commission, where the patient is unable or unwilling to give consent.[171] Thus, as at present, medication could be imposed on a detained, but competent, patient during the first three months of his or her detention[172] at the behest of a single psychiatrist, and the Bill does not state whether treatment would be permitted during the proposed 24-hour holding period pending the making of a hospital order.[173] Furthermore, no attempt is made to define the term 'unwilling'[174] or 'unable' in a coherent way, and the decision to impose treatment or ECT will be decided from the subjective viewpoint of a consultant psychiatrist who is likely to hold the same values as the treating psychiatrist. The doctor's sense of what the patient's best interests require may therefore dictate how he or she tests the patient's competence, and devalue what the patient perceives to be in her best interests.[175] As noted above in relation to the 1983 Act, the second medical opinion is an inadequate safeguard which legitimizes coercion and control of female patients by the medical profession. As the Irish courts seem to take a benign approach to the non-disclosure of risks by the medical profession,[176] any reform should ensure that, where consent *is* given, written information has been provided to patients and relatives on the nature and side effects of ECT and medication, to ensure that a given consent is a genuine and informed one. The Bill's stipulation that a consultant psychiatrist making an admission order will be required, *inter alia*, to give a statement in writing to the patient to the effect that he or she will be given a *general* description of the proposed treatment to be administered to him or her during the course of his or her detention[177] will therefore be an inadequate safeguard.

A charter of civil rights for detained psychiatric patients was promised in 1994,[178] but this has never materialized. Under the 1945 Act every health board must appoint a visiting committee whose duties include a requirement to hear the complaints of any patient and, if requested to do so, see him or her in private.[179] However, the 1999 *Report of the Inspector of Mental Hospitals* found a need among patients for more information on how to make a complaint.[180] Some consolation may be drawn from the watchdog powers of the Inspector of Mental Hospitals who is required, under the 1945 Act, to visit all institutions[181] at stated intervals,[182] and whose annual report highlights areas of concern relating to the standard of accommodation and quality of care in Irish psychiatric hospitals.

Nonetheless, the Inspectorate's independence and efficacy is thrown into doubt by its practice of giving several days' notice to the institutions about to be inspected and the fact that the Inspector feels obliged to give the responsible authorities every opportunity to consult on the report before its publication.[183] Once the Inspector has written his version of the annual report he sends it to the Department of Health which 'edits' it and returns it to the Inspector for approval. It is then sent to the various health boards for their comments and, when these are received, the Inspector amends his report. It is then sent for a second time to the health boards and, when a response is received from them, the Inspector writes a further draft which is sent to the minister for his 'approval'. When 'approval' has been given, the report is sent to be printed and then again forwarded to the minister whose consent is required for its publication.[184] For 19 years the Irish Department of Health did not publish this report, even though the 1945 Act required its submission to the president of the High Court.[185] In addition, even the Inspector's effectiveness as a watchdog over standards of care and conditions is dubious, given the failure of some psychiatric hospitals to react to recurrent criticisms outlined in the Reports. Finally, the Inspector's Reports are gender-neutral and have failed to recognize the particular needs of women in Irish psychiatric hospitals. It is disheartening to read of the Inspector's acceptance of integrated wards when, in the United Kingdom, separate sleeping accommodation, toilet and washing facilities for women have been recognized as essential to a successful therapeutic regime.

Some improvement in the current system of inspecting psychiatric hospitals may be signalled by the number of unannounced inspections made by the Inspectorate in 1999. The Inspector has promised that this number will increase in the coming years and that the locations of the unannounced inspections will vary.[186] Furthermore, a number of mental health patients were interviewed in 1999 to ascertain their views on service provision. As noted by the Irish government in 1992, 'the need to examine services from the consumer's view point is critical in the psychiatric services because so many psychiatric patients are unable to express themselves and their families cannot always be relied upon to be advocates for their welfare'.[187] While patients generally indicated that they were informed about the nature of their condition and treatment, some felt that it could have been better explained to them and that more information could have been provided.[188] Tellingly, a number of female patients complained about aspects of dignity and privacy in relation to their care,[189] such as the lack of single-sex toilets, the absence of locks on toilet doors, the existence of integrated accommodation and the need for curtains around beds. Furthermore, many patients felt that additional occupational activity was required during their stay in hospital as their days tended to be long and boring, leaving them with too much time to think.[190]

The Inspectorate's Code of Practice, *Guidelines on Good Practice and Quality Assurance in Mental Health Services*, has now have been circulated to all mental health service providers in Ireland[191] with a view to setting standards and encouraging service providers to improve the quality of care delivery.[192] The Code states that patients should be informed of diagnosis on request and provided with suitable documentary literature on their condition, as deemed appropriate.[193] This suggests that documentary information on the patient's condition need not be provided to him or her if not requested or if not deemed appropriate. The *Guidelines* add that treatment plans should be *discussed* with patients, the nature of treatment fully outlined and the treatment plan, including any medication, clearly recorded in the case notes. They promote fully informed consent by requiring that patients be given reasonable time to consider whether to accept the treatment plan outlined for them, including any medication and possible side effects, and that they be given time for discussion with relatives before accepting. The *Guidelines* do not make it clear whether documentary evidence must be provided on treatment plans, as the accompanying checklist only requires documentary evidence in relation to medication and its side effects. Furthermore, it is also unclear whether evidence of treatment plans and side effects of medication needs to be provided if not requested or not deemed appropriate.

As well as setting down stringent requirements in relation to the administration of ECT, the *Guidelines* lay down minimum standards for residential settings.[194] These include single-sex toilet facilities but do not stipulate single-sex sleeping accommodation; integrated accommodation is assumed, and only curtains and rails are required.[195]

Under the Mental Health Bill 1999 the inspection of psychiatric hospitals will be performed by the Inspector of Mental Health Services[196] who will be required to furnish his or her written report to the newly created Mental Health Commission. The Commission will submit a written annual report to the Minister, including the Inspector's report, to be laid before both houses of parliament.[197] The Mental Health Commission's functions will be 'to promote, encourage, and foster the establishment and maintenance of high standards and good practices in the delivery of mental health services and to take all reasonable steps to protect the interests of persons detained in approved centres'.[198] The Commission will, *inter alia*, appoint persons to be members of tribunals and prepare a code, or codes, of practice for the guidance of persons working in the mental health services.[199] Allied with this will be the Minister's requirement, after consultation with the Commission, to make regulations for the purpose of ensuring proper standards in relation to centres, including adequate and suitable accommodation, food and care for residents being maintained in centres, and the proper conduct of centres.[200] In this way the Commission:

... has the potential to introduce positive changes for individual patients in both the rights area and in the supervisory role in relation to services. Further it has potential to foster future developments in relation to service provision, research and more appropriate legislative developments.[201]

Although two members of the Commission shall be representatives of voluntary bodies, promoting the interests of persons suffering from mental illness,[202] the Commission's constitution will not contain any representation from service users or their families,[203] whose perspective would surely be invaluable when regulating standards of care and conditions.

At present, as a result of the current emphasis on developing community services and competing demands on scarce resources, expenditure on the existing large Irish public psychiatric hospitals that may soon be closed is not a priority in many health board regions.[204] This is likely to remain the case, despite the government's promise of an additional £12.2 million to fund the mental health service in 2000.[205] It is lamentable that the Mental Health Bill 1999 has not provided for a charter for psychiatric patients and the real promise of improvement, therefore, lies in sections 63–65 of the 1999 Bill. First, the Commission will be obliged to maintain a register of all hospitals and inpatient facilities and may remove a centre from the register if the premises or regime does not comply with the regulations.[206] Second, a person who fails or refuses to comply with a provision of the regulations shall be guilty of an offence and may be disqualified from practising in any centre.[207] However, when formulating the regulations it is vital that the Mental Health Commission and Minister for Health and Children develop a greater awareness of women's particular needs within the Irish mental health system than the minimal amount that exists at present. The Irish government's current strategy for health care, *Shaping a Healthier Future*, stresses three underpinning considerations which are fundamental to the satisfactory delivery of health care – quality of service, accountability and equity.[208] However, equal treatment does not always ensure equity. As noted by the EU Commissioner for Social Affairs, '[t]he challenge in improving the health of women ... is not to place their needs ahead of men's, but first to acknowledge that, because of biological and social conditions, their needs are different'.[209]

Conclusion

Recent reports issued by the MHAC have highlighted the plight of female patients who are detained in psychiatric hospitals against their will. However, the *Reports of the Irish Inspector of Mental Hospitals* remain gender-neutral, and recommendations for improving the conditions of psychiatric hospitals have failed to recognize the particular needs of women. In the United Kingdom, criticism has been directed at the poor conditions for women in psychiatric hospitals and the unsatisfactory treatment received by them. Despite the presence of in-built safeguards in England and Wales, paternalistic attitudes are still reflected in the inappropriate conditions, treatment facilities and programmes, the male-dominated environments and male-oriented regimes in hospitals. This is particularly evident in relation to the position of female patients detained in secure conditions.

Furthermore the broad definition of mental illness and medical treatment in the United Kingdom, and the failure to provide any definition of these terms in the 1945 Act, enable psychiatry to control women's non-conforming and abnormal behaviour.

In Ireland, the 1945 Act's paternalistic ethos permits the enforced treatment of women without regard to their capacity or values and without any legal obligation to provide information to psychiatric patients or their relatives on the nature or side effects of their treatment. This unsatisfactory situation for female detained patients is compounded by appalling conditions in some of Ireland's public psychiatric hospitals.

Reform proposals in both jurisdictions suggest that the position of female detained patients may be strengthened. The Irish Mental Health Bill's proposed Code of Practice and enforceable regulations for the purpose of ensuring proper standards in centres in which psychiatric patients are detained may lead to improved conditions in Irish psychiatric hospitals. Since the time of writing this chapter, further improvements have materialized in the committee stage of the Mental Health Bill.[210] At least one of the two representatives of voluntary bodies promoting the interests of persons suffering from mental illness, sitting on the Mental Health Commission, must be someone who is experiencing, or has experienced, mental illness. This will enable the perspective of service users to be reflected in future developments. Furthermore, under an amendment to section 65, the Minister will prescribe requirements as to the setting up and running of psychiatric hospitals as far as practicable in consultation with each patient, and of an individual care plan for that patient, including the setting of goals. Additionally, the Inspector of Mental Health Services will be required to furnish a report to the Mental Health Commission on the degree and extent of compliance by approved centres with any code of practice prepared by the Commission. An amendment to section 58 of the Mental Health Bill will impose a statutory obligation on the Mental Health Commission to make rules governing the use of ECT. It is envisaged that these rules will draw on the protocols and guidelines already in existence. The fact that the rules will have the force of law, as opposed to the voluntary codes currently in existence, should ensure additional protection for those undergoing ECT. However, the proposal in the 1999 Bill for a second medical opinion or consent is unlikely to go far enough in this direction, as it will simply mirror the current defects in England and Wales.

The UK White Paper on reforming the 1983 Act is also deficient as the criteria for the use of compulsion are broadened and the proposals governing the administration of compulsory treatment are unlikely to strengthen the position of female detained patients. However, these concerns may be counteracted by the White Paper proposals to introduce a number of new safeguards to protect patients, such as independent tribunals, a new Commission for Mental Health and the provision of independent specialist advocacy services for patients. Coupled with the introduction of the National Service Framework and the mental health strategy, this may hold the promise of improvement, although the position of female patients detained in secure conditions is still worrying.

The lack of privacy, dignity and security experienced by female patients in some mental health units, as well as the inappropriate and undignified treatment received by some of them has major human rights implications. In particular, they may be susceptible to challenge under the Human Rights Act 1998. Detained female patients may seek to challenge current practices and conditions under Article 3 (alleging inhuman or degrading treatment) or Article 8 (alleging breaches of the right to private life) of the European Convention on Human Rights.

Reform is urgently required, but it is vital to ensure that, as well as providing legal mechanisms to protect rights, appropriate facilities are provided, which meet the special needs of female patients. Increased public awareness through media coverage of the Inspector's 1998 Annual Report may result in more pressure being brought to bear on the mental health service providers to improve treatment regimes and the conditions of Irish public psychiatric hospitals. However, the mental health services will continue to face a dilemma relating to expenditure on hospitals which have no long-term future.[211] Improvement will require considerable resources and this may be the biggest obstacle in ameliorating the position of female detained patients. In the final analysis '... all the watchdogs in the world, all the fine legal safeguards, will not prove a substitute for the resources so often found wanting in this field'.[212]

Notes

1 Department of Health (2001), *In-patients Formally Detained in Hospitals under the Mental Health Act 1983 and other Legislation, England: 1990–91 to 2000–2001*, Statistical Bulletin 2001/28, London: Department of Health.
2 *Green Paper on Mental Health*, Pl.8918, Dublin: The Stationery Office, 1992, p.14, para. 2.3. Cf. Browne, C., Daly, A. and Walsh, D. (2000), *Activities of Irish Psychiatric Services 1998*, Dublin: Stationery Office, p. 67.
3 Browne *et al.*, *Activities of Irish Psychiatric Services*, *op. cit.*, n. 2, p. 107.
4 *Green Paper on Mental Health*, *op. cit.*, n. 2, p. 12, para. 1.6.
5 Showalter, E. (1981), 'Victorian Women and Insanity', in A. Scull (ed.), *Madhouses, Mad-doctors and Madmen: The Social History of Psychiatry in the Victorian Era*, London: Athlone Press, p. 316. See also the recent study and report by the Social Services Inspectorate (2001), *Detained: Inspection of Compulsory Mental Health Admissions*, London: Department of Health, p. 16, which demonstrates that, although more males than females were assessed by social workers, women were more frequently detained under the Mental Health Act 1983 than men.
6 See Fegan, E.V. and Fennell, P. (1998), 'Feminist Perspectives on Mental Health Law', in S. Sheldon and M. Thomson (eds), *Feminist Perspectives on Health Care Law*, London: Cavendish; Ussher, J. (1991), *Women's Madness: Misogyny or Mental Illness?*, Hertfordshire: Harvester Wheatsheaf; Penfold, P.S. and Walker, G.A. (1984), *Women and the Psychiatric Paradox*, Milton Keynes: Open University Press; Showalter, E. (1987), *The Female Malady: Women, Madness and English Culture 1830–1980*, London: Virago.
7 See for example the writings of Thomas S. Szasz (1970), *The Myth of Mental Illness: Foundations of a Theory of Personal Conduct*, New York: Harper and Row; and (1970), *The Manufacture of Madness*, New York: Harper & Row.
8 See Howell, E. and Bayes, M. (eds) (1981), *Women and Mental Health: New Directions for Change*, New York: Basic Books.
9 Department of Health (1995), *Developing a Policy for Women's Health: A Discussion Document*, Dublin: The Stationery Office.

10 Department of Health (1997), *A Plan for Women's Health*, Dublin: The Stationery Office, p. 44.

11 Penfold and Walker, *Women and the Psychiatric Paradox*, *op. cit.*, n. 6, p. 172.

12 See works cited in n. 6 *supra*.

13 See Boland, F. and Laing, J.M. (1999–2000), 'Out of Sight and Out of Mind? A Feminist Perspective on Civil Commitment in Britain and Ireland', *Contemporary Issues in Law*, p. 257.

14 *RTE Guide*, 10 April 1992; *Woman's Way*, **6**, 17 July 1992, p. 18; *Irish Press*, 5 May 1992.

15 Boland and Laing, 'Out of Sight', *op. cit.*, n. 13.

16 Department of Health/Welsh Office (1999), *Mental Health Act 1983 Code of Practice*, London: HMSO, para. 6.1.

17 Mental Health Act 1983, s. 3.

18 DoH/Welsh Office, *Code of Practice*, *op. cit.*, n. 16, para. 30.5.

19 See Laing, J.M. (1999), *Care or Custody: Mentally Disordered Offenders in the Criminal Justice System*, Oxford: Oxford University Press, pp. 4–15.

20 Heginbotham, C. and Elson, T. (1999), 'Public Policy via Law: Practitioner's Sword and Politician's Shield', in N. Eastman and J. Peay (eds), *Law Without Enforcement: Integrating Mental Health and Justice*, Oxford: Hart Publishing, p. 67.

21 This means that medication may be imposed against the patient's will in the absence of consent/second medical opinion during the first three months of detention.

22 Mental Health Act 1983, s. 145(1); see also *R* v. *Mersey Mental Health Review Tribunal, ex p. D* (1987), *The Times*, 13 April.

23 Hoggett, B.M. (1996), *Mental Health Law*, London: Sweet & Maxwell, p. 144.

24 Ibid. This was exemplified in the case of *R* v. *Mental Health Act Commission, ex. p. W* (1988), *The Times*, 27 May. The case involved the surgical implantation of hormones to reduce the sex drive of a compulsive paedophile. The judge in that case found that, where the patient was mentally disordered and sexually deviant, '[i]n practice, … it seems likely that the sexual problem will be inextricably linked with the mental disorder, so that the treatment for the one is treatment for the other'. This is despite the fact that sexual deviancy cannot of itself amount to a mental disorder under the 1983 Act. See, further, Fennell, P. (1988), 'Sexual Suppressants and the Mental Health Act', *Criminal Law Review*, pp. 660–76 for criticism of this decision and the 'nebulous' inextricable link between the sexual deviancy and the mental disorder.

25 See, for example, the comments of Fennell, P. (1995), 'Medical Law', *All ER Annual Review*, pp. 354, 381.

26 *Re KB (Adult) (Mental Patient: Medicine Treatment)* (1994) 19 BMLR 144.

27 *B* v. *Croydon Health Authority* [1995] 1 All ER 683: 'It would seem strange to me if a hospital could, without the patient's consent, give him treatment directed to alleviating a psychopathic disorder showing itself in suicidal tendencies, but not without such consent be able to treat the consequences of the suicide attempt', *per* Hoffman LJ. See also Lewis, P. (1999), 'Feeding Anorexic Patients who Refuse Food', *Medical Law Review*, **7**, pp. 21-37.

28 *Re MB* (1997) 38 BMLR 175.

29 *Re KB (Adult) (Mental Patient: Medical Treatment)* (1994) 19 BMLR 144.

30 *B* v. *Croydon HA* [1995] 1 All ER 683.

31 *Re MB* (1997) 38 BMLR 175.

32 Fegan and Fennell, 'Feminist Perspectives', *op. cit.*, n. 6, p. 93.

33 Lewis, 'Feeding Anorexic Patients', *op. cit.*, n. 27, p. 33.

34 Fegan and Fennell, 'Feminist Perspectives', *op. cit.*, n. 6, p. 96.

35 Lewis, 'Feeding Anorexic Patients', *op. cit.*, n. 27, p. 37.

36 Mental Health Act Commission (MHAC) (1999), *Eighth Biennial Report 1997–1999*, London: HMSO, para. 6.46, p. 183, Table 14.

37 Most recently, the use of psychosurgery has been questioned by the Council Of Europe (2000) in its *White Paper on the Protection of Human Rights and Dignity of People Suffering from Mental Disorder, Especially Those Placed as Involuntary Patients in a Psychiatric Establishment*, DIR/JUR (2000) 2, Strasbourg: Council of Europe, para. 7.3.

38 Tomkin, D. and Hanafin, P. (1995), *Irish Medical Law*, Dublin: Roundhall Press, p. 131.

39 Ibid.

40 Department of Health (1999), *Electro-Convulsive Therapy, (ECT): Survey Covering the Period from January 1999–March 1999*, London: HMSO. See also MHAC, *Eighth Biennial Report, op. cit.*, n. 36, para. 6.30, p. 177, Table 2.

41 Penfold and Walker, *Women and the Psychiatric Paradox, op. cit.* n. 6, p. 172.

42 See, for example, ECT Anonymous, *Response to the Government Green Paper*, located at <http://markwalton.net>; Clare, A. (1980), *Psychiatry in Dissent: Controversial Issues in Thought and Practice*, London: Tavistock, ch. 6, pp. 252–56; Anonymous (1965), 'The Experience of ECT by a Practising Psychiatrist', *British Journal of Psychiatry*, **3**, pp. 365–67.

43 Rogers, A., Pilgrim, D. and Lacey, R. (1993), *Experiencing Psychiatry: Users' Views of Services*, Basingstoke: Macmillan/MIND, pp. 142–45; Siddall, R. (1994), 'A Shock in the Dark', *Community Care*, 26 May, pp. 23–24; Council of Europe, *White Paper, op. cit.*, n. 37, para. 7.2; O'Leary, D.A. and Lee, S.A. (1996), 'Seven Year Prognosis in Depression: Mortality and Readmission Risk in the Nottingham ECT Cohort', *British Journal of Psychiatry*, **169**, p. 423, which suggested that there are increased readmission and long-term mortality risks for patients subjected to ECT, especially amongst the elderly and female patients.

44 Duffet, R. and Lelliott, P. (1998), 'Auditing Electroconvulsive Therapy. The Third Cycle', *British Journal of Psychiatry*, **172**, p. 401. See also Brookes, G., Rigby, J. and Barnes, J. (2000), 'Implementing the Royal College of Psychiatrists' Guidelines for the Practice of Electroconvulsive Therapy', *Psychiatric Bulletin*, **24**, p. 329.

45 Pippard, J. and Ellam, (1981), *Electroconvulsive Treatment in Great Britain*, London: Royal College of Psychiatrists, quoted in Cohen, D. (1988), *Forgotten Millions: The Treatment of the Mentally Ill – A Global Perspective*, London: Paladin Grafton Books, p. 28.

46 Showalter, *The Female Malady, op. cit.*, n. 6, p. 207; Ussher, *Women's Madness, op. cit.*, n. 6, p. 108.

47 Prior, P. (1999), *Gender and Mental Health*, Basingstoke: Macmillan, p. 132.

48 Rogers *et al.*, *Experiencing Psychiatry, op. cit.*, n. 43, pp. 122–23. See also Chernomas, W.M. (1997), 'Experiencing Depression: Women's Perspectives in Recovery', *Journal of Psychiatry and Mental Health Nursing*, **4**(6), pp. 393–401 for an account of the experiences of women suffering from depression.

49 Cooney, T. and O'Neil, O. (1995), *Psychiatric Detention in Ireland*, Wicklow: Baikonor, p. 254.

50 Ibid.

51 Ibid. p. 250.

52 Ibid., p. 254.

53 Richardson, G. and Thorold, O. (1999), 'Law as a Rights Protector: Assessing the Mental Health Act 1983' p. 126 in Eastman, N. and Peay, J. (eds), *Law Without Enforcement: Integrating Mental Health and Justice*, Oxford: Hart Publishing; see also Rogers *et al.*, *Experiencing Psychiatry, op. cit.*, n. 43, p. 168.

54 DoH/Welsh Office, *Code of Practice, op. cit.*, n. 16, paras 15.8–15.12, 15.14–15.17.

55 Rogers *et al.*, *Experiencing Psychiatry, op. cit.*, n. 43, p. 172.

56 DoH/Welsh Office, *Code of Practice, op. cit.*, n. 16, paras 1.1, 1.6, 2.6, 19.5.

57 See, for example, the comments of the (UK) Health Select Committee (2000), *Fourth Report: Provision of NHS Mental Health Services*, Session 1999–2000 HC 373. The Committee members were '*very disturbed*' (emphasis added) by the evidence they received 'on the quality of in-patient care ... natural justice and the principle of reciprocity demand that those who are detained on such wards without their consent should be provided with accommodation which affords reasonable privacy and dignity' (para. 99). See also (1998), *Not Just Bricks and Mortar*, London: Royal College of Psychiatrists.

58 Bean, P. (1986), *Mental Disorder and Legal Control*, Cambridge: Cambridge University Press, p. 183.

59 MHAC, *Eighth Biennial Report, op. cit.*, n. 36, pp. 148–50, 160–61. See also Kaye, C. (1998), 'Hallmarks of a Secure Psychiatric Service for Women', *Psychiatric Bulletin*, **22**(3), p. 137.

60 MHAC (2001), *Ninth Biennial Report 1999–2001*, London: HMSO, paras 6.33–6.38. See also MHAC, *Eighth Biennial Report, op. cit.*, n. 36, paras 10.57–10.73.

61 MHAC, *Eighth Biennial Report, op. cit.*, n. 36, paras 10.57–10.73.

62 See Prior, *Gender and Mental Health, op. cit.*, n. 47, pp. 173–74.

63 Health Select Committee, *Fourth Report, op. cit.*, n. 57.

64 Fortunately, however, the government has also recognized the need to consider the particular needs of women in the secure services and, as part of its programme to take forward its proposals for dangerous and severely personality disordered individuals, it has pledged to commence work to ensure that services '*are developed in a coherent and non-discriminatory way*'. Home Office, Prison Service, Department of Health (2000), *Managing Dangerous People with Severe Personality Disorder: Taking Forward the Government's Proposals*, London: HMSO, p. 5 (emphasis added).

65 MIND (2000), *Environmentally Friendly? Patients' Views of Conditions on Psychiatric Wards*, London: MIND.

66 Ibid., p. 17. See also Social Services Inspectorate, *Detained, op. cit.*, n. 5, p. 34, which stressed that a number of women reported some negative experiences in being nursed in mixed-sex wards.

67 Ibid., p. 3.

68 Department of Health Press Releases 98/311, 29 July 1998 and 98/580, 8 December 1998, London: DoH. See also Session 1997–98 *H C Debates*, Wednesday 29 July 1998.

69 Department of Health (1998), *Modernising Mental Health Services: Safe, Sound and Supportive*, London: DoH.

70 Department of Health (2000), *Safety, Privacy and Dignity in Mental Health Units: Guidance on Mixed Sex Accommodation for Mental Health Services*, Leeds: DoH.

71 Ibid., para. 3.1.

72 Ibid., paras 4.2.1, 5.3.1.

73 Ibid., para. 1.2. It is encouraging to note that the first women-only mental health residential crisis centre in the UK – Drayton Park in London – opened in 1995. A study into the operation of the centre has demonstrated that it has proved to be an unqualified success in providing a safe alternative to hospital admission for women with severe and enduring mental health problems: see Royal College of Psychiatrists, Press Release, 1 March 2000, located at <http://www.rcpsych.ac.uk>.

74 Department of Health (2000), *Mental Health Czar Begins the Process of Reform for Mental Health Services*, Press Release 2000/0319, London: DoH.

75 MHAC, *Ninth Biennial Report, op. cit.*, n. 60, para. 6.35.

76 DoH *Modernising Mental Health Services, op. cit.*, n. 69 Foreword by the Secretary of State – the Government has pledged a total of £700 million over the next three years to fund these reforms.

77 Ibid.
78 *Report of the Expert Committee, Review of the Mental Health Act 1983* (1999), London: HMSO.
79 *Reform of the Mental Health Act 1983 Proposals for Consultation* (1999), Cm 4480, London: HMSO. For further discussion of the reform proposals see Laing, J.M. (2000), 'Rights versus Risk? Reform of the Mental Health Act 1983', *Medical Law Review*, **8**(2), pp. 210–50.
80 *Reforming the Mental Health Act 1983* (2000) Cm 5016, London: HMSO.
81 Ibid., paras. 3.28–3.36. The White Paper envisages that the first stage of formal procedures will be triggered by a request which will normally be from a patient, a patient's carer or GP, or from criminal justice agencies for a preliminary examination. Two doctors and a social worker or another approved mental health professional will visit the patient to carry out the examination. Once the examination is complete, if the professionals decide that the conditions for assessment and initial treatment are met, the social worker will be responsible for coordinating the next steps and arranging for the patient to be admitted to hospital, if necessary.
82 Ibid., paras 3.10, 3.44–3.51. The new tribunal will have a legally qualified chair and two other members with experience of mental health services. All members will be required to undergo training and will be able to seek independent expert advice from an approved panel. The tribunal will be able to seek an opinion from the members of the panel in addition to the report from the medical expert. The task of the tribunal will be to decide, on the basis of the evidence put to it, whether the conditions for continuing care and treatment under compulsory powers are met. If it is satisfied that these are met, it will have the power to approve a care and treatment order.
83 Ibid., paras 3.3–3.7, 3.18.
84 *Reform of the Mental Health Act 1983*, *op. cit.*, n. 78, p. 56.
85 *Reforming the Mental Health Act 1983*, *op. cit.*, n. 79, paras 5.16–5.23.
86 Ibid., para. 5.18.
87 Ibid., para. 5.19.
88 *Review of the Mental Health Act 1983*, *op. cit.* n. 77, paras 6.18–6.21.
89 *Reforming the Mental Health Act 1983*, *op. cit.*, n. 79, para. 5.21.
90 Ibid.
91 DoH., *Electro-Convulsive Therapy*, *op. cit.*, n. 40.
92 *Reforming the Mental Health Act 1983*, *op. cit.*, n. 79, paras 7.5–7.20. The remit of the new Commission will be similar to that of the existing MHAC but without its current responsibilities for regular visiting. Instead there will be a fresh emphasis on monitoring the implementation of the safeguards which ensure that the compulsory powers and compulsory treatment provisions are properly used. It is intended that issues of quality and consistency of services and visiting arrangements will fall within the remit of the Commission for Health Improvement or the National Care Standards Commission.
93 MHAC, *Eighth Biennial Report*, *op. cit.*, n. 36, para. 3.38; MHAC, *Ninth Biennial Report*, *op. cit.*, n. 60, paras 3.31–3.35.
94 *Reforming the Mental Health Act 1983*, *op. cit.*, n. 79, para. 5.22.
95 Hoggett, *Mental Health Law*, *op. cit.*, n. 23, pp. 143–47.
96 See notes 29, 30, 31 *supra*.
97 The United Kingdom Psychiatric Pharmacy Group (2000), *Response to Reform of the Mental Health Act 1983* at <http://www.ukppg.co.uk/mha-review-2000.html>.
98 Ibid.
99 The National Service Framework has been developed in relation to all aspects of health care, although a specific framework for mental health will determine service models and quality provision in that area. It aims to improve consistency across the country and ensure

that high-quality services are available locally, which meet national standards. It has been complemented by the establishment of the National Institute for Clinical Excellence to provide clear guidance for clinicians on the most effective drugs and therapies.
100 These are: mental health promotion; primary care and access to services; effective services for people with severe mental illness; caring about carers; and preventing suicide.
101 HSC 1999/223: LAC (99) 34.
102 Department of Health (1996), *The Patient's Charter and You: A Charter for England*, Leeds: DoH.
103 See, further, Kaye, 'Hallmarks of a Secure Psychiatric Service', *op. cit.*, n. 59.
104 Private communication with the Department of Health and Children.
105 Newman, C. (2000), 'Survey Reveals Extent of Prison Health Problems', *Irish Times*, 1 August.
106 Mental Treatment Act 1945, s. 189(1)(b) as amended by the Mental Treatment Act 1961, s. 18(1)(a)(ii).
107 Mental Treatment Act 1961, s. 18(1)(a)(i).
108 Mental Treatment Act 1945, s. 172(1) (chargeable) and s.181(1)(b) (private).
109 Department of Health (1995), *White Paper: A New Mental Health Act* Pn.1824, Dublin: Stationery Office, p. 30, para. 3.2. An application for admission may also be made by a community welfare officer, or, in certain circumstances any interested person. Relative is defined to exclude in-laws.
110 Mental Treatment Act 1945, s. 184(4).
111 Ibid., s. 163(2)(b).
112 Cooney and O'Neil, *Psychiatric Detention in Ireland*, *op. cit.*, n. 49, p. 100.
113 Boland and Laing, 'Out of Sight', *op. cit.*, n. 13.
114 Cooney and O'Neil, *Psychiatric Detention in Ireland*, *op. cit.*, n. 49, chs 2 and 4. The Irish Supreme Court in *Re a Ward of Court (Witholding medical treatment)(No.2)* [1996] 2 IR 100 has noted that: 'The loss by an individual of his or her mental capacity does not result in any diminution of his or her personal rights recognised by the Constitution, including the right to life, the right to bodily integrity, the right to privacy, including self-determination, and the right to refuse medical care or treatment.'
115 Carey, T. *et al.* (1993), 'Involuntary Admissions to a New District Mental Health Service – Implications for a new Mental Treatment Act', *Irish Journal of Psychological Medicine*, **10**(139), p. 143.
116 *In re Philip Clarke* [1950] IR 235 p. 250.
117 Webb, M. (1995), 'A Psychiatrist's Comments on the White Paper on a New Mental Health Act', *Medico-Legal Journal of Ireland*, **83**, p. 83.
118 Mental Treatment Act 1953, s. 5.
119 Keys, M. (1998), 'Mental Treatment Legislation: Are the White Paper Proposals Adequate?', *Dli*, **51**, p. 52.
120 *RTE Guide*, 10 April 1992, p. 6; *Woman's Way*, 17 July 1992, p. 18; *Irish Press*, 5 May 1992; *The Big Issue*, October 1994, p. 6.
121 *Woman's Way* 17 July 1992, p. 18 at 20; *RTE Guide*, 10 April 1992, p. 6.
122 Boland and Laing, 'Out of Sight', *op. cit.*, n. 13.
123 Casey, P. and Craven, C. (1999), *Psychiatry and the Law*, Dublin: Oak Tree Press, p. 501.
124 DoH, *A New Mental Health Act*, *op. cit.*, n. 108, p. 62, para. 6.7.
125 Keys, 'Mental Treatment Legislation', *op. cit.*, n. 118, p. 52.
126 O'Shea, N. (1993), 'Some Thoughts on the Law Relating to the Admission Procedures to Psychiatric Hospitals in the Republic of Ireland Today', *Dli*, **77**, p. 78.
127 Casey and Craven, *Psychiatry and the Law*, *op. cit.*, n. 122, p. 502.
128 This criterion does not apply to a temporary patient detained on the grounds of addiction.

129 Supreme Court, Unreported Judgment, 31 July 1996 (272/1995).

130 Casey and Craven, *Psychiatry and the Law, op. cit.*, n. 122, p. 502.

131 Ibid., pp. 502, 503.

132 Cooney and O'Neil, *Psychiatric Detention in Ireland, op. cit.*, n. 49, p. 213.

133 Webb, 'A Psychiatrist's Comments', *op. cit.*, n. 116, p. 83.

134 Cooney and O'Neil, *Psychiatric Detention in Ireland, op. cit.*, n. 49, p. 45.

135 Ibid., p. 239.

136 DoH, *A New Mental Health Act, op. cit.*, n. 108, p. 61, para. 6.5.

137 Ibid.

138 Lynch, T. (1981), 'ECT', *Irish Medical Journal*, 74, p. 29.

139 Tomkin and Hanafin, *Irish Medical Law, op. cit.*, n. 38, p.134.

140 Webb, 'A Psychiatrist's Comments', *op. cit.*, n. 116, p. 84.

141 Browne, V. (1999), 'Unanswered Questions on Mental Institutions', *Irish Times*, 1 December.

142 Tomkin and Hanafin, *Irish Medical Law, op. cit.*, n. 38, p. 133.

143 *Report of the Inspector of Mental Hospitals, for the Year Ending 31st December 1997* (1998), Pn. 6230, Dublin: The Stationery Office, p. 107.

144 Ibid., p. 123.

145 Ibid., p. 124.

146 Department of Health and Children (1998), *Guidelines on Good Practice and Quality Assurance in Mental Health Services*, Dublin: Department of Health, p. 9, para. 4. 4.

147 *Report of the Inspector of Mental Hospitals for the Year Ending 31st December 1999* (2000), Pn. 8606, Dublin: The Stationery Office, pp. 202, 203.

148 Connolly, L. (1996), 'Consent and Involuntary Treatment in Anorexia Nervosa', *Medico-Legal Journal of Ireland*, **55**, p. 55.

149 'For the Benefit of the Child', *Irish Times*, 25 May 1998.

150 Walsh, D. (1999), 'Deaths in Mental Hospitals', *Irish Times*, 26 November.

151 *Report of the Inspector of Mental Hospitals for the Year Ending 31st December 1998* (1999), Pn. 7706, Dublin: The Stationery Office, p. 3.

152 Ibid., p. 4.

153 *Report for the Year Ending 31st December 1999, op. cit.*, n. 146, p. 2.

154 *Report for the Year Ending 31st December 1998, op. cit.*, n. 150, generally.

155 *Report of the Inspector of Mental Hospitals for the Year Ending 31st December 1996* (1997), Pn. 5050, Dublin: The Stationery Office, pp. 43, 115, 117. Also, *Report for the Year Ending 31st December 1997, op. cit.*, n. 142, pp. 37, 38, 107, 110, 118, 129, 137; *Report for the Year Ending 31st December 1998, op. cit.*, n. 150, pp. 39, 43, 44, 70, 107, 115, 128, 141, 150.

156 *Report for the Year Ending 31st December 1997, op. cit.*, n. 142, p. 99. Cf: *Report for the Year Ending 31st December 1996, op. cit.*, n. 154, pp. 39, 42.

157 *Report for the Year Ending 31st December 1998, op. cit.*, n. 150, pp. 2, 8, 10, 12, 22, 40, 43, 48, 52, 53, 54, 90, 94, 109, 122, 124, 140, 149; *Report for the Year Ending 31st December 1997, op. cit.*, n. 142, pp. 7, 8, 10, 48, 60, 61, 62, 66, 81, 89, 107, 108, 114, 118; *Report for the Year Ending 31st December 1996, op. cit.*, n. 154, pp. 6, 7, 29, 39, 46, 57, 115, 128, 148.

158 *Report for the Year Ending 31st December 1998, op. cit.*, n. 150, p. 52.

159 Ibid., p.22.

160 Ibid., pp. 16, 64, 69, 75, 90, 95, 104, 109, 114, 118, 131, 133, 150; *Report for the Year ending 31st December 1997, op. cit.*, n. 142, pp. 36, 58, 62, 76, 81, 87, 91, 101, 102, 108, 120, 145; *Report for the Year Ending 31st December 1996, op. cit.*, n. 154, pp. 42, 57, 59, 65, 76, 85, 102, 103, 105, 109, 128, 135, 148.

161 *Report for the Year Ending 31st December 1998, op. cit.*, n. 150, pp. 89, 109, 118, 122,

140; *Report for the Year Ending 31st December 1997, op. cit.*, n. 142, pp. 46, 48, 57, 81, 97, 99, 101, 102, 108, 135, 148.

162 *Report for the Year Ending 31st December 1998, op. cit.*, n. 150, pp. 12, 13, 24, 36, 109, 149; *Report for the Year Ending 31st December 1997, op. cit.*, n. 142, pp. 11, 28, 81, 87, 139; *Report for the Year Ending 31st December 1996, op. cit.*, n.154, pp. 41, 44, 46.

163 *Report for the Year Ending 31st December 1997, op. cit.* n. 142, p. 24.

164 Ibid., p. 149.

165 Mental Health Bill 1999, s. 2(1).

166 Ibid., s. 57(1).

167 Ibid., s. 57(3)(a).

168 Ibid., s. 47(2), (10).

169 Ibid., s. 57(5).

170 Cf. Webb, 'A Psychiatrist's Comments', *op. cit.*, n. 116, p. 84.

171 Mental Health Bill 1999, ss. 58, 59.

172 Cooney and O'Neil, *Psychiatric Detention in Ireland, op. cit.*, n. 49, p. 254.

173 Cf. Keys, 'Mental Treatment Legislation', *op. cit.*, n. 118, p. 54.

174 Cooney and O'Neil, *Psychiatric Detention in Ireland, op. cit.*, n. 49, p. 45.

175 Ibid., p. 254.

176 Casey and Craven, *Psychiatry and the Law, op. cit.*, n. 122, p. 523. Cf. McCarthy J in *Murphy* v. *Greene* [1990] 2 IR 566, who commented that: 'The standard of reasonable care under the [1945] Act may be quite different from such standard in ordinary medical practice.'

177 Mental Health Bill 1999, s. 15(2)(c).

178 'Bill to Protect Mental Patients Pledged', *Irish Times*, 27 May 1994.

179 Mental Treatment Act 1945, s. 97.

180 *Report of the Inspector of Mental Hospitals for the Year Ending 31st December 1999* (2000) Pn. 8606, Dublin: The Stationery Office, pp. 36, 48, 52, 61, 81, 85, 95, 100, 111, 123, 128, 132, 136, 140, 157, 161, 168.

181 Mental Treatment Act 1945, s. 235.

182 Ibid., s. 236.

183 Browne, V. (1999), 'Scandal in our Mental Hospitals is Revealed', *Irish Times*, 10 November.

184 Browne, V. (1999), 'Protecting the Rights of the Most Vulnerable', *Irish Times*, 11 August.

185 Browne, V. (1999), 'Has Official Malevolence Created a Health Crisis?', *Irish Times*, 17 November.

186 *Report for the Year Ending 31st December 1999, op. cit.*, n. 179, p. 1.

187 DoH, *Green Paper on Mental Health, op. cit.*, n. 2, p. 52, para. 12.4.

188 *Report for the Year Ending 31st December 1999, op. cit.*, n. 179, pp. 2, 33, 36, 43, 48, 52, 61, 81, 95, 100, 111, 125, 128, 136, 161, 165, 169, 177.

189 Ibid., pp. 33, 36, 48, 62, 128, 132, 140, 144, 147.

190 Ibid., pp. 33, 36, 40, 43, 48, 52, 76, 81, 86, 136, 140, 144.

191 *Parliamentary Debates*, 6/4/2000, p. 1002.

192 *Report for the Year Ending 31st December 1999, op. cit.*, n. 179, p. 3.

193 Department of Health and Children, *Guidelines on Good Practice, op. cit.*, n. 145, p. 5, para. 3.2.

194 Ibid., pp. 13–15.

195 Ibid., p. 14, para. 5.4.

196 Mental Health Bill 1999, s. 50(1).

197 Ibid., s. 41.

198 Ibid., s. 32(1).

199 Ibid., s. 32(3)
200 Ibid., s. 65.
201 Keys, M. (2000), 'Guarded Welcome for Mental Health Bill 1999', *Medico-Legal Journal of Ireland*, **6**, p. 28.
202 Mental Health Bill 1999, s. 34(1)(g).
203 Ibid.
204 *Report for the Year Ending 31st December 1997*, *op. cit.*, n. 142, p. 4.
205 Walsh Cowen, J. (1999), 'Pledge on Mental Health Services', *Irish Times*, 16 December.
206 Mental Health Bill 1999, s. 63.
207 Ibid., s. 65(3).
208 Department of Health and Children, *Guidelines on Good Practice*, *op. cit.*, n. 145, p. 3.
209 Quoted in Smyth, P. (1997), 'Study Raises Concern Over Women's Health Care', *Irish Times*, 2 June.
210 At <http://www.irlgov.ie/committees-00/c-health/001025/Page1.htm>.
211 *Report for the Year Ending 31st December 1998*, *op. cit.*, n. 150, p. 3.
212 Prins, H. (1984), 'Attitudes towards the Mentally Disordered', *Medicine, Science and Law*, **24**, p. 181 at 190.

Chapter 8

Body Beautiful? Feminist Perspectives on the World Health Organization

Susan M. Nott

Analyses such as those in *Well Women* demonstrate that the health-care policies of individual states can, despite their apparent neutrality, adversely affect women. There are numerous reasons why this is so. Laws and policies are criticized for taking a male perspective on women's needs and behaviour and for overtly and covertly discriminating against women. Such actions affect women whether they are the providers or the recipients of health care and, clearly, strategies are needed to address these problems. However, health care is not only a national but also an international concern. When compared with their male counterparts, women throughout the world are badly served by the medical profession and by health-care policies in general. One way of persuading states to see women's health concerns as more than a peripheral issue is to use international organizations and international law to apply pressure on them.

The purpose of this chapter is to consider the contribution made by one such international organization, the World Health Organization (WHO), to improving women's access to health care. The WHO was formally established in 1948 and its constitution sets out its functions and how they are to be performed. Its objective is 'the attainment by all peoples of the highest possible level of health', health being defined as a 'state of complete physical, mental and social well-being and not merely the absence of disease or infirmity'.

The WHO has a wide range of functions which include:

- acting as coordinating authority on international health work
- assisting governments, on request, in strengthening health services
- stimulating and advancing work on the prevention and control of epidemic, endemic and other diseases
- promoting research
- promoting improved standards of teaching and training in the health, medical and related professions
- promoting, in conjunction with other agencies, improved standards of nutrition, housing and sanitation.

Membership of the WHO is open to states and, currently, 191 states are members. Any state which is a member of the United Nations may become a member of the WHO by accepting its constitution. Arrangements are also in place to allow states that are not members of the United Nations or territories that are not responsible for the conduct of their own international relations[1] to join the organization. The work of the WHO is financed by its member states which make annual contributions to the WHO's budget, but some states also make additional voluntary contributions. In 1998–99 the WHO's budget was $1.8 billion. The WHO has its headquarters in Geneva but maintains regional offices in Africa, the Americas, south-east Asia, Europe, the eastern Mediterranean and the western Pacific. The presence of these regional offices allows the development of programmes and policies that are specific to the health problems and concerns of that region. For example, WHO/Europe[2] (WHO's regional office for Europe) has to tackle the health issues faced by the inhabitants of developed industrial societies. These particular problems will not necessarily be similarly encountered elsewhere in the world.

It would be impossible, in the space of a few thousand words, to analyse a body as complex as the WHO. Instead, this chapter takes as its starting point the lack of comment, or more specifically the lack of feminist comment, on the WHO's activities. This seems surprising since there is a growing body of feminist research into international human rights,[3] such as the right to health,[4] and the use that can be made of these rights at a national level.[5] International law has also been the target of feminist analysis, which has revealed its deeply gendered nature.[6] Health-care policy and health-care law and the ways in which they discriminate against women is another well-researched area.[7] Since health care and international issues are clearly of concern to feminists, the apparent lack of interest in the WHO seems an anomaly. Part of the problem may be the absence of a framework within which to conduct a feminist analysis of international organizations and a lack of guidance on what criteria to use.[8] In order to address this omission, this chapter aims to develop a set of criteria designed to evaluate, from a feminist perspective, the WHO's contribution in securing improvements to the standard of women's health care. Reference will be made to feminist theory, as well as feminist analyses of international law, in determining what these criteria should be. Once these are in place, the WHO's performance[9] will be measured against this critical framework and, if necessary, ways suggested of improving that performance.

Setting the Scene

Feminism is difficult to define since it does not comprise a single feminist theory but rather a collection of theories[10] on how the status of women may be enhanced in any given society. This would be problematic if our purpose here was to set out the practical steps the WHO should take in order to feminize its activities. However, the multifaceted nature of feminism is not a particular problem in the context of this chapter since its objective is simply to analyse the WHO's current activities from a feminist perspective and to assess how woman-friendly that organization is. Adopting a feminist standpoint requires certain enquiries to be made of whatever body or activity is under examination. In the case of an organization, particular attention must be paid to whether it focuses on men and marginalizes women by regarding male experience and attitudes as representing the norm. Questions must also be asked about its commitment to eliminating gender inequality and enhancing the status of women. Hence, in order to analyse the WHO from a feminist perspective, criteria should be adopted which relate to these issues. Logically, the extent of women's representation (in the broadest sense of that term) within a particular organization is a measure of whether or not they are marginalized by it. Moreover, the strategies an organization adopts to identify and eliminate gender inequality institutionalized within its processes and policies provide further evidence of its commitment to enhancing women's status. Finally, there must be some effort to determine how a body relates to other organizations and to identify its political and social culture. No organization is totally autonomous nor can it be totally objective in its actions. This means, therefore, that an organization's ability to enhance the status of women may be inhibited by other organizations. Moreover, the actions of that organization in determining what is in women's best interests will be shaped by its internal culture. This raises one of the recurring themes of feminism – namely, the danger of essentializing women and presuming that all women's needs are alike. The extent to which an organization recognizes this problem and takes steps to address it is another indicator of its capacity to enhance the status of women.

On the basis of these criteria, this chapter will analyse the WHO's contribution to facilitating women's access to health care. It will do so initially by examining the significance of these criteria in greater detail and then by evaluating women's representation within the WHO, its policies for dealing with gender inequality and its independence of action in promoting equality.

Representation

Writing in 1991, Charlesworth, Chinkin and Wright[11] drew attention to the 'masculine world of international law' and sought to explain why it was significant that all the major institutions of the international legal order were staffed by men: '[l]ong-term domination [by men] of all bodies wielding political power nationally and internationally means that issues traditionally of concern to men become seen as general human concerns, while "women's concerns" are relegated to a special, limited category.'[12] This suggests a correlation between the numbers of women within an organization and the extent to which that organization pays proper attention to the needs of women. If the WHO's agenda is set by men, and if it acts on what men perceive as women's health needs, then it is difficult to see how it could be regarded as truly responsive to women's needs. Feminists have often roundly condemned organizations, such as national legislatures, for failing to be representative.[13] The notion that the sex of a representative is immaterial and that a white middle-class male can successfully represent the views of a working-class woman has been rejected in the context of national politics.[14] If few women have access to an organization in order to express their views, to influence policy-making and the allocation of resources and to monitor the impact of its actions on women, that organization is likely to reflect male priorities, male values and, above all, a masculine perception of women's needs. Hence evidence must be sought that the WHO gives women the same degree of access to its deliberations as it does men.

It does not suffice, however, simply to look for equal numbers of men and women within the WHO's management structure. In addition, it should have links with women's grassroots organizations or non-governmental organizations (NGOs). Commentators in other contexts[15] have argued that such links are important for a variety of reasons. Links with NGOs offer international organizations a way of interacting with individuals as opposed to governments. In this manner, international organizations can claim to be more responsive and representative, and hence they can claim greater legitimacy for their views. Furthermore, NGOs can provide international organizations with a wider knowledge base and an alternative view to that of national governments. These positive features of cooperation with NGOs would seem to have a great deal to offer the WHO. In the first place it would allow the WHO to discover whether its, or indeed national, health-care policies are working satisfactorily in practice and, in particular, whether (and if so how) women are being adversely affected by such policies. Second, feminists constantly warn against the danger of essentializing women – that is, treating women as if each and every one had the same needs and aspirations and as if their experiences of life were identical.[16] This is a considerable problem in a state context, but it is magnified in the context of an international organization which deals with women worldwide. The preoccupations of women in the developed countries may be very distinct from those of women in the developing world. For example, to most Western feminists, abortion represents a right to be fought for and won. In other countries, however, abortion may be used as an instrument for limiting family size and can therefore represent a means of oppressing women. Thus, care must be taken that the concerns of women in one part of the world are not allowed to predominate or to speak for women as a whole. Contacts with organizations representing a cross-section of women's views would help to counteract any essentializing tendency and affirm that, whilst feminism is concerned with addressing women's subordinate status, the factors which contribute to that status are not fixed but vary between regions and between states. Third, the WHO's membership consists of state representatives who may wish to present their state and its actions in relation to health care in the best possible light – emphasizing what is positive and glossing over more negative aspects. This certainly occurs in other contexts when states are reporting to international organizations.[17] Moreover, representatives on some WHO bodies[18] have to possess medical knowledge or medical qualifications, and the essays in *Well Women* serve as a warning on how stereotypical the medical profession's view of women can be. The WHO may, therefore, wish to provide itself with a counterbalance to such views, and NGOs would seem ideally placed to fulfil this role.

Besides the positive aspects of cooperation between NGOs and international organizations, there are other, negative, factors which have to be taken into account. It is sometimes argued that many NGOs represent a particular group of individuals or point of view. By allowing such special-interest alliances access to international organizations there is a danger that policies will be manipulated in ways that are not helpful to citizens as a whole. Clearly, it is possible to address this fear by ensuring that views are canvassed from a cross-section of NGOs designed to represent a variety of opinions. However, this is an issue of which international organizations have to be aware and deal with in a satisfactory manner.

The notion of representation, besides requiring women's presence either as individuals or as members of NGOs, would also seem to require their visibility within any data collected by the WHO. Unless statistics are disaggregated according to sex, then it is very easy to assume that the effect of a particular event or action on men and women will be the same. In the sphere of health care this is particularly pertinent since there are marked differences in how women, as compared with men, are affected by illness. Women are more susceptible to certain diseases, such as arthritis, and less susceptible to others, such as smoking-related illnesses.[19] If this is not appreciated when allocating resources to fight disease, inequality can result. What is true of diseases is also true of treatments. Research into potential remedies must therefore explicitly monitor for possible variations in men and women's reactions in any research design.[20] Finally, women are providers of health care as well as its recipients. Any decisions taken on the training and working practices of health-care professionals need to acknowledge this as well as the fact that male and female patterns of work are not necessarily identical.

Hence the first criterion for evaluating the WHO's performance in facilitating women's access to health care is the extent to which it is accessible to women and acknowledges the circumstances of their lives.

Equality Policy

In order to be considered truly responsive to the needs of women, an organization must have in place the machinery and the policies to ensure that its actions do not discriminate against women. There is a considerable body of research on how discrimination occurs and how best to go about eliminating inequality.[21] The easiest form of discrimination to identify and address is that which is overt and uncompromising, such as a refusal to employ women in certain posts. However, discriminatory behaviour is often far subtler. Policies or practices which, on the surface, appear even-handed and gender-neutral may, on closer analysis, be shown to be advantageous for men but disadvantageous for women. This is because discrimination is not simply based on sex, but on gender – that is, on the way in which society constructs what it regards as appropriate roles or behaviour for men and women. Indeed, the WHO has itself acknowledged the adverse effects of gender which it defines as follows: 'Gender refers to women's and men's roles and responsibilities that are socially determined. Gender is related to how we are perceived and expected to think and act as women and men because of the way society is organised, not because of our biological differences.'[22]

Actions or policies which are based on those social constructions can be just as discriminatory as deliberate discrimination against women. However, this form of discrimination is more difficult to eradicate. For example, a policy on an individual's eligibility for free health care may require that they have contributed to a work-based fund for a period of years. Women may be far less likely to qualify because of society's expectation that they will give up work in order to care for their family, and this will make it difficult for them to establish an appropriate contribution record. Alternatively, rather than base policy on a male lifestyle, policy-makers may adopt what is sometimes referred to as a gendering strategy[23] in which the (male) policy-maker assumes that women behave in a particular fashion and structures the policy accordingly. For those women who fit within the stereotype that has been adopted, the policy may prove helpful, but it may have very undesirable consequences for those women who are outside it. Such stereotypes often represent how men expect women to behave or how they choose to categorize women's behaviour. To take a simple example, women are often inextricably linked with their reproductive capacity. Health-care policies may, therefore, focus on safeguarding that capability by restricting where women can work, their hours of employment and their exposure to certain substances. In principle, policies of this nature may seem sensible – until their effects on women in general are appreciated. They may make no exceptions for women who are beyond childbearing age, who are infertile or who simply do not wish to have children. The use of gender stereotypes as a basis for policy-making once again makes women the targets of discrimination.[24]

Because of the subtle forms that inequality can assume, an organization needs to have the means in place to eliminate overt and covert discrimination and promote equality between the sexes. In a state context, this can be achieved in a variety of ways. First, a ban may be placed on discriminating against women, which will be legally binding and may allow women who have been the target of sex discrimination to take action against the guilty party to recover damages for any harm suffered.[25] States quite often choose to supplement anti-discrimination legislation with constitutional guarantees of equal treatment for men and women. This may allow challenges to be made to laws and policies which breach this undertaking. In order, however, to transform a formal commitment to equality between the sexes into a strategy for substantive change, states will need to embark on a programme of positive action or positive discrimination. The concept of positive action or positive discrimination acknowledges that women face barriers to their progress in society that are not experienced by men and aims to 'compensate' women for these disadvantages. For example, in many societies women are seen as suited to certain kinds of work (such as nursing) and not to others (such as building). Positive action programmes authorize employers to train women for occupations where they are underrepresented, whilst positive discrimination will, in certain circumstances, permit women (as opposed to men) to be offered employment in these sectors.[26] More recently, states have begun to use an equality strategy known as mainstreaming, which is designed to assess whether apparently gender-neutral policies will, in reality, have an adverse impact on women but not on men.[27]

In a national context it is common to make use of a combination of these strategies in order to combat gender inequality. Most states then oversee their equality strategies by putting in place equality agencies whose task it is to monitor equality legislation, pursue claims of sex discrimination or promote good practice.[28] The extent to which international bodies can, and indeed should, adopt similar mechanisms and policies is problematic.[29] At the very least, however, there is an expectation that an international organization would have in place first the means of ensuring that internally it does not discriminate on the grounds of sex in relation to its employees, its members or those individuals with whom it may have dealings. Second, since it is one of the tasks of international organizations to produce policies, another necessity would seem to be some procedure for ensuring that those policies do not discriminate on the grounds of sex or gender. Third, an international organization needs to give careful thought to the concept of equality to which it aspires. In a national context, the most frequently employed notion of equality is equality as equal treatment. Feminist commentators have frequently pointed out that equality as equal treatment is a deeply flawed concept likely to produce little more than formal equality since it does no more than demand that women and men receive the same treatment.[30] It makes no attempt to address the fact that women's lives are, for biological, cultural and social reasons, very different from those of men. In order to promote substantive equality between the sexes a concept of equality has to be employed which is far more sensitive to the reasons for inequality between the sexes. Finally it is not sufficient simply to have an equality strategy or procedure however well thought out: a way of monitoring its effectiveness in promoting policies which respect gender equality is also required. At a national level this task is performed by equality agencies, the academic community and women's organizations. An international organization, however, would need to establish some alternative machinery for this purpose.

The second criterion on which the WHO's ability to facilitate women's access to health care should be judged is the existence of suitable mechanisms for eliminating gender inequality and for monitoring their effectiveness.

Independence of Action

The role of an international organisation is at least partly to agree policies or action programmes among its membership and then to ensure that those initiatives are acted upon. In securing compliance with its decisions, the key to success would seem to be policies or programmes that 'fit' well with the political systems and national aspirations of an organization's membership. This is an issue that has been analysed in the context of the European Union (EU). The EU is a supranational organization with considerable powers to compel member states to comply with its decisions. Yet, if what the EU proposes does not 'fit' well with its member states' political and institutional landscapes, little may be accomplished.[31]

An international organization, such as the WHO, whose task it is to raise standards of health, would seem to face a particular dilemma. On the one hand, there is the need, already mentioned, to secure a 'fit' between the WHO's policies and the political and institutional landscapes of its membership. On the other hand, those member states may support practices that deliberately discriminate against women. In order to ensure acceptance of its policies and programmes, the WHO may come under pressure to accommodate or 'respect' such discriminatory practices. The extent to which the WHO is prepared to assert its autonomy and oppose such demands may offer another measure of its commitment to promoting gender equality. Clearly the WHO does not function in a political, cultural or economic vacuum, yet its willingness to establish a set of autonomous internal values, including respect for equality between the sexes, and to adhere to them despite external pressure, is an important measure of its feminist credentials.

States may also invoke the notion of autonomy in order to create a divide between the public and the private – a distinction that is familiar to feminists[32] and refers to the division of issues into those that a state regards as a legitimate target for regulation and those that are not. Whether an issue falls into the public or private sphere can change over time,[33] and practice can vary from state to state. What is significant, so far as feminists are concerned, is that matters that are of importance to women are regularly assigned to the private, unregulated sphere. This has been the case, for example, with the issue of domestic violence; it may be regarded as inappropriate for the state to interfere with what happens within the home. The way in which the boundary between the public and the private is drawn can have a bearing on the work of an organization such as the WHO. The public sphere will be identified with those areas of activity open to its influence, whilst the private sphere will be equated with matters of national autonomy. As a consequence, states may claim that cultural or social customs that jeopardize or restrict women's access to health care are outside the legitimate influence of the WHO.

Therefore the third criterion for judging the extent to which the WHO facilitates women's access to health care is to consider the degree to which the WHO's membership and their claims to national autonomy inhibits that body's independence of action.

Evaluating the WHO's Performance in Facilitating Women's Access to Health Care

Having established a variety of criteria with which to assess the WHO's performance, the concluding sections of this chapter will use those criteria in order to evaluate the extent to which the WHO has facilitated women's access to health care.

Representation

The first criterion for consideration is representation – that is, the extent to which the WHO is accessible to women and acknowledges the circumstances of their lives. In order to reach a view on this issue it is necessary to start with a brief description of the manner in which the WHO is organized. The supreme decision-making body of the WHO is the World Health Assembly which comprises delegations from member states and meets once a year in May. The World Health Assembly is charged with the task of approving the WHO's budget and making major policy decisions. The body responsible for putting the World Health Assembly's decisions into effect is the Executive Board which has 32 members who are nominated by member states specifically selected to perform this task by the World Health Assembly. The seats on the Executive Board are allocated among the WHO's six regions. As well as the Executive Board, which meets twice a year, there are regional committees made up of representatives of the member states and associated members in that region. These committees meet once a year and deal with matters of significance for that specific region.

The WHO also possesses a secretariat which is headed by a Director-General and has 3800 employees. The Director-General is appointed by the World Health Assembly on the nomination of the Executive Board. There have been five Director-Generals to date. The current Director-General, and the first woman to hold the post, is Dr Gro Harlem Brundtland who was formerly a Norwegian politician. Beside the Director-General there are eight executive directors who are responsible for specific aspects of the WHO's work. For example, there is an executive director for social change and mental health and another for sustainable development and healthy environments. The Director-General also has four senior policy advisers to keep her in touch with developments at the WHO's headquarters and in the regions. Several of these key posts have been held by women, although this is no guarantee for the future. The WHO has been praised in the past, however, for its treatment of women. It has been said of the WHO that, in the context of UN specialized agencies, it 'has had the best record on recruiting and retaining women staff and promoting women to the managerial level as well as addressing the needs and concerns of women in its field programs'.[34]

As part of the WHO's task of directing and coordinating international health work it actively cooperates with NGOs. Article 71 of the WHO's constitution authorizes such activity and there is a set procedure for initiating such cooperation.[35] The objectives of the WHO's collaboration with NGOs is said to be:

> To promote the policies, strategies and programmes derived from the decisions of the Organization's governing bodies; to collaborate with regard to various WHO programmes in jointly agreed activities to implement these strategies; and to play an appropriate role in ensuring the harmonizing of intersectoral interests among the various sectoral bodies concerned in a country, regional or global setting.[36]

The WHO divides its contacts with NGOs into two categories – formal or official relations and informal relations. In order to maintain formal relations with the WHO an NGO has to satisfy certain criteria and has to go through what might best be described as a probationary period of cooperation. During this probationary period, mutual interests are identified and arrangements may be made to collaborate on specific projects (so-called working relations). It is possible that the relationship between the WHO and the NGO may not be taken beyond the stage of informal contacts or working relations or may cease altogether. Alternatively, an NGO may apply to the Executive Board of the WHO to enter into official relations with it. In order to do this the NGO in question must be international in its structure or scope,[37] must have a constitution, a headquarters and a management structure[38] and, finally, its area of interest must fall 'within the purview of WHO'.[39] According to the WHO's policy document, the types of organization that are likely to satisfy these criteria include 'various types of international NGOs with a federated structure (made up of national or regional groups or having individual members from different countries), foundations that raise resources for health development activities in different parts of the world, and similar bodies promoting international health'.[40]

Those NGOs whose application for admission into official relations with the WHO are approved normally collaborate with the WHO on specific schemes or objectives. The success of such arrangements are reviewed every three years and the Executive Board of the WHO may decide to terminate its official relations with an NGO.[41] Given the relative stringency of the conditions for establishing official relations with the WHO, it might seem curious that NGOs go to the trouble of doing so. The explanation for this may rest on the fact that, by maintaining official relations with the WHO, an NGO obtains certain privileges, including access to WHO documentation and the ability to participate in the WHO's policy-making process.[42]

Apart from maintaining relationships with international NGOs, the WHO also has contacts with regional and national NGOs. These are not necessarily bodies affiliated to an international NGO with official relations with the WHO. Such contacts are usually with the WHO's regional offices and involve collaboration at that level in joint activities.

Clearly, the WHO takes its relationships with NGOs very seriously but, equally clearly, it sees the prime purpose of those relationships as collaboration in order to further its policy objectives. There is little sense that the WHO encourages such contacts in order to receive feedback on how its policies are affecting specific groups of individuals or on what the unmet health-care needs of those groups may be. Although it is, of course, perfectly possible that, in the course of its cooperation with an NGO, the organization may be made aware of the fact that its policies or programmes are having unforeseen effects on women or not meeting their needs. In particular those NGOs that maintain official relations with the WHO do have the right to participate in the organization's decision-making process and to communicate with the Director-General. An NGO could use this as an avenue for raising concerns about the gender impact of a particular programme or policy.

The NGOs that are most likely to voice such concerns are those which have as their focus the health care of women. The WHO maintains official relations with a number of such bodies,[43] for example, the International Council of Women (ICW) and the International Alliance of Women (IAW). The ICW was founded in 1888 and has maintained official relations with the WHO since 1981. Its objective is to bring together women's voluntary organizations from all over the world for consultation and action to

> ... promote the welfare of mankind, the family and the individual; support all efforts to achieve peace through negotiation, arbitration and conciliation; promote recognition and respect for human rights and work for the removal of discrimination, such as that based on birth, race, sex, language or religion; promote equal rights and responsibilities for both sexes in all spheres; encourage women to recognize their responsibilities in the community and train and stimulate them to participate in public life on local, national and international levels; deepen the understanding and increase the mutual sympathies of women through international contacts.[44]

The ICW has collaborated in disseminating information about the WHO and its policies, and participates in meetings relating to such matters as traditional practices, breastfeeding and the health of the elderly. The IAW was founded in 1904 and has maintained official relations with the WHO since 1993. Its prime objective is to secure 'all such reforms as are necessary to establish a real equality – of liberties, status and opportunities – between men and women and to work for equal partnership between men and women in all spheres of life'.[45] The collaboration which has taken place between the IAW and the WHO aims to improve curative and preventive health care for women. The IAW also disseminates information on behalf of the WHO and communicates the views of its affiliates to the WHO.

The very fact that the WHO has formal relations with organizations such as the ICW and the IAW means that women have some degree of access to the WHO and its decision-making process. In no sense, however, is the WHO making a systematic effort to obtain the views of women through its links with NGOs. This is merely the by-product (to the extent that it does occur) of a process which is meant to implement the WHO's policies rather than shape them. Indeed, the very formal nature of the procedure for establishing official relations with an NGO may well mean that only well-established women's organizations have a chance of satisfying the relevant criteria. Yet it would appear that maintaining official relations with the WHO gives an NGO the most influence. On this basis, radical women's groups that do not possess the management structure or the international character that the WHO requires for establishing official relations would be excluded. There is the possibility, however, that they could institute contacts with the WHO's regional committees and make their views felt in this manner.

Another important aspect of ensuring that women are adequately represented within an international organization is for the body in question to assemble statistical data on women. If data is disaggregated by sex then a body can appreciate the effect its decisions will have on women rather than assume that their effect on men and women will be identical. The Fourth World Conference on Women held in Beijing in 1995 stressed the importance of disaggregating data by sex in its Declaration and Platform for Action.[46] In its turn, the WHO has acknowledged that 'it is essential that the situation of women is more accurately reflected in routinely collected health statistics'.[47] Without this information it is conceded that it will be difficult to appreciate 'the specific situation of women (or men) and to plan in ways that take these differences into account'.[48] However, although it is vital that any statistical data should take account of sex, the WHO's ability to ensure that this need is met is more debatable. Statistics on the incidence of disease and issues such as maternal mortality are collected by states and their systems may, as the WHO's Women's Health and Development programme concedes, not give an accurate picture.[49] The WHO, therefore, needs to encourage the collection of accurate disaggregated statistical data by states. As the current Director-General said in a speech to the United Nations Commission on the Status of Women:

> To be able to look through the gender lens, we need information. The basis for a gender approach is sex disaggregated data. ... You must contribute to the global knowledge base in this regard. The data that your countries collect on major health issues must be sex differentiated. By providing us with this information, WHO can produce information about men and women separately that will allow you to more equitably and effectively address health needs.[50]

In addition, the WHO needs to be proactive in ensuring that the data states do provide covers health issues, such as domestic violence, that are of importance to women.[51] In some states there may be social or cultural pressures to ignore certain subjects or regard them as private or family matters. Such omissions can be damaging since they give a misleading picture of the state of women's health.

Judged on this first criterion of representation, therefore, the WHO seems to be becoming more aware of the importance of taking heed of women's views and needs. The appointment of the first female Director-General may have contributed to an appreciation that the presence of women is a vital aspect of gender equality. She has committed the WHO to being a 'partnership organization' and has emphasized that 'the time is over for using women as instruments of public policy without being participants in a process of consensus building for social change'.[52] Yet, despite this commitment to the 'feminization' of the WHO, this may prove a short-lived shift in policy. Broadening the representation of women must be a permanent feature of the WHO's activities, and this may not be achieved until member states are persuaded to take this message seriously and to abandon the outmoded view that the sex of their representatives does not greatly matter.

Equality Policies

The WHO[53] came into being in 1946 when 61 states signed its Constitution. Since Article 55 of the United Nations Charter commits it to promote 'solutions of international economic, social, health, and related problems', the WHO functions under the auspices of the United Nations. Indeed, the decision to establish an international health organization was taken at the United Nations Conference on International Organizations held at San Francisco in 1945. This is a significant factor so far as women's representation is concerned. Article 8 of the United Nations Charter provides that: 'The United Nations shall place no restrictions on the eligibility of men and women to participate in any capacity and under conditions of equality in its principal and subsidiary organs.' As a 'subsidiary organ' the WHO is bound by this commitment to equality. However, the wording of Article 8 does not place a positive obligation on the United Nations and its subsidiary organizations to ensure that men and women *are* equally represented because, as commentators have pointed out in the past, it is 'phrased in the negative, rather than as an affirmative obligation to include women, as the right to choose delegates and representatives to international organisations was thought to belong to nation-states, whose freedom of choice was not to be impeded in any way.'[54] As a consequence the WHO is under no strict obligation to observe the equality imperative. This means that it will be necessary to explore what steps the WHO has taken to ensure that gender equality has been integrated into its administrative and decision-making processes.

So far as its personnel is concerned, the WHO has acknowledged that there is a 'gender gap' which it is seeking to redress. As the current Director-General said in 1999, 'as you may know, I have strongly increased the number of senior women at the highest levels of the Organization as well as at other senior levels. I shall continue to close the gender gap in my Organization'.[55] This commitment on the part of the Director-General seems to have been acted upon so far as senior office-holders are concerned,[56] although there must be some doubts about an equality policy that rests on a personal guarantee rather than upon a specific policy built into the organization's working practices.

With regard to promoting gender equality in its policies, until comparatively recently, the WHO does appear to have adopted generally applicable health-care policies supplemented by specific women-centred policies. Whilst it was appreciated that, for biological reasons, men and women might be differently affected by disease, little attention was paid to the effect that gender might have on health. For example, the 'preponderance of male patients in malaria clinics in many countries has led to the assumption that males are more exposed to infection for occupational reasons'.[57] Research has demonstrated, however, that women experience similar rates of exposure, but do not attend the clinics because of lack of time, problems with transport and other social constraints.[58] In addition, those health programmes specifically aimed at women largely focused on women's reproductive capacity. The 'women as mothers' stereotype was allowed to dominate what were perceived as women's health needs. The WHO has now acknowledged that, in the past, it may have overemphasized women's role as mothers and that it needs to look at women's health care needs throughout their lives.[59]

Undoubtedly the WHO has become more aware of the effect of gender on health-care policies. It has a Working Group on Gender (GWG)[60] that was established in 1996 by the Women's Health and Development Programme. The purpose of the GWG is said to be twofold:

- to raise awareness and understanding of the importance of a gender perspective to public health programmes; and
- to promote, expand and guide the integration and/or application of gender perspectives in the work of WHO and in health research, policy and programmes.[61]

The GWG published a technical paper in 1998, *Gender and Health*,[62] which was designed to familarize the WHO's personnel which the effect which gender can have on health-care policies.

In order to ensure that the effects of gender on the WHO's health-care policies are properly addressed, the organization has committed itself to integrate or to mainstream gender into its policies. The strategy of mainstreaming gender has attracted a great deal of attention at a national and international level during the past few years: it featured prominently at the Beijing World Conference on Women, and the UN Economic and Social Council agreed a measure on 'gender mainstreaming in all activities of the UN system'.[63] The WHO defines gender mainstreaming as the 'integration of gender concerns into the analyses, formulation and monitoring of policies, programmes and projects, with the objective of ensuring that these reduce inequalities between men and women'.[64] It is committed to mainstreaming gender equality into the WHO's policies and programmes by 2002. Moreover, the WHO has identified the following key elements as essential to successful gender mainstreaming:

- an organizational policy that mandates the incorporation of gender equity and equality considerations into all policies, programmes and projects
- a commitment from senior management to implementing such a policy
- the existence of a core group of in-house gender experts that can support the process of gender mainstreaming
- a capacity-building strategy that is specifically tailored to the area of work of those being trained
- the opportunity and guidance provided to staff to incorporate gender concerns into their work.

Clearly, the WHO is still in the process of integrating gender mainstreaming into its organizational structure. At present, therefore, it is possible to comment only in very general terms on the likely success of its efforts, based on experiences elsewhere of mainstreaming. Feminist commentators seem to agree that gender mainstreaming has the potential to address aspects of gender inequality that other equality strategies currently leave untouched.[65] In the past, equality has been regarded as requiring no more than treating women and men in the same fashion. If, however, that equal treatment is based on men's needs or men's experiences of life, then it will not promote equality between the sexes. Rather, it will simply maintain the status quo. In addition, the promotion of equality has, in the main, been centred on the workplace, leaving other areas of activity untouched by the equality imperative. Mainstreaming, however, is applied to all aspects of policy-making and requires a policy-maker to consider whether a proposed policy will have an adverse gender impact. If the answer is 'yes', then the expectation is that the policy in question will be modified or some other adjustment made.

The obvious sophistication of gender mainstreaming is its strength as well as its weakness. Experience at national level has demonstrated that states often commit themselves to mainstreaming without investing the resources necessary for success.[66] A body which is truly committed to gender mainstreaming must consider who is to be responsible for the procedure – gender experts or administrators. If the latter, then consideration has to be given to what training they will receive. Simply providing an administrator with a definition of gender and telling them to evaluate proposed policies for their gender impact is totally inadequate. An evaluation of gender impact requires statistical data as well consultation with agencies or organizations with a specific knowledge of the policy area under consideration. It requires a clear conception of how adverse gender impact is to be defined. Furthermore, gender mainstreaming requires internal and external monitoring so that the accuracy of assessments can be observed over time.

Gender mainstreaming has been used not only at national level but also at an international level[67] and in health-care contexts.[68] The same factors appear to restrict the success of mainstreaming in these contexts as is the case at a national level. If gender mainstreaming is to improve the WHO's performance in delivering health care to women, the mainstreaming process has to be carefully thought out and integrated. Clearly, the WHO has already identified some key elements of the process but others, such as the need for consultation and monitoring, are not mentioned. In addition, the WHO's efforts to mainstream gender may be thwarted if other international organizations, or indeed its member states, do not attach similar importance to the procedure. It is commendable if a body such as the WHO takes account of the impact of its health-care policies on women. Any impact will, however, be limited should other organizations in other contexts ignore gender matters. The all-embracing effect of gender means that it has to be addressed at all levels and in every context. Whilst making a commitment to gender mainstreaming is easy, it is far more difficult to act on that commitment in a meaningful fashion.

Judged on the second criterion – namely, the existence of suitable mechanisms for eliminating gender inequality in its health-care policies and for monitoring their effectiveness – the WHO appears to have made some positive progress. Whereas, in the past, it has tended to ignore the significance of gender in perpetuating inequality, it now seems to be taking steps to rectify this situation, although only time will tell whether those steps will prove to be effective.

Independence of Action

Earlier in this chapter the notion of autonomy was discussed as a factor affecting the WHO's ability to promote gender equality. Reference was made to the WHO's need to preserve its autonomy in the face of claims by its member states that their national autonomy was threatened by the organization's health-care initiatives. In these circumstances, the WHO has the choice of either opposing national practices if they are perceived as compromising women's health (and the promotion of equality) or adjusting its health-care policies to take account of such practices. In order to illustrate this point, it is possible to cite a variety of examples. These would include cultural practices, such as female genital mutilation (FGM), the use of methods of contraception that jeopardize women's health to limit population and religious restrictions on women's ability to access competent health care.

FMG, which involves 'partial or total removal of the external female genitalia or other injury to the female genital organs', is often referred to as a traditional practice. The motives behind the practice vary but include religious[69] and social reasons,[70] reasons of hygiene and as a way of reducing a woman's sexual desire. It is estimated that over 130 million women worldwide have undergone FGM. The consequences of the procedure for a woman's health can be extremely serious and can include infection, painful intercourse and complications in childbirth. The WHO's stance on FGM has changed over the years. As Charlesworth and Chinkin record, 'When the WHO was asked, in 1951 and again in 1961, to undertake a study of the health effects of traditional practices on young girls, it refused to do so on the basis that the practices were ritual and cultural and beyond its sphere of competence'.[71] More recently, however, the WHO has condemned the practice:

FGM is a deeply rooted traditional practice that adversely affects the health of girls and women. It is a form of violence against them that has serious physical and psychosocial consequences, and is a reflection of discrimination against girls and women.[72]

Despite this, the WHO has noted that progress towards eliminating the practice is slow. One reason for this is the fact that, where FGM is common, national governments are reluctant to invest time and money in discouraging it. Indeed, governments may fear that, if they were to attempt to do so, they would risk unpopularity. As a consequence, the WHO's efforts to eliminate FGM are likely to achieve results only if the WHO and other international agencies, which oppose FGM, apply pressure to these states.

This last fact is an important consideration in any discussion of the WHO's independence of action. The WHO is part of the 'family' of international organizations, many of which also take an interest in health-care issues. This could work to the advantage of the WHO (and women) in the fight for gender equality. States frequently have to report national progress on a variety of issues to international organizations. For example, Article 12 of the Convention on the

Elimination of all Forms of Discrimination against Women (CEDAW) requires states to take all appropriate measures to ensure that women have equal access to health-care facilities and to submit regular reports to the CEDAW Committee. This might, therefore, represent a way of exerting additional pressure on states to eliminate discriminatory practices.

The example of FGM demonstrates the WHO's readiness to assert its independence and to censure a practice even though, at a national level, it may be supported on religious or social grounds. This willingness to condemn behaviour that discriminates against women is very welcome. Rather than accept claims by some states that FGM is a matter for national autonomy, and hence within the private sphere, the WHO has been prepared to stand its ground. It also illustrates the fact that, in asserting its autonomy, the WHO should ally itself with other likeminded international organizations.

This third criterion of autonomy is particularly problematic. Whilst it is essential that the WHO condemns discriminatory practices that some states claim to be matters of religious conviction or local culture, this is done at a cost, since the states taking such a stance are unlikely to cooperate and modify their behaviour. Yet it does seem crucial that the WHO sets its face against discrimination wherever it is identified as failure to do so would put at risk any claims made by the organization of being gender-sensitive.

Conclusions

The extent to which the WHO facilitates women's access to health care has been assessed on the basis of the framework developed at the outset of this chapter. In recent years the WHO appears to have taken the issue of gender inequality and its adverse effects on health-care provision more seriously than in the past. This has led it to address the issue of women's representation and the gender impact of its health-care policies. That said, however, the interface between the WHO and its membership still remains a very real obstacle to progress. Many of the initiatives that the WHO has taken are to be welcomed although there may be reservations over the rigour with which it will pursue its strategy of mainstreaming and over its apparent reluctance to integrate some reforms within its own organizational structure. With regard to promoting gender equality, the possibility that apparent gains could disappear or be no more than paper exercises is an ever-present fear. The WHO's performance, therefore, needs to be constantly monitored for evidence that its commitment to addressing gender equality produces positive and permanent results.

Notes

1   Such territories become associate members. There are currently two associate members: Puerto Rico and Tokeiau.
2   Who/Europe's website is at <http://www.who.dk/>.
3   See, for example, Cook, R.J. (ed.) (1994), *Human Rights of Women*, Philadelphia: University of Pennsylvania Press; Byrnes, A., Connors, J. and Bik, L. (eds) (1997),

Advancing the Human Rights of Women, London: Commonwealth Secretariat; Charlesworth, H. and Chinkin, C. (2000), *The Boundaries of International Law – A Feminist Analysis*, Manchester: Manchester University Press, ch. 7.

4   The right to health is acknowledged in a variety of international human rights instruments – some general and some with a particular relevance for women. See, for example, Article 12 of the International Covenant on Economic, Social and Cultural Rights which recognizes the right of everyone to the enjoyment of the highest attainable standard of physical and mental health; Article 11 of the European Social Charter in which the Contracting Parties undertake, *inter alia*, in pursuance of the right to protection of health, to take appropriate measures to remove as far as possible the causes of ill-health, to promote health and to prevent epidemics; and Article 12 of the Convention on the Elimination of all Forms of Discrimination against Women which requires states to take all appropriate measures to ensure that women have equal access to health-care facilities.

5   Byrnes *et al.*, *Advancing the Human Rights of Women, op. cit.*, n. 3.

6   See, for example, Charlesworth and Chinkin, *The Boundaries of International Law, op. cit.*, n. 3.

7   See, for example, the essays contained in Bridgeman, J. and Millns, S. (eds) (1995), *Law and Body Politics*, Aldershot: Dartmouth. Chapter 1 of *Well Women* also contains comprehensive references to the feminist literature on health care, women and the medical profession and women's bodies.

8   Although tools do exist to assess the gender-sensitivity of health sector institutions including international health organizations. See Baume, E., Juarez, M. and Standing, H. (2001), *Gender and Health Equity Resource Guide*, Brighton: Institute of Development Studies, p. 38.

9   It should be stressed, however, that this analysis of the WHO is limited to the organization's public activities. This is not an insider's perspective of the organization nor will it consider the impact of specific health initiatives.

10   Not all of which are compatible with one another.

11   Charlesworth, H., Chinkin, C. and Wright, S. (1991), 'Feminist Approaches to International Law', *The American Journal of International Law*, **85**, p. 613.

12   Ibid., p. 625.

13   Statistics compiled by the Inter-Parliamentary Union (IPU) suggest that although women comprise roughly half of the world's population they account for only 13.7 per cent of the world's elected representatives. See the IPU's website <http://www.ipu.org/wmn-e/world.htm> for detailed national and regional statistics. For feminist comment on the consequences of women's exclusion from national legislatures see, for example, Phillips, A. (1995), *The Politics of Presence*, Oxford: Clarendon Press and Norris, P. (1996), 'Women Politicians: Transforming Westminster?', *Parliamentary Affairs*, **49**(1), pp. 89–102.

14   Phillips, *The Politics of Presence, op. cit.*, n. 13, p. 13, argues that, if policies are put in place for a politically excluded constituency, they are unlikely to engage with all that constituency's relevant concerns. The research undertaken by Norris, 'Women Politicians', *op. cit.*, n. 13, suggests that the presence of women in parliament can lead to greater prominence being given to gender issues.

15   For example, in relation to the World Trade Organization (WTO). See Esty, D. (1998), 'Non-Governmental Organizations at the World Trade Organization: Cooperation, Competition or Exclusion', *Journal of International Economic Law*, p. 123; Marceau, G. and Pedersen, P. (1999), 'Is the WTO Open and Transparent? A Discussion of the Relationship of the WTO with Non-governmental Organisations and Civil Society's Claims for More Transparency and Public Participation', *Journal of World Trade*, **33**(1), p. 5.

16   For a discussion of essentialism see Barnett, H. (1998), *Introduction to Feminist Jurisprudence*, London: Cavendish Publishing Ltd.

17 On this point, see Donnelly, M., Mullally, S. and Smith, O. (2000), 'Making Women Count in Ireland', in F. Beveridge, S. Nott and K. Stephen (eds), *Making Women Count*, Aldershot: Ashgate, pp. 44–47.

18 Such as state representatives on the WHO's Executive Board. The Executive Board is the body entrusted with putting into effect decisions of the WHO's supreme decision-making authority, the World Health Assembly.

19 World Health Organization (1998), *Gender and Health: Technical Paper*, Geneva, World Health Organization, pp. 12–18.

20 Ibid., p. 43.

21 Townshend-Smith, R. (1998), *Discrimination Law: Text, Cases and Materials*, London: Cavendish Publishing Limited.

22 World Health Organization, Gender and Health, *op. cit.*, n. 19, p. 10.

23 Chunn, D. and Lacombe, D. (eds) (2000), *Law as a Gendering Practice*, Oxford: Oxford University Press.

24 Townshend-Smith, *Discrimination Law*, *op. cit.*, n. 21, pp. 210–23.

25 Anti-discrimination legislation is, however, usually limited to certain contexts, such as employment, rather than being generally applicable.

26 Questions have arisen in Europe regarding the legitimacy of positive discrimination and whether it amounts to sex discrimination. The use of all women shortlists in the United Kingdom to select Labour Party candidates for the 1997 General Election was held to discriminate against men in *Jepson and Dyas-Elliot* v. *The Labour Party* [1996] IRLT 1166. Within the European Union, the European Court of Justice has, despite some initial problems, been more positive in its treatment of such schemes provided they do not automatically and unconditionally give priority to women – contrast the decision in *Kalanke* v. *Freie und Hansestadt Bremen*, Case 450/93 [1995] IRLR 660 with those in *Marschall* v. *Land Nordrhein-Westfalen*, Case 409/95 [1988] IRLR 39 and *Application by Badeck*, Case 158/97 [2000] IRLR 432.

27 For a discussion of mainstreaming see Council of Europe (1998), *Gender Mainstreaming: Conceptual Framework, Methodology and Presentation of Good Practices, Final Report of the Activities of the Group of Specialists on Mainstreaming* (EG-S-MS (98) 2), Strasbourg, Council of Europe.

28 Stephen, K. (2000), 'Catalysts for Change? The Effectiveness of State Agencies in Promoting Equality' in Beveridge, *et al.*, *Making Women Count*, *op. cit.*, n. 17.

29 Certain equality strategies (for example, the use of anti-discrimination legislation) require the existence of enforcement machinery; others, however (such as gender mainstreaming), do not, and can work well at an international level.

30 Rees, T. (1998), *Mainstreaming Equality in the European Union*, London: Routledge, pp. 29–34.

31 On this point see Maher, I. (1998), 'Community Law in the National Legal Order: A Systems Analysis', *Journal of Common Market Studies*, **36**, p. 237.

32 Thornton, M. (ed.) (1995), *Public and Private Feminist Legal Debates*, Oxford: Oxford University Press; Pateman, C. (1987), 'Feminist Critiques of the Public/Private Dichotomy', in A. Phillips (ed.), *Feminism and Equality*, Oxford: Basil Blackwell Ltd.

33 O'Donovan, K. (1985), *Sexual Divisions in Law*, London: Weidenfeld and Nicolson, ch. 4.

34 Meyer, M. and Prugl, E. (eds) (1999), *Gender Politics in Global Government*, Maryland: Roman and Littlefield, p. 37.

35 *Principles Governing Relations Between The World Health Organization and Nongovernmental Organizations*. For the text of this document see <http://lynx.who.ch/ina-ngo/ngo/princ-e.htm>.

36 Ibid., 1.3.

37 In other words, it must represent 'a substantial proportion of the persons globally organized for the purpose of participating in the particular field of interest in which it operates': ibid., 3.2.

38 This must include voting rights for the members of the NGO in relation to its policies or actions. Ibid., 3.3.

39 Ibid., 3.1. This means that its interests must centre on development work in health or health-related fields. The NGO must also be free of concerns which are primarily of a commercial or profit making nature.

40 Ibid., 3.4.

41 If, for example, it considers that such relations are no longer appropriate or necessary in the light of changing programmes or other circumstances or if the NGO no longer meets the criteria applied when official relations were first established or if the NGO has failed to play its part in a programme of collaboration. Ibid., 4.7.

42 Ibid., section 6.

43 The following website, <http://lynx.who.ch/ina-ngo/ngo/ngo055.htm>, contains a list of these NGOs.

44 Ibid.

45 Ibid.

46 See Strategic Objective C.4 – 'Promote research and disseminate information on women's health'. The action to be taken includes the introduction of systems that allow the use of data collected, analysed and disaggregated by, among other factors, sex and age.

47 Women's Health and Development (1998), *Gender and Health*, Geneva: World Health Organization, p. 42.

48 Ibid.

49 Ibid. Either because their system for gathering data is less than perfect or because of non-reporting of, for example, maternal deaths arising from abortion.

50 Speech delivered in New York on 3 March 1999 by Dr Gro Harlem Brundtland. For the text of this speech see the following website: <http://lynx.who.ch/inf-dg/speeches/english/19990303_un_commission_women.html>.

51 Women's Health and Development, *Gender and Health*, *op. cit.*, n. 47, p. 43.

52 Ibid., p. 41.

53 The WHO succeeded the Health Organization of the League of Nations. This body was set up in 1919 and ceased to function with the setting up of the United Nations.

54 Charlesworth *et al.*, 'Feminist Approaches', *op. cit.*, n. 11, p. 622.

55 Speech delivered by Dr Gro Harlem Brundtland to the Commission on the Status of Women, United Nations, New York, 3 March 1999. For the text of the speech see website in n. 50.

56 Of the current eight executive directors four are men and four are women.

57 WHO, *Gender and Health*, *op. cit.*, n. 47, p. 20.

58 Ibid.

59 The current Director-General has acknowledged the 'reality' that 'for long, and rightly so, the focus has been on the reproductive period [of women]. Primarily women have been considered as synonymous with "mothers". However, the time has come to focus beyond the sexual and reproductive health of women and view the different needs in the entire life-span': Women's Health and Development, *Gender and Health*, *op. cit.*, n. 47.

60 The Group consists of individuals working on gender and/or women's issues within a variety of the WHO's programmes.

61 See the following website: <http://www.who.int/frh-whd/GandH/mainstre.htm>.

62 WHO, *Gender and Health*, *op. cit.*, n. 47.

63 Reanda, L. (1999), 'Engendering the United Nations – The Changing International Agenda', *The European Journal of Women's Studies*, **6**, p. 49.

64 WHO, *Gender and Health*, n. 47, p. 56.
65 Beveridge *et al.*, *Making Women Count*, *op. cit.*, n. 17.
66 Ibid.
67 Reanda, 'Engendering the United Nations', *op. cit.*, n. 63.
68 Baume *et al.*, *Gender and Health Equity Resource Guide*, *op. cit.*, n. 8.
69 There is a belief in some quarters that female genital mutilation is demanded by the Islamic faith. The practice is, however, found in other religious communities.
70 As a sign that a girl has made the transfer to womanhood.
71 Charlesworth and Chinkin, *The Boundaries of International Law*, *op. cit.*, n. 3, p. 226 (footnote omitted).
72 World Health Organization (1995), *Women's Health*, Geneva: World Health Organization, p. 17. *Women's Health* was a position paper prepared by the WHO for the Fourth World Conference on Women, Beijing, China, 4–15 September 1995. The World Health Assembly condemned the practice in 1994 whilst at the same time affirming its support for local culture and tradition that was positive in its impact.

Index